If Ever a Man Suffered

Bernie Comaskey

Best Wishes,
Bernie

A Journey ...

From the Soft Bogs of Westmeath
to the Hard-Rock Canadian Mines:

From Collinstown to Costa Blanca:

From ten-shillings-a-week bar apprentice
to Business Entrepreneur:

From Pioneer to battling the Booze.

Told with honesty, humour
and without ever a hint of self-pity

For Pamela
Who read the odds
But gambled anyway.

ISBN: 09553686-0-X
978- 09553686-0-X

Published by:
Deel Publications,
Graftonstown, Bracklyn, Mullingar.
Tel: 044 9664776

Printed by Leinster Leader Ltd.
18/19 Main Street,
Naas, Co Kildare, Ireland.

Cover by: Sean Kelleghan

CONTENTS

Preface

I wrote this book in long-hand, in just over three months. I started it on 4 July 2005 – appropriately enough, Remembrance Day! This is "take one". After I finished writing, nothing got changed, other than to leave out a couple of petty little things, which had little relevance to the story.

It is very much stating the obvious, to say it could be better written. I have since thought of more descriptive ways for putting things, or episodes I should have included, but as I always hated having to make the same field of hay twice, I didn't go back on it. I decided against change or restructuring.

It is written as if I were just telling you the story – which is what it is. If you are looking for grammatical errors you will find them. Let's just call it "The Common Vernacular".

In telling the story, I did not spare anybody, least of all myself. If it comes across as being overly hard on some people, I make no apology. This is how it was in my shoes – or bare feet, as the case might be. When the prospective publishers told me it would be at least another year before the book would hit the shelves, my impatient streak prompted me to self-publish. I formed "Deel Publications" and here we are. The River Deel borders my lands now, as it did in my home place.

I wish to thank all the family, especially my mother, for their understanding of the bits they might not necessarily like to see written.

Thank you, dear reader, for buying the book. I hope you will feel it was worth the money!

CHAPTER 1

I am now in my sixty-first year and I have a long memory. I have such a long memory that I don't really need to tell this story yet – only I don't know what twist or turn the story takes next, or how much longer the story lasts! This is my story – the story of an ordinary man.

I was born on 18th September 1944, in the North Westmeath village of Drumcree. I don't remember this event – but there is documented evidence that it took place exactly as I tell it. Now, to the long memory; I have two vivid memories of incidents that happened when I was about two years old. My Granny lived with us until I was two and a half and I clearly recall the day she left to live in another house, four miles away in Ballinock. She travelled in a neighbours pony and trap, with her few personal belongings. I can imagine now how she must have been lonely leaving to go live on her own – but the second house was there, and room was scarce in a two bedroom house, where I had two younger brothers before I was twenty eight months old. I finished up with five brothers, Camillus the last born, when I was seventeen. As you can guess, I was the first born.

The other oldest memory I have is sitting on my father's knee, when I was about two and a half. That is the only time I ever remember being on my father's lap – so it must have been a huge emergency involving my Mother, with either or both of my younger brothers, Willie and Seán.

Our house at The Derries, Drumcree,
where my 5 brothers and I were born and reared

My father, John Comaskey, was not a 'touchy feely' or demonstrative sort of man. He came from a school where children should be seen and not heard and that's how it was. A small 'wirey' man he worked hard for small reward. My father dealt with every crises, big or small, real or imaginary, by turning his eyes up to heaven and "saying the words", "If ever a man suffered", or "Good Jaysus, if ever a man suffered".

His most often spoken utterance, which was a threat to us and also adapted by Mammy was "The last of yer bread is baked" if you don't do such'n'-such. We had a small farm of bogland and Daddy worked his day with Westmeath County Council. He was employed as a "Carter", with his own horse and cart drawing gravel from sand-pits and tipping it along the sides of the road, where it was spread for repairs and the filling of pot-holes. As he often bemoaned "The so'n'so horse gets paid more than I do". He got loads of hardship and abuse from petty gangers and foremen: Five minutes late on slippy roads meant not being allowed start for two and a half hours, load "boxed" or measured, after leaving pit; sent to a pit further from home on the whim of ganger etc., little wonder that I grew up believing that the only sentence worse than Belsen or Austwich was Westmeath County Council!

In the early 1950's the miracle of rural electricification came to our area. Daddy left "The Council" for a couple of years to pull E.S.B. poles into the fields with his two horses. He still complained, ("If ever a man suffered!") but I think he was happy enough working for the E.S.B.

After a couple of years, or so, when all the poles stood upright, bringing much light into our lives, Daddy was out of work. For the next couple of years he did short stints with neighbouring farmers and Bord na Móna.

Eventually though he returned to his "hell-hole"(!) Westmeath County

My Parents, Martha and John

On the old grey mare – about age three

Council. By now, things were changing, lorries drew the gravel and "Carters" were a thing of the past. My father was content to work as a labourer and also, the new breed of gangers and foremen were much more human than previously, and these men became his best friends.

Through all of above and ongoing it must be remembered that my father had to come home each evening and deal with our few cows, calves, cattle, hay, turf etc.

My mother worked inside and outside the house (Father never lifted his finger indoors – except to give orders – or give us a belt!) and all of us boys had a never ending list of chores to do including milking, both before and after school.

My father had a great wit when "out". He was great company and known as a great man to tell a story. An only son, with six sisters who "spoiled" him all his life, he expected things to happen for him. He had no ambition to improve his lot. My mother used crave him to exchange our poor land for a land commission farm and once, she applied for land in his name, was successful, but when he found out, there was another row and he wouldn't budge.

Playing the bodhrán in the pub was his only pastime, or being in the pub, without the bodhrán. As they say, "He took a drink!"

Daddy was hard and contrary at home, but strangely I never had any resentment against him for this – unlike my feelings towards my Mother, whose human faults I often couldn't accept.

It must be remembered that the 'fifties' was a harsh, cruel time to grow up in – at home, at school and in the community. If I tell it like it was, it is not intended to contain a drop of self-pity or, a grain of regret. I was lucky and life was good to me.

CHAPTER 2

My Mother

My mother, Martha Mulligan was a strikingly good looking woman who married my father, nine years her senior, when she was twenty. After national school she got one year's convent school education, before the money ran out. Today, in her eighty third year, her brain is as sharp as the most intelligent person, half her age. She is so well read on every imaginable topic, that she can carry on a stimulating conversation with anyone.

In a way, I suppose, her brain was wasted, to some extent (whilst not implying that any part of her life was wasted). If she were starting off now, she could be anything she wanted to, be it in the professions or such. Her grandmother was a school teacher and I think that she wanted to be a teacher when growing up. Often, when we were kids, she would become enthused with some money making idea, such as selling clothes or other items.

For a variety of reasons, lack of capital, "what the neighbours might say", or more especially my father's aforementioned lack of enthusiasm for anything, nothing got past the planning stage - although after twenty years she managed to succeed in opening a sort of "caravan park" for well off Dublin people with mobile homes.

Keeping the wolf from the door was an ongoing battle. Having six sons and three miscarriages, while all the time longing for a daughter, wouldn't have

Poor quality, but the only photo of Granda Comaskey, shortly before his death.
Back L to R: Granda, Granny, Aunt Greta and an unknown visitor
Front L to R: Daddy and Aunt Terry

been easy - even if you had enough money to do it on. Mammy could get the big things done but couldn't deal with the humdrum daily family - management things. Later, we were the first in our neighbourhood with a bathroom, first with a television, most modern churn for butter making, new range (stove) etc. etc., but the grocery bill in Briodys was an on-going festering problem. Even though my father got paid every two weeks, the grocery bill was always going up and up. When the shopkeeper, Ganey (Eugene) Briody felt it was getting "dangerously" high he would tell me to tell my father he needed money. This is where the worry started for me. I would tell my mother first and she would tell me to say nothing to my father! Eventually he would find out the size of the bill. The ensuing row would keep us kids awake half the night. – blame and counter–blame for how the groceries could have created such a debt. Anyway, next stage would be for a couple of cattle or calves to be sold - and we started the pattern all over again.

Mother was a bit of a hypochondriac, - always had to have an ailment. Two things she couldn't be without, when I was going to school, "Cullen's Powders", and a book. Later she progressed from the "Cullen's Powders" to the cure for almost every ailment known to man – or woman! She read books well into the night and come morning she most often would not get up to get us out to school. This huge responsibility for getting myself and the younger boys ready and out fell to me. Of all the things, this is the one resentment I carried with me for a very long time. However, mother instilled a pride, ambition and vision in her six sons. There was no doubt in her mind, but that her lads would "get on". When my first job was "serving my time" in a pub, for ten shillings a week, to her and therefore to me, it was the first step in becoming a publican. Her optimism in the ability of her family, starting from nothing, has, I suppose not been misplaced. Willie, or Bill as he is now called, is the Mayor of the Canadian City of Thompson, as well as a government mines inspector. In spite of my fathers dire warnings Sean (having left a factory quality control job, for health reasons) finished up with the dreaded Westmeath County Council, where he is a ganger. Fechin is currently a director of our property company in Spain. Anthony has his own business in Denver, Colorado and Camillus has a posi-

On Granny's knee in Ballinock

tion of responsibility with a pharmaceutical company in Westport. I have business and interests in Spain and Ireland.
Again, above is just to tell it like it is and to show how happy a woman my mother was when we all gathered for her eightieth birthday.
Sadly my father died at the age of sixty nine, in 1984. If 'doul' drink didn't get him, the 'fags' did. A heavy smoker, he died from lung cancer. We had many a "session" when I would come home from abroad, during my drinking days. I was settled at home for the last dozen years of his life. Only then did I sort of learn what made him tick, as we engaged in long chats and I asked about his young days, when his father died whilst he was still a kid. He absolutely adored my wife Pamela, and we became close. This didn't stop him complaining, however, "I have all the money I can drink now and I'm not able to drink it and when I was able to drink it, I didn't have the price of it!!"

On a rare trip to Dublin
Auntie Kathleen, Myself, Willie and Mammy

CHAPTER 3

School

In the most prominent position in my house, hangs an oil painting, by local artist Sean Kelleghan of a two-room stone built schoolhouse. This is Johnstown N. S. where I, along with generations of boys and girls from Killulagh, Rickardstown, Glaxtown, Clondelever and Johnstown got our education, between 1880 and 1969. Both my parents attended school there. In 1993, I, along with Ann Dugdale, Pat Fox and Dessie Kiernan initiated a Johnstown school reunion which turned out to be a huge success. The reunion took place in my Sports and Leisure Centre in Mullingar. Three hundred and fifty past pupils converged from the four corners of the world for a night of music, banter, nostalgia and chat. It was a wonderful moving experience to meet old school friends – many of whom hadn't met since schooldays. The bond, the feeling of "my place" was just incredible.

The school produced a conveyer belt of solid hard working citizens and people who distinguished themselves in all walks of life, throughout the world. It was also the nursery for the great Rickardstown hurling team.

From our house in The Derries to Johnstown school was a mile. One bright sunny morning, when I was five, my mother lifted me on to the carrier of her bicycle and took me to school for the first time. I wore a new cardigan, which she had knitted for me, which had a big reindeer on the back. Mammy

Johnstown School After it closed,
it has since been restored as a dwelling house

only came the once. Next day I walked with the Fordes – Kitty having been told to mind me! There was no crying from me, I loved being off to school. Mrs McCormack, the teacher, gave me a jotter and pencil and a stick of white chalk. I remember that in the school-yard, in my first days, I preferred to play with the girls. Eventually the girls told me to run off and play with the boys, which I did but I would return to play with the girls a dozen or so years later!

I settled in to the learning which I found easy. My mother marvelled at how much I was learning and she helped me at home with old school books, with the result that I was ahead of the class at most things – especially reading. I was reading sixth class books in second class. This didn't mean that I got any less "belts" from Mrs. McCormack. Books not covered, "blot" on copy book, talking or laughing in class, copying or letting someone copy etc. etc., were all grounds for a slap of the ruler on the hand, a cheek pinched, or even a knuckle in the jaw. Parents accepted this and we got on with it. Most of the kids I knew then were grand kids and they are grand people today. There was one exception, which I'll touch on later.

Having settled into school I began to learn lots from the other pupils about the "outside" world – all simple, quaint, innocent stuff. So many of the pupils would have brothers and sisters in England, Canada and America. Home on holiday, or what they wrote home, would be carried and discussed around the play-ground. Pictures were planted in my mind of far-away places and I think the travel bug was planted at that early stage. Stories in our English reading books conjured up pictures of another world, far removed from the Johnstown to Drumcree gravel road. Most of the families were poor, some very poor and a few well off. We were in the first category I suppose. All kids were equal at school in Johnstown and I don't remember any snobbery or distinctions – very little of the kettle calling the pot black. Johnstown N. S. was one of four schools in the parish of Delvin. The others being Killough, Crowenstown and the Delvin school, situated at Ballinvalley.

In the school playground
L to R: Willie, Oliver Kiernan & Myself aged 12.
Note the new hurling boots and socks, courtesy of Aunt Betty

As I said, all us kids were "the same" and being different in any way, was not a good idea. At home we often got parcels from America, or, more often, England and I hated having to wear any of the contents to school. The jeering would last for days.

From the first of May every pupil turned up for school in bare feet. Our feet got so hard that we could run a mile on the gravel road and feel no effect on the feet. Thorns, however, were an on-going hazard – as well as the occasional stone bruise. For whatever reason, the doctor in Delvin, Dr. Cox, choose to drive his family to school in Johnstown, rather than have them attend the local school in Ballinvalley.

They weren't allowed leave home in bare feet, like the rest of us. It was funny to see Olga, Mary and the twins stand outside the school gate until their fathers' car had gone, so that they could hide their shoes in the ditch and be the same as everybody else!

A school photo

In first class, I shared a desk with Mary Cox. One day she was chewing away – chewing and chewing. Eventually I asked her what she was eating. Mary took this pink, sticky substance out of her mouth. "It's chewing gum and it lasts forever" she told me. I couldn't believe it, here we had a sweet that didn't finish. "Here" said Mary, "I'll give you a loan of it". Right enough, after chewing for half and hour I gave Mary back the same amount for she to resume her chewing. I wonder what her father, the doctor, would have though of that!

The Big Room

In Johnstown N.S. there was "The Little Room" and "The Big Room". Both rooms were of similar size but were so called because "The Masters' Room" contained the big pupils.

In my time, the total roll averaged around eighty although more than a hundred had attended in my parents' time. It was a cold, drafty building, with an open grate being the only form of heating. Some parents brought in a horse-load of turf, but often we each had to carry a couple of sods to school – which warmed no one except the teacher.

A hundred yards from the school was Hynes' shop, where you could purchase a penny bar, or a packet of lozenges for a penny-halfpenny. I think it was thirteen lozenges were in the packet, which made great value, as they were easy to share – and we were great sharers in Johnstown.

As well as bringing sods of turf to school, carried along with the school-bag and the most important item of all – the hurley, we often had to gather elder berries to manufacture ink for the inkwells on each desk. A long way from the school computer!

Even though our house was in Collinstown parish, Killulagh, in the parish of Delvin is our regular church and family burial ground. Killulagh is a good three miles away and, as kids, we travelled by foot or bicycle to Mass. I served Mass there. As we had to be fasting from midnight, looking back now, it must have been a strain, but cold or hunger seemed to bother us little.

I got my first communion when I reached seven. Along with my mother I rode a bicycle the three miles to Killulagh. Hynes' shop was our stop on the way home, after calling to see Granny Mulligan. I had nearly two shillings in the pocket of my new suit and Mrs Hynes gave me a present of a sixpenny bar of chocolate, which I brought home to divide with my brothers. I was in with God now and the world was a wonderful place!

My brother Willie started school a year after me and Seán the following year. Willie was just an average scholar, not as brainy as I, but he was better than me where it mattered most – in the playground. He was a gifted hurler. Seán was not into sport, although he had to take part. Delicate as a child he didn't fare out well in the robust games of the playground. It bothers me that Willie and I didn't take greater care of him than we did, both at school and at home. All we knew was the hard competitive edge of the jungle that is a growing boys' world.

On reaching fourth class, I moved into the Master's Room, or "The Big Room". This was a big move up in the world. The Master was a Kerryman, Seámus Lawlor (father of Eamon Lawlor of RTE). The same as everybody else, I had a certain amount of fear of him, but I always liked and respected him and that never changed. A tough disciplinarian, he was hard but fair and a good teacher, while he was in Johnstown. Steeped in the footballing tradition of Kerry, that didn't prevent him from enthusiastically embracing hurling (there was no football in our area of North Westmeath) and Johnstown became the Kingpins of "Comortas na Mbun Scoil".

I absolutely loved hurling. The school playground was where we fought our way onto the team and where skills were honed. Some of the best under-fourteen hurlers I have ever seen, such as Peter Loughlin, played in that school. I remember a school final in Mullingar, where, from the puck-out, Des Kiernan, playing mid-field, doubled overhead on the ball and Loughlin in the forwards, doubled again, to send it over the bar. Willie and I were never without a hurley; (or hurl as we call it) going for the cows, going to the shop, Saturday mornings, all day Sunday – and any other time. I'm sure there are neighbours who can still hear my fathers' "Lave down the hurls and pull them weeds!" ringing in their ears! Getting hurleys was a problem – the odd one subsidised through the school, but most came from going to senior games, prowling the side line waiting to pounce when a hurl broke. Often the broken hurl was in two halves, with two boys, with a half each. Then, either a bargain or a row, left one lucky junior with two pieces of a hurley, ideally with a long splinter break, to take home and get banded.

Michael O' Hehir inspired us with the exploits of the Rackards and Christy Ring. How could I ever have dreamed that when Willie Rackard received the Texaco Hall of Fame Award in 2002 I would sit next to him for the dinner and presentation at the Burlington Hotel. A few times our hearts swelled with pride when our own "Jobber" McGrath made it onto the radio.

At best, I was never more than an average hurler. However, I am a better than average sports fanatic and that has served me well all my life!

One Rotten Apple

To this day, I have a strong bond of friendship with everyone I went to school with, except for this one exception. There was this family who seemed to me to be a bit different. They were the only ones I ever knew who fought with the teachers. This family of kids were all well informed on every bit of adult scandal and who to task what with. Most of it was stuff I, or most others I imagine, couldn't understand. I got it for my father's drinking – simple enough stuff, but there were a few unfortunate kids who had much worse to listen to.

Jimmy was a class ahead of me and as big for his age as I was small for mine I learned early in life that it's made up of balances and counter-balances. I was happy at school but Jimmy was the counter-balance to that. He was the bane of my school-life. For whatever reason, he hated me. He rarely left me alone, to such an extent that I enjoyed a great sense of freedom any day he was absent. I got poked and pinched, taunted, ink rubbed on my neck "bored" with the hurling ball, until I would finally retaliate and then I got the shit beaten out of myself. That was the water-shed; then I would have peace for a couple of weeks and the cycle started over again.

There was a strict code for fighting in the playground. It had to be just one to one and the ring of boys made sure nobody else jumped in – including brothers. Sometimes a fight would be brooding for days, other times, it could start in a second. "Drop the hurl" was the challenge. You couldn't hit a fellow "when he wasn't looking" and you couldn't use the boot or have anything in your hand. It didn't give the small fellow any chance of an 'equaliser' but I suppose, in fairness, little damage was done. I admit that later I fantasised well into adult life as to how I should have fixed Jimmy, but isn't it a good job you cannot put an old head on young shoulders, or I would have finished up in a reformatory like my class-mate Ollie Fitzsimmons. Poor Ollie was reared by his overly strict Grandmother, because his mother had died. He wasn't allowed go hurling or anything. Eventually he rebelled. Did nothing wrong but his Granny said she couldn't control him and he was sent off to a reformatory. He was my pal and I never saw him again. I believe he is in England. Even when I was getting abuse, I knew I wasn't too badly off.

One day, we had what appeared to be a grumpy old inspector in the school. He was talking about words which weren't pronounced as they are spelled. He mentioned pneumonia and, like a shot, my hand went up. As luck would have it my mother had taught me the spelling of it: p_n_e_u_m_o_n_i_a, P_N_E_U_M_O_N_I_A, SIR! The inspector called me up, put his hand in his pocket and gave me a shilling. I was so 'choked' I couldn't get out the words "go raibh maith agat".

Master Lawlor used sometimes read out my English compositions for the class. I never heard him read anyone else's. Like I said, I got on great with him. I still got many a 'belt', some earned, some not. There was only one thing I never forgave him for and I told him this, over a couple of pints, years later. We were in a county semi-final against Kilallon. We had won all our previous games easily and were certainties for the title. The master had brought in a rule that no boy could play an evening match, who hadn't been to school that day. Our best player was Petey Loughlin, the best hurler for his age, in his last year at school. On the day of the match, Pete was at home "picking spuds" or something. He turned up for the game. The Master gave out the jerseys and there wasn't one for Loughlin. We were beaten by two points with our star on the sideline.

A decade later, over the drink; Lawlor said "Bernie, I hoped you wouldn't remember that. I brought ye to matches, in my car all your school life. I trained with ye in the playground. That was one of the hardest decisions of my school life. Peter had become big-headed. He knew what he was doing. He took me on and left me with no choice". "All I know", I said, "is that you left the rest of us without a medal".

Only now can I appreciate the 'hard call' that must have been for "The Master" to make.

That year, in sixth class I got the highest marks in the school for the Primary Certificate.

CHAPTER 4

Holidays

"Holidays" could conjure up a lot of different feelings in my young mind. There were different sorts of "holidays". The happiest days of my childhood were going on holidays to my Granny in Ballinock. Then, when I was nine, Granny took ill, and Auntie Betty, with her son, Seán, home from England for three weeks "couldn't leave her" and to the eternal credit of her husband J.B., the three weeks became three years, until Granny died when I was twelve.

My cousin, Seán Jefferies, became like another brother to us and we are still close. Two years younger than I, he came from London – as you can imagine, with loads of new ideas and devilment. I remember those holidays fondly, where the days were always sunny and life seemed to be one adventure after another.

The only other "away" holiday was twice to Dublin with my auntie Kathleen; once with my Mother and Willie, when I was around four and the other for a few days when I was eleven.

The word "holidays" to most of us attending Johnstown N.S. simply meant no school and more work. During the Summer months there would be a demand for strapping, hard-working young lads to pick-spuds, thin turnips, toss turf, etc – all back-breading work for usually nine hour days – and then

Around 1959
Willie, Myself, Seán with Fechin in front

do your own chores when you got home; it was a badge of approval to be asked to work for these "Bully" farmers, as they were "affectionately" called! Daddy was always giving out about something and he gave Willie and I a hard time over the fact that our neighbours, The Harris', hired the Nolans and the Mulvanneys – two miles away and didn't rank us worthy of working for them. (You never went looking for work, you had to be "picked"). "Is it any wonder, when they never see yiz doin' a 'Crossa Christ' – except hurling a ball up against the back of the house!" Then one day, I learned a story which told us why Harris' didn't pick Willie and me – and guess who's fault it was? Pat, Neddie and Johnny Harris, all bachelors and middle-aged at that time, along with their spinster sister Nanny, lived two doors from us. As well as owning a good 'swipe' of land, they were well known and highly successful calf and pig dealers. They were rich, in poor times. People, naturally looked

up to them – especially to Pat, who was a wise old man who had spent some years in America. Nothing ever changed in Harris'.
Anyway, my father worked for them in his teen years. One of his duties was to come in on Sunday evenings to milk the three cows. It was up to Nanny to have three clean enamel buckets ready in the dairy (woman's work!) Nanny, until she finally left, when she was near sixty, never got on with the boys (as she called the brothers) and was always pulling against them. Anyway to annoy "the boys" and my father; one Sunday she fed the pigs food to the bonhams, in the milking buckets and left them back in the dairy – dirty. Daddy just took the buckets, coated with an inch of pigs "vittles", milked into the buckets and went home. His temper never failed him!
Local grocer, 'Ganey' Briody hired Willie and I to pick spuds a couple of seasons. Ganey always reminded me a bit of my father – both small, wirey, contrary men. Unlike my father, Ganey had quit the booze and became a successful shopkeeper and farmer. We were well treated by Briodys; Ganey was a fair man and the fact that they had a shop ensured that Mrs. Briody fed us well.
The summer of my thirteenth birthday, Willie and I worked the holidays with Hugh Macken. Mackens were the most important people around Johnstown, by their own admission! They say that you can teach people how to treat you and the Macken family were a good example of promoting the fact that they were more than a cut above the rest.
There was no harm in Hugh – and indeed his wife was a nice woman also. Hugh was always "in a hobble" and generally presided over one farming disaster after another.
We worked six days a week, for six shillings a day – 36/= per week. The work was tough and the food was not nearly as good as Briodys. At meal times we were segregated, so as that no family member might be contaminated by eating near the hired help. Of the 36/= earned, the deal was that we would "give up" 30/= to mammy and keep the remaining six shillings. Saturday evening was pay day and half the time it proved to be a heart-breaking, frustrating experience for us young lads. After bursting ourselves all week; come Saturday, Hugh Macken wouldn't have the money to pay us: - sometimes half, sometimes less. It had to be, at best, bad management or at worse, sheer contempt, because, eventually we would get paid.
Willie and I saved our money and in September purchased two wrist watch-

es at £2.13 each from Dores of Dame Street (by post). The worth it. No purchase ever gave more joy or excitement and th a wonderful place!

Neighbours

We were blessed with the most wonderful neighbours. On either side of us we had Fordes and Reillys – all large families of course! Tom Forde was a quiet man and one of the few daddies I knew who wasn't always shouting at his children. The land around us was all poor, but Tom was shrewd and made money from the bog, by way of cutting turf (peat) and setting turf-bank. Most significantly, Tom "didn't take a drink!" Mrs Forde was a real old-fashioned

My Mother with Mrs. Reilly

country woman; hard-working, strong willed and as they say; "a good neighbour".

Reillys were a bit worse off than us. As well as the bit of poor land around the house Jody had a few acres of good land in Killulagh but the lack of a steady wage coming in showed. Mrs Reilly, another great neighbour, was kind, quiet, patient and considerate. She never went anywhere other than to mass. When I was seven, Andy Reilly, aged nine, died. It was my first exposure to loss and grief.

In the boreen from Reilly's the Harris' lived, whom I have mentioned already, and behind them, brother and sister; John and Madge Malone. It's amazing that we all lived in almost perfect harmony. Ok, there would be the odd row among us children, but I only remember one adult argument. That was between Jody Reilly and my father, over fencing. Jody was a lot older than Daddy and as we, the respective off-spring, gathered round this is how the shouting match finished! "You have had your day Jody, you're finished telling the people what to do"! "Ah, but Thank God I left three sons after me to do it!" "You did, but thank God I left four (at the time)!" My father had to have the last word!

Next day Jody and Daddy were talking as if nothing had happened and they each fenced their half of the 'maring'.

We literally begged or borrowed anything we didn't have, from our neighbours. When our cows were 'dry' we got milk until a cow calved. We could go out in Fordes' field and get "greens" or a turnip for the dinner, without the least compliment. One evening Willie and I, on our way over to "Barber", to cut fishing rods, were handed a can of milk to leave into Malones. It just so happened that Madge had hung out several pairs of knickers on the clothes – line. Later, when we were home mammy overheard the two of us making some "sneer" about this. She gave us a serious lecture about respect etc etc., and finished up by saying; "What you two ámadáns are giggling about is just a "bit of material". From that day on, Willie and I never referred to that item of ladies apparel as anything other than "The Bita Material!"

Once a year we killed a pig, as did also Fordes, Reillys and Harris; when the pig was "boned" we were then sent to each neighbour with a bucket of "greeshgeens" (fresh pork) and when the others killed they reciprocated.

No part of the pig was wasted; "crubeens" (feet, or hocks) were much sought after. My job would be to keep the crock of blood stirred until it cooled, so that black-puddings could be made. We even dried, and then blew up, the bladder and used it as a football.

Half a mile down the road lived the Bell family – a large family on equally limited acreage. Mrs. Bell was a nice quiet woman and Tom was a harmless hard-working man. However Tom had one comical trait – a massive illusion of grandeur! This wasn't taken seriously by the people and every so often the jokes would do the rounds about Tom discovering, once again, how much better off he was, than what he had previously thought. He was always finding extra pigs, or calves he forgot he had! But Tom passed this on to his children – especially the girls. They were told to hold their heads up and not to speak to any of the locals – and that's how it was.

As well as the neighbours mentioned, there were so many other great people within a couple of miles radius and then of course, there were the characters. Tom Bartley, the "Shot" Henry. Jack Murtagh, Patchín Flanagan, The Blacksmith McCabe. Ireland was full of characters in those days, and there was a great acceptance of people as they were.

Confirmation
L to R: Myself, Seán and Willie

Confirmation

In a most unusual happening three of us; Willie, Seán and myself got our confirmation together. We were probably the best dressed at the ceremony. In our house it was "the whole hog or nothing" – usually nothing – but this time it was "the whole hog". Mammy went to Dublin to buy the suits; she was met by Aunt Kathleen and they probably lost the run of the budget because when Daddy heard how much it cost, he took to the pub for three nights in a row. He had sold three store bullocks and he told me later he never got over the buying of the three outfits. Maybe he didn't!

Three well cut, matching suits, with a hint of green in them. Three cream shirts, three green ties, three pairs of fawn socks and three pairs of brown shoes. Everybody was admiring us, as my Mother hovered round, beaming with pride – and didn't she deserve it. Daddy was delighted with us and he had a few pints, to celebrate. We all had a great day!

CHAPTER 5

Christmas Pudding

Telling it like it was, might give the impression that we were miserable growing up. Nothing could be further from the truth. Children have a much greater grasp of "the now" than adults give them credit for. I was content and happy most of the time. Certainly, we were never bored. As well as the never ending list of chores, we engaged in hurling (of course), hunting, fishing, athletics, all sorts of games and the great thrill of listening to sport on the radio. We got a radio early on – with its outside aerial, wet battery, dry battery and a valve ready to blow! I followed Ronnie Delaney around Santry Stadium – just breasting the tape ahead of him. The morning the word came through that he won the gold medal in Melbourne, we ran the mile to school. Again, the younger brother beat me by about fifty yards.

But, above all, it was the magnificent spectacle of the world of GAA that the radio opened up for me, through Michéal O'Hehir. Everyone remembers where they were when President Kennedy was killed; well, I remember where I was when Kevin Behan won the All-Ireland for Louth in 1957. I remember Christy Ring in 1954, and I remember where I was for the Rackards in 1956, for Frankie Walsh of Waterford in 1959 and for Kevin Mussen of Down in 1960.

Daddy's bark was much worse than his bite and most of the time we could "get round him" easier than Mammy – if we wanted to be let go somewhere, or the like. I recall many funny bits when he made a "bags" of things. One day he was shouting at us in the kitchen – blaming us in the wrong for something Willie ventured to say "Daddy, you're making a mistake". Father rounded on him, shouting at the top of his voice; "I don't make mistakes!" Then, the absurdity of this statement hit us all and everyone burst out laughing including both parents.

When he was nine, Willie nearly died. He was rushed into Mullingar hospital and operated on in the middle of the night. He had a burst appendix and a life-threatening ulcer on his stomach. We said prayers, and prayers were offered up in the school, and Thank God he got better. The day we heard he was coming home, Seán and I spent most of it jumping up and down, cheering on the road, waiting for the ambulance to appear. When he arrived, he was laden down with "goodies" that patients and their visitors had given him. He introduced me to grapes and we all feasted to our hearts content. For ever more, if not before, Willie was Daddy's favourite and I don't believe he ever spoke a seriously cross word to him again.

There is one other episode where we might have lost Willie and even now, thinking about it gives me goose-pimples and makes my blood run cold. Our parent's never knew about this. One Sunday, when I was thirteen and he twelve, we got involved in a wrestling match. I know it was Sunday because we had the shirts and tie on. Our contests were always robust and vigorously fought. I grabbed him by the tie as we rolled on the ground. I was pulling half the tie then I heard a 'gurgle' and saw his lips were blue. I fumbled feverishly to loosen the tie and it is only just that I managed it. If I hadn't succeeded, that tie would have been the death of both of us.

I have a sweet tooth all my life, but I can't eat Christmas Pudding – and here's why. It was the week before Christmas and Mammy was gone to second Mass in Collinstown. The previous day, she had just finished boiling the Christmas Puddings and they were hanging up in the customary "pudding bags", over the mantle piece. The muslin bag in which the pudding was boiled (for about six hours) was made from a cut-up cotton type flour bag. (Sheets were also made from these bags). The "ingredients" for the pudding were mixed and mixed and mixed – not forgetting the couple of bottles of stout my father would have been commissioned to bring from Drumcree. The bag would be coated with lard and flour; to make it waterproof; and then placed in the boiling pot. Mammy did two together – one for us and one for Ballinock.

I was about ten years old. Daddy was in a good mood and myself, Willie and Seán got around him to give us a taste of the pudding. He took down one bag and opened it. Fechin, who would have been about three, had joined the chorus and he got the first slice. Daddy didn't do things by half; one slice led to another … and another … I got the most awful sickening I have ever had in my life and from that day to this, fifty years later, I have never eaten a slice of Christmas pudding.

Roots

Today I live on a hundred acre farm at Graftonstown, Mullingar. On the maternal side of my family, I am the eighth generation to be here and no other generation ever felt more privileged or happier here than I do. Pamela and I had built a house here a few years ago and my Mother lives next door. I had however, paid for a share of the farm in 1990. At that time Uncle Paddy, my mother's brother, owned about fifty of the acres; when the other half came up for sale and we bought it between us. My mother sold her house and moved here to a lovely house on the farm. They were both so anxious to put the farm back together again – as half of it had passed out of the family some generations back. I was the "favoured Nephew" and Paddy had willed his land to me anyway. Is all that clear!?

A young Granny Mulligan

Uncle Paddy was the smartest man I ever knew. After national school he went to night school and, in fact, he never stopped learning. He was so well read and incredibly well informed on almost every subject you wanted (or didn't want!) to discuss. No

car, no TV, no luxuries of any description, he could very fairly be described as eccentric. Very few people are one hundred percent honest. Paddy was.
Granda and Granny Mulligan lived at Battstown, near Killulagh. As long as they were there we always called in on our way home from mass. Granny always welcomed me with the same greeting; "Ah, did you come, a mhic". She was a good, kind woman who lived for her family, and she was noted for being a great neighbour. An indication of the sad part of her life is the following piece.
She was an excellent musician and her pride and joy was a pearl-key melodeon which she played at house-dances and at home in her own house, after the rosary, when all the work was done. I never heard her play, because her eldest son, my uncle Willie, died at the age of thirty two. My granny never opened the melodeon case again – ever.
Granny Mulligan was a large woman and Granny Comaskey was tiny. When I was very small I differentiated between them as "Little granny" and "Big Granny". That stuck and they were never known as anything else!
My Granda Comaskey died when the family was young. "Little Granny" had come home from America to marry him and I think she always carried a bit of disillusionment with life after that. No need to say that life was tough for a while, but the family she reared, six daughters and my father, were very good to her. She "took a drink" – unlike Big Granny who was a teetotaller.
Granda Mulligan was a gentleman. Proud, intelligent, witty

Granda Mulligan

and well spoken. He was a stone mason by trade. I don't remember him working at this, but in Mothers' youth, when he worked they had lots of money and when he couldn't get work, which was often, they had none. Granda was in his mid nineties when he died in 1963.
Big Granny died in 1960 and I was surprised at how Granda grieved for her. In my youthful ignorance I couldn't understand why a ninety year old man would cry so much for an old woman.
Both of them died in our house, as Mammy brought each one to live with us during their final illness, so that she could look after them. She was a great daughter to do this and full credit to my father, who was fully supportive. Granda too "took a drink" and it's many a time I saw Daddy slip him a baby power, after he came in from Drumcree. Indeed, when I came home I always brought "a drop" to Granda – which he would then proceed to hide on my Mother – although she knew well.
My Mother's only sister, my Aunt Maria, lived in Dublin. She was comfortably off and became well-off by virtue of an inheritance. I could never understand why she contributed neither time nor a shilling to looking after her parents. It all fell to my Mother, as poor as we were, and of course, Uncle Paddy did his bit. Uncle Tony, who also lived nearby gave his time and stayed up at night during the last weeks or months of Granda and Grannie's life.
Aunty Marie was so friendly and great conversation ensued whenever – which was seldom – she called; but in all my life, she never as much as gave me one sweet. This was the total opposite to all my father's sisters – especially Auntie Kathleen, who lived in Dublin and Auntie Betty who lived in England. Nobody had more caring or more generous aunts than had the six of us. They looked after Santy Claus, bikes, hurling boots and just about every occasion; "Dear Auntie Betty/Kathleen", I hope you are well. I will be nine on the eighteenth of September" … love …! By return came the birthday card with the crisp ten shilling note inside.
Kathleen died a few months ago, suddenly, in the best of health – just the way she wanted. She was ninety three. Betty in her ninety eight year is the last of that family. By the way, both my great grandmothers lived to be over one hundred.

The Aunts

The aunts "took a drink". The family was good at "taking a drink!" We loved

The last photo of aunts Betty and Kathleen together

the aunts, but I hated the smell of drink off them when they were on holidays. I hated drink – for what it did at home and I vowed I would never drink!

Betty and Kathleen came home on holidays regularly, together. They were very close, but a row would be building up and every few days, they would fight like dogs – or cats! Not physically of course, but the verbal onslaught was fantastic entertainment for us kids! Auntie Terry lived in California. The youngest of that family, Betty had paid for an education for her and she had done well. Married to a wealthy American dentist, Terry came home – not as often as the other two naturally, but fairly often nevertheless. The rows were even better when those three were home together. Here is my favourite of them all. First of all, you need to know, Betty is very "grand" – wouldn't even use the word "damn". Kathleen, is middle of the road and Terry is typical American "call it like you see it".

It was Saturday afternoon and the crowded house had just finished lunch – sorry, I mean dinner. All, including Daddy, were hung-over and he headed upstairs for bed. It was clear to us that a row was simmering and ready to erupt. Kathleen carried the dinner plates and planked them in the sink. "Oh no, no, no "said Betty, "you must not do that! John is trying to sleep". Terry, coming behind Kathleen, threw a few cups in the sink and said, in her best American drawl: "Ah – fuck John!" Betty is totally horrified, puts her two hands over her ears and screams "Oh my God, if J. B. (her husband) only knew I had to listen to that". Terry: "Fuck J. B. too!" Betty screams again and heads for the door, hands still over ears. Terry calls her back "Hey Betty". Betty takes down the hands, thinking Terry is going to apologise. "One more time", says Terry, "Betty, fuck you too!!" Like I said, we weren't depending on "The Foley Family" or "Dinjo" for our comedy!

I had the happiest days of my childhood in Ballinock, with Little Granny, Auntie Betty and as I said cousin Seán Jefferies. They had great neighbours also. Murrays and Cruises, who kept them in plentiful supply of fresh milk and indeed, frequently, eggs and vegetables. At night they all came in to play cards and tell yarns.

Sean's father sent the Beano and Dandy every week. We learned a lot from those also. We made catapults, slings and bows and arrows. We cut and learned how to make stilts. At first we were only a few inches off the ground, but soon they were six feet high. We could cross rivers and even play football on stilts. Seán and I started a craze and soon all the kids in Collinstown were walking on stilts.

Little Granny died in 1956, when I was twelve. She died at home in Ballinock, after a long illness. In her final few weeks she wouldn't let anybody touch her except my mother – who was incredibly good to her at that time. Granny had pain and bed-sores. Every day Mammy rode the bicycle the four miles to Ballinock to wash, sooth and dress the sores. She did the same for her husband's Mother as she did for her own parents. She would have made a great nurse.

Granny "snorted" snuff and anytime afterwards, when I got that smell I thought of Little Granny and how she loved to spoil me in Ballinock.

Rover

We got Rover and Fechin the same year, when I was seven. Rover was lovely and fluffy and soft, with brown, black and white hair. Fechin was red faced and ugly. I knew that Fechin wasn't found under a head of cabbage. They

A dogs life!
An aging Rover, glad to see me home

couldn't fool me. I knew he came in the big black bag, carried in by the mid-wife; Mrs. Lawlor, the Master's wife. Rover was a Collie pup, given to Daddy by Ganey Briody. Fechin turned out to be just an ordinary pup.
I loved Rover from the moment I saw him and he loved me in return. He actually turned out to be a good cattle dog, in spite of the type of training my father gave him. Daddy used him principally for revenge, when cows or calves had broken into meadow or the garden. Daddy would run, in a temper, whistling for Rover as he ran. Rover loved this, scattering calves in all directions – usually onto the road. It was difficult for the dog to understand my father's frenzied instructions which went something like this, "Go on, Rover, put them out, go on Rover, good dog, behind – behind, lie down, come back – go home ya fuckin' mongrel of a dog" – "Jazus, if ever a man suffered!" Like the rest of us, poor Rover had a tough life. He survived, mange, fits, a broken leg and a meagre diet and lived for thirteen years. If ever a dog suffered!
Rover wasn't allowed in the house and he knew it. Extraordinarily, though if any of us boys were getting a 'belt' in the kitchen, faithful Rover rushed in, bared his teeth, barked and if there was a stick being used, he grabbed it in his mouth.
What games we had out in the rushes in Hynes field. Rover would duck and dive, with the ball in his mouth, while we tried to catch him. When we got tired, he dropped the ball and pretended to be unable to pick it up until one of us got to within a foot of him – and off we went again.
I have a particular memory which tickles me to this day. We were seated at the kitchen table looking out into the yard. Fechin and Rover were three

years old. Fechin was eating a nice fresh slice of bread and jam. His guard and his hand dropped and suddenly the slice of bread was in Rovers' mouth. Fechin was enraged; he dived on Rover, wrestled the dog's mouth open and before Mammy could get out, the tasty morsel was recovered and eaten by its rightful owner; so much for modern sterilisation!

In the horse-stable was a clippers for cutting off horse hair. (Horse hair made a good price). One day, Willie and I deduced that if Judy the mare was regularly shaven, why not Rover? We brought Rover into the shed and set to work. God Almighty, the sight of him when we were finished was awful. He didn't look a bit like Rover. Not even his own mother would have known him.

Daddy wasn't often speechless, but this time his mouth just opened and closed and no sound came out for a couple of minutes. "Martha, Martha", he squalked first and then screeched. Mammy came running out of the house, sensing it was serious this time. "Jazus, will you look at what they done to the hoor of a dog?" Up went the eyes in his head and he wailed: "If ever a man suffered". Not a word of sympathy for poor Rover, who in all fairness was taking it very well. He sat, looking up at Daddy, the stump moving back and forth, where his tail used to wag. Mammy burst out laughing and I knew we had survived this one. "What will the Harris' think of yiz, yiz pair of whelps, when they see what yiz done to the eejit of a dog, that let yiz!" was all he said.

But for a couple of months his "suffering" returned every time he saw Rover. The excited welcomes Rover gave me on my returns home are still fresh in my mind. He didn't bark. He had this special sort of whine of utter delight and pleasure and his eyes could only be described as laughing. He was getting old, had pains and was going blind. I was working in Ballinasloe, and on a visit home I was shocked at how much Rover had failed. His once sparkling brown eyes were dull and coated. He came to meet me, his body stiff with pain, his coat matted and scraggy. But tail still wagging for me. Father and I went for a pint to Bartleys. "I don't want to see Rover again", I said. I didn't and I wouldn't say his name was mentioned by me, or in front of me for years afterwards.

The red faced ugly baby turned out to be and still is, the character of the family. Sharp, witty and great company, Fechin went through life believing that life is for living today and not for worrying about tomorrow.

The Bog

Ours was "the Bog Road" and come summer it was busier than O'Connell Street in Dublin, with hoards of men passing by on their mission of cutting, saving and drawing home the year's supply of fire. It was a family operation, with all ages involved in the tossing, footing, clamping and loading of the turf. The sods were cut by a slane – a two-sided spade like tool. A good slanesman was highly thought of and much sought after. In one flowing movement he cut and threw the sod to a barrowman, who caught and loaded the turf and then wheeled it out and dumped it on the spread-bank, where it was left for a couple of weeks to be firm enough to be "tossed", or spread. It was hard work, especially for the slanesman; we were all barrowmen!

There was a wonderful atmosphere on the bog. Neighbours chatted, fires were lit and tea made. No tea in the world ever tasted as good as the tea made on the bog. A plentiful supply of drinking water and also fresh butter milk was also very popular, for the thirst.

Most of the turf was cut from turf-bank or virgin bog. Then, on cutaway bog, which our bog was, there was the more difficult procedure of cutting out the dams. You cleaned off the top of the bank – maybe 3M2 (three metres square) and cut sods, layer by layer until the slanesman reached marl, a soft white substance, at the bottom of the pit. The ensuing bog-hole was a death-trap, about twenty feet deep, I would say. There was excellent stone turf in our bog – "like coal", my father would brag. As well as saving our own turf, Willie, Seán and I made money from saving other peoples' supply as well. A price would be agreed for tossing or clamping the bank of turf and we got paid on completion. We always got paid, but it was sometimes a hassle to get it. "I have no money on me now, but I'll see yiz after mass etc., etc … and then he'd go to a different mass!

As Willie and I got stronger our work load and responsibility increased. Soon Father didn't have to take time from "The Council" for the turf-cutting, all that was required now was a slanesman, two turf-barrows and Willie and myself. Our slanesman was Jack Murtagh.

Jack was one of those characters who are still regularly talked about. A bachelor, he came from a highly respected family. He had inherited the home place, which was now gone, and Jack lived in a little two room house, in a boreen near us. Mad with brains, an avid reader, totally intolerant, not a child lover, Jack was even more contrary than my father. Jack "took a drink"! He was a periodic alcoholic – could be off it for months and when he drank, he drank.

No problem this summer, Jack was off the beer, the weather was fine and the three of us were on the bog. Jack didn't talk much to us, but I knew we had earned his approval cause after a few days he told Daddy we were "two great men". Each of us had to be back in with the empty barrow, before the other pushed out, so that the slanesman didn't have to stop. The most important thing was to catch every sod and not let it back down on top of the slanesman – especially Jack! We, of course, were in our bare feet. Jack was getting near the bottom of the hole. Water was seeping in, making everything, including the bank where the barrowmen stood, very slippy. It was half-way through the second week and like everything else we did, the competitive edge between Willie and I came into play. We were counting the sods to see who could wheel out the most. We were wheeling out a man's load at twelve or thirteen years of age. Then, disaster struck. I had gone out with twenty two sods. As you caught your last sod – actually when it was on its way up; you always shouted "That'll do" to the slanesman. I pulled my empty barrow in behind Willie and waited; twenty two … twenty three … twenty four … twenty five … twenty six … "That'll do", said Willie, as he

Our own "Hells Angel" –
Da on his motorbike

gave me a triumphant smirk. He lifted the handles, no problem. The wet muck squelched up between his toes. He pushed and nothing happened – couldn't get traction, with the bare feet and then, as if in slow motion, the barrow of turf tilted to one side and the turf returned from whence it had come – down on top of Jack. The only other time I had heard such a roar was from Tormey's bull. "Run", I shouted to Willie. We ran at our best across the bog, towards home. When we made five hundred yards I ventured to look back. Jack was running too – but in the opposite direction, towards Drumcree. Jack needed a drink!

We never let on what happened and were terrified that Jack would tell on us. After a fortnights' drinking and in need of money, he called to the house on a Saturday morning to get paid. We were shaking in our boots. "You didn't give me any notice you were quitting", said Daddy. "I didn't know", said Jack; "It came on me, just like a cow coming abullin'!"

Another quote illustrates the wit of Jack. He was a long time "dry" but a neighbour knew the break-out was imminent when he heard Jack say to the pig he was fattening to kill; "God direct me, whether I'll eat ya or drink ya!"

It's many a cow, calf or bullock we had drowned in the bog. We had no choice but to take the chance and let the cattle graze it. A week would rarely pass but that either ourselves, Fordes, Reillys or Harris's would have some animal in a drain or boghole. We were all experts on how to pull them out; how to put the rope on their head, so as not to break the animal's neck. Also, everybody downed tools for the search and 'pull-out' – so there was always loads of help.

Last Autumn I drove down to the bog, hoping to find a couple of birch trees to dig up for planting around the house. Finding a suitably small one, I drove the spade down and prised the roots up. Then, that magical smell of bog hit me. I was never before aware of it. I closed my eyes and memories flooded back. I was "on the bog" again!

CHAPTER 6

The Show

Every so often, a travelling show would arrive in the village. The anticipation and excitement for us was almost unbearable. The type of "show" varied enormously; from movies, to singing, to drama. I remember every act from the play, "Murder in The Red Barn" and how in the final scene as Maria Martin lay dead on the ground and as the perpetrator, full of remorse, turned to the audience and with overplayed dramatics wailed "What'll I do" ... What'll I do"... and a "bucko" from the back of the marquee shouted up "Tip her while she's hot".

Other "shows" would just show films, usually "Cowboys and Indians" but the one I remember most in this category was a whole series of George Formby films. A lot of these had to do with horse racing and stories about jockeys and the 'nag' who turned into a champion racehorse winner, when the right jockey got him. George played the ukulele and I never hear "I'm standing at a lamppost" ... without thinking of the show.

Other shows were singing, comedy and music – usually an accordion. These shows always had a talent contest and this created huge interest. There was this character in Drumcree, by the name of Tom Grimes. Tom was the greatest spinner of tall yarns in the parish; such as the fact that he had a waistcoat made from the hide of his favourite departed dog and every time he met a dog on the road, the hair stood on the waistcoat. Tom always entered the talent contest and he was such a favourite with the locals, that he usually won. This show would then finish up with a sketch. This beautiful girl had three suitors, all vying for her hand in marriage. In the final showdown all three shot each other and lay dead on the stage. The beautiful woman struts the stage and looks down on each body in turn. "I'm glad you are dead... and I'm glad you are dead.... and I'm glad you are dead.... because now, I can marry my one true love!".... Enter stage left - Tom Grimes! The place erupted. I couldn't catch my breath with the laughing. Tom Grimes was no Clarke Gable. Innocent times!

Daddy at his happiest - with his 'aul Bodhrán

Sometimes the shows would have wild animals, or a dwarf, or "the strongest man in the world".

The best shows were the ones which had "amusements". This was swinging-boats and dodgem cars. The swinging-boats cost two pence each and the cars were six pence. We got very good at the swinging-boats – standing up to pull the rope at our best and driving each other up in the clouds. The show stayed for two weeks and we walked the mile to Drumcree and home in the dark – maybe one bad flash lamp between us. All the neighbours, young and old walked together and our glee at what we had seen carried on the frosty air as we trudged light footed back up the log road. Madge Malone, Mick Forde, Paddy Reilly, Mena Crone, Joe Bartley and others. Mammy went to some of the shows, but Daddy wasn't into that sort of thing.

As always, money was a problem and a worry for the show. Of course we didn't get going – nor did we expect to, every night, but we would get around three shows in, in the week. We worked on both Mammy and Daddy; sometimes together, but more often separately, to get the money. Admittance was usually six pence (a tanner!) for kids and maybe 1/6 for adults.

Our parents knew how much the show meant to us and to their eternal credit, the money was usually found. Once there just wasn't any and Mammy sent up to Big Granny and she gave us the money – Willie, Sean and myself. Another time, the well was totally dry and the prospects looked bleak. Then Willie displayed some of the ingenuity he was to show in later life. Bottles! At the back of the house was a pile of bottles – not just any old bottles, returnable bottles from Briodys shop! Off with us, two bags full. That night, we brought Mammy to the show.

Nobody enjoyed the shows more than Sean. We are all musical (I could rasp a tune on a mouthorgan, accordeon or piano – which was good for the Wren!) but Sean was the only one of us who could sing. He later played the drums in a band and to-day he has one of the finest collections of original records in the country.

Laddie

I learned how to fish, when I was about ten. Daddy had no interest in fishing either. With my Hazel rod and line, I could pluck Perch out of the river Deel all evening. The Deel mared our land, but the fishing was better over around Mooretown Bridge. I also caught the odd roach and pike. A stream flowed past our yard and was the source of endless pleasure in our youth. First catching "pinkeens", racing self-made toy boats, bathing etc. "The Tinkers" taught Willie and I how to catch eels under the bridge. You got a fish-hook, with a two-foot piece of line and a two-foot length of stick. After putting on the worm, you stuck the top of the hook into the end of the stick. Next you "muddied" the water and held the stick, with the worm in the water, at the mouth of a hole, or divide of the stones. Soon the eel's head would appear out. Heart beating, you waited. The slightest movement and he was gone. Sometimes he would look at the worm for several minutes, before making any move. Then, with more than a bit of luck, he took the worm and swallowed the hook. The eel was incredibly difficult to kill. A local character "Small Johnny" Bartley, used tell us that when he tried to fry an eel with a piece of bacon; the eel ate the bacon!!

But it was in hunting rabbits that I had my most enjoyable, carefree outings. I was a bit envious of the lads at school who were expert hunters, had their own "half-greyhounds" for the job and some of them even had ferrets. My envy increased to undiluted jealousy when next door neighbour Paddy Reilly got a hunting dog. We went hunting through the furze and through the bushes, over bogs and over hills. Whilst the rabbits were in a state of constant retreat, it has to be said that their casualty list would have been of no concern to them!

Willie and Seán with Rover

Then one evening a friend of my Father's, Tom Brown, called in and what had he running alongside his bike, only a greyhound? It soon became obvious to all that this twelve year old boy had fallen in love with the hound, who's name was "Laddie". To the eternal credit of my father and to Tom, they did a deal and I got to keep the dog. I couldn't sleep at night with excitement! I was now a serious hunter!

Nothing is simple and, from the start, Laddie caused problems. Rover was beside himself with jealousy and resentment at the new canine acquisition. Rover went on strike and wouldn't do a tap of work for my Father. He spent his time stalking Laddie and as soon as he got a bite at Laddie, Laddie ran the three miles back to Brown's and Daddy would have to go for him.

One Sunday morning, after walking from Killulagh Mass, Willie and I headed off down "the bottoms" with Laddie, full of the joys of the hunt. The place was awash with rabbits and surely it was only a matter of a short while before Laddie has his first kill. Paddy Reilly, on his way home from Collinstown, heard the commotion and came running, calling his dog as he came towards us. Paddy had a brand new navy suit which he would normally have changed out of first, but his fear of Willie and I having any advantage in the rabbit hunt, clouded his otherwise extremely cautious nature.

The two dogs, neck and neck, were closing on a rabbit. All three jumped the river, out into Fordes' bog. Willie, ever the superb athlete, cleared the river without any difficulty. It was in reality a deep, dirty boggy drain and I was relieved when I took the leap and felt the firm bank under my feet, the far side. Paddy, five years older than me, would normally have no problem in jumping the river – but he was so conscious of the new suit. The excited yelping of the dogs, now out of sight, made up his mind. Paddy went back for a long run at the jump. He commenced his run, accelerated and then he again thought of the suit. Paddy tried to "abort" the take-off, but his momentum took him right to the edge, where he hovered for ten seconds, his right leg raised … and then, he simply stepped into the river, up to his neck. There he was, specks of bog-dirt on his nice clean face and a red tie gently floating on top of the water. Now I was laughing so much that I had to lie down. Willie was ditto. Paddy's brother, Joseph had now arrived on the far bank and he helped Paddy out of the river and off they went home. That was the end of the hunt for that day – how could you improve on that!

On a Saturday, Daddy, Willie, Sean and myself were working on the bog. Walking home for the dinner and nearing the house, we could suddenly see Mammy, standing on the middle of the road, waving her apron in the air. Then we recognised the cause of her agitation; coming towards us, down the middle of the road, in definite record-breaking mode was Laddie. Having been bitten by Rover he was "going home" again. Only this time it was different. This time Laddie had had enough, because wedged firmly in his jaws was a cake of bread which mammy had baked and put out on the windowsill to cool. We spread ourselves across the road to block the runaway hound. Laddie, as Michael O'Hehir might describe it, was on a solo run and going straight through. "He pretends to go left, goes right, his opponent goes the wrong way, falls and Laddie has nobody else to beat – it's all over …!

"If ever a man suffered!" I said nothing, but I knew that was the end of Laddie. That evening Rover withdrew his industrial action and went back to work.

Dodgey Pursuits

Things like snaring rabbits, killing a pig, killing turkeys by ringing their necks, cock-fights, skulling cattle, seem terribly cruel now, but all, and worse, seemed perfectly natural in those harsh times.

Patchín Flanagan used snare rabbits for a living – or rather for a drinking. A half crown he charged for a pair of rabbits. Mammy would often buy them, but more often, she wouldn't have the half crown and Patchín didn't do credit! Rabbit stew was great and also we would fry the thighs, which were gorgeous with home-made bread.

Ours was the area for cock-fights – although I never got to one. In later life I could have, but wasn't that bothered. The exact location of the cock-fight would be known to only a handful of men, until the last minute. The hoards of "exhibitors" and gamblers, many from the North, would gather in or around Bartley's Pub, until "the word" was given. I knew many of those involved, including Andy Cosgrove. I was very fond of Andy. He had a piece of land beside our house so I knew him all my life. A great sportsman, he played hurling and was a boxer in his youth. Horses and "anything that gave persecution" – Andy was into it. On this remote piece of land he had a railway wagon, where he fed a fighting cock. A patent was in place whereby the gamecock could get in or out, but it was small enough to prevent the fox getting the cock. Andy told me this one was going to be the best ever – big, mean, loud and mad for fight. One day I walked up the field with him and there six feet from the entrance, was a small pile of feathers – all that remained of the cock. "There yar now" said Andy "the fecker was so good that he came out to take on the fox!"

Another gruesome pastime we enjoyed as kids was killing rats; with the hurleys during a threshing. As the stack of oats was moved, rats scurried in all directions. Every mongrel dog and ourselves formed a ring away from the action and pulled right, left and centre, as the rats fled the scene. Joseph Reilly and a huge big happy dog, belonging to Bill Price, were the slowest two on the pitch. This day, the game was ended when Joseph connected under the jaw of Price's dog and knocked him unconscious.

Something which I find surprising now is that neither Willie, Sean or myself ever "swore" at home, or outside the home. It is surprising because Daddy cursed – on account of his "suffering" and Mammy did also – though not as much, and in a more "refined" sort of way!

The Handball alley in Drumcree was another of our favourite haunts. There wouldn't be a blade of grass on the roadside for a hundred yards, with the crowds on a Sunday waiting to play handball. Generally there was money involved, a "tanner" (six pence) a corner – or something like that. There were some top class handballers in Drumcree. A choc-ice or a mineral in Briodys and then funds permitting, we finished off the day playing Pitch'n'Toss at the crossroads.
I didn't smoke till I was eighteen (bar the odd puff) but Willie was "at it" from the age of ten. One day, he crawled in under the parents' bed, looking for a 'butt'. Next he came running excitedly for me; under the bed was a cache of toys! First thing Mammy knew was she heard a scooter, with iron wheels, being driven on the wooden floor upstairs. We had found Santy's store and we both got a few belts for our trouble!
Regrets are the most futile of exercises and I don't have any regrets to-day. Maybe I have a few "little ones" and one of these is that I never got to play hurling for Rickardstown – our team; the team of "Jobber" McGrath, Phil Reilly, The O'Farrell's, Williams', and Fordes – for me, the best club team the county ever produced. As I wrote in a piece in a County Final Programme a few years ago; "I was always either too young, too bad, or too far away".
We used travel to the matches in Mullingar in 'Harris' lorry – a covered-in calf and pig lorry. Fair play to the Harris', they would carry us all, from us kids to old age pensioners, picked up along the way. The wooden door at the back could only be opened from the outside and Pat would hop out of the cab to open the rear door at every stop along the way. We couldn't see out, so a lot of time was spent guessing where we were. We sat on a thin bed of nice clean straw and some of the old men would have a bag of straw as well. Most of the adults would be smoking, pipes and cigarettes. Can you imagine it? What sort of an insurance quote would you get for that mode of transport today?!! Those were some of the best days out we ever had.
One of the worst bits of news for us boys was to hear, or see that a cow was "Round". Other peoples' cows were Bullin' or a'Bullin', but ours were "Round," because my mother couldn't bring herself to say the other word. Anyway the condition was the same. The cow, or heifer stood there and the other cattle rose on her and the fact of the matter was that this cow would have to be brought to Tormey's Bull. It was our job to walk the cow the mile to Tormeys and rarely was the cow in favour of this arranged union. Breaking

back, running through the bog, breaking out to other cattle, jumping into bog-holes. These and much more were some of the hazards along this obstacle course. Worse, as well as our own, Willie, Sean, myself, or all three of us would be "commissioned" to bring Harris' or Madge Malone's cows to the bull as well. We normally got paid a shilling each, with a ceiling of two shillings, no matter how many of us. If ever a boy suffered!

We lived half way between the village of Drumcree and Johnstown School. How many times I pounded every inch of that two mile stretch of country road. There were so many markers, or place-names along the way. When people walked, or travelled by horse or bicycle the world was bigger and greater use was made of townslands and milestones. Starting from Drumcree, we had first, Miller's Hollow, then "Seagrave's Gate", "Mullacroy Boreen", "Leavy's Road", "Malone's Road"; "Comaskey's Bridge" (our house) "The Railroad"; (a bog boreen and I don't know how it got it's name – perhaps from the continuous trail of carts of turf coming out) Betty "Fay's Crossroads", (Betty Fay was murdered as an informer in the nineteenth century) "Johnstown Boreen"; "Hynes' Shop" and then Johnstown School. Halfway between Leavy's Road and Malone's Road somebody dumped a load of old bicycles, dynamos, farm implements, tins and household rejects. Paddy Reilly saw it first. "There is a sale down the road", he told me. Over the next year we scavenged and put to use just about everything from this unexpected deposit. To Reilly's and ourselves, that spot was forever more known as "The Sale Gap!"

All this on as rural a road as you will find in Ireland.

Cavan Connection

A few years back I was in a Mullingar Office one day when some talk about Cavan came up. "You know, I have a few drops of Cavan blood in me", I said to the lady, with whom I was doing business. "Aye", she replied "and I have always seen that it done you no harm!"

My Great Grandfather came from Mullahoran. Not only that, but he went back there for a wife. Not only that, but he married a Comaskey - albeit with a different spelling of the name. My father never had any contact with the second cousins that he must surely have had around Mullahorn. Twice I have met, by chance, people from that area, by the name of Comaskey. Absolutely lovely people (naturally!) and no doubt distant cousins of my own.

For the above reasons, I always had a soft spot for Cavan on the football field. I felt they were the "tail-end of ourselves" and I had every right to be there cheering them on.
This affiliation was dented in 2003 when Westmeath played Cavan, in a "friendly". Young Finian Newman, due to captain Westmeath under 21s the following week-end, had his jaw made smithereens of, off the ball by a Mullahoran man. Enough said!
My Grandfather "took a drink". He was comparatively well off when my Granny came home from America to marry him. Having lived in New York she expected more from life than boiling pigs pots. "Small Johnny" Bartley told me that while my Grandparents would be gone to the races, the workmen would spend the day fishing in the Deel. Little Granny's expensive tastes, Granda's bad management, ill health and early death meant that the acres of good land were sold and he left an impoverished family.
Granda Comaskey had two brothers – my fathers' uncles. Tom lived at Killulagh. He had the name for being one of the best carpenters of his era. I don't know much else about him, except that word has been passed down that he married an awful bitch of a wife.
The other uncle was Dinny (my grand uncle) and I know lots about him. He was an out and out character, who is still talked about for his wit and devilment. He was also a bit of a rogue – always watching to pull a fast one. Dinny had a farm in Glaxtown, two miles from us. I was about ten when he died, so I did see him a couple of times, as a very old man.
"Dinny took a drink!" Dressed in the proper gear; three quarter jacket with split, and two shiney buttons at the back; leather boots and whip in hand, he rode his horse to Delvin for drink. Therefore, my grand uncle had to live on his wits! He was always in money trouble. One time he went to a solicitor in Mullingar to see how he might get out of paying a debt. The solicitor examined every detail and announced; "There is no way out of this, just go and pay". As Dinny was standing up, the solicitor added; "and my advice is worth ten shillings". "I'm sure it is", replied Dinny "but I'm not going to take it"!
His ability to talk himself out of a fix or in having the last word is legendary. Once he went to confessions to a missionary in Killulagh and told the priest he missed Mass. After several minutes of verbal lashing about not keeping the Sabbath, at the top of his voice, Dinny was finally able to escape the con-

fessional. As he opened the door he saw that the short-isle was full and all his neighbours were looking at him with smugness. Dinny turned back, reopened the door of the confessional-box and in a good loud voice exclaimed; "And another thing, Father; I only meant yourself to know about it!" Dinny had the last word!

He married late in life. A Miss Holloway from Delvin – Lizzie. Holloways had a restaurant in the village and I suppose "Uncle Denis", (as proper speaking Auntie Betty used call him,) got a bit of an appetite after a few drinks.

My Aunts had more money than my father so Dinny dangled the leaving of the farm a bit more to them. They brought him baby Powers, cases of stout, tobacco and bit of furniture. When he died he left the farm to a man whom himself and Lizzie had fostered as a young boy. Daddy was very bitter, we being the only Comaskeys left. As far as I am concerned, Dinny was entitled to do whatever he wanted with what was his and besides, there was such a debt on it that it wasn't much good to anyone.

News

How simple the way of life was in those days. There seemed to be very little national headlines and anything of interest was talked about by the ordinary people when they met. Ruby Murray sang "Oh to be in Dunaree". We had an outbreak of national pride when one of our own, Grace Kelly, married her Prince and became an Irish Princess! If a murder took place, as far away as Cork or Kerry, everybody talked about it and followed the investigation with ongoing interest – murder being such an infrequent occurrence.

I remember a cargo ship "The Flying Enterprise" listing for several days, before it went down, as the country listened to every news bulletin. The Captain stayed with the ship as it continued to list and he was rescued just before she sank. It's funny that I remember a cartoon in "Dublin Opinion" showing the captain, after coming ashore and walking with a tilt of about forty five degrees. The importance of the postman cannot be overstated at that time. Not only did he bring letters with news of loved ones in England, America or Canada but he carried the local news from house to house that such'n'such a person "got a turn". How they are to-day. Somebody else is home from England; news of births, marriages and deaths.

Even more welcome were the parcels from America or England. Huge excitement when we got a parcel, but I always hated wearing any of the clothes to school or Mass. They had "parcel" written all over them from a mile away and we got teased – the same way we teased the others when it was their turn. When I was fourteen Auntie Betty sent me a new jacket and trousers from England for my birthday. The trousers was a "drain-pipe". Can you imagine? I was Drumcree's first Teddy-Boy!

The first postman I remember was Jack Daly. A really nice man he did the rounds for donkeys years until one day he died by the side of the road, at the church in Drumcree. The relief postman was Mick Ivory. Mick took a drink! Jack was replaced by Joe Masterson – another harmless, easy-going, most obliging man.

We knew when the postman was approaching because Rover would get into serious barking. I heard a theory recently that the reason dogs don't like postmen is, because they see the postman come to the door, time after time, without ever getting into the house, and therefore the dog sets out to clear him off as quickly as possible.

Our postman rarely had to come to the door. Forewarned by Rover, we watched and waited. Most often, the feeling of hope was followed by a sinking feeling, as "the post" sailed by on his bike. We did have our good days. I used write to J. Ashton Freeman who did a nature programme on Radio Eireann. On radio, or in magazines, I entered every children's competition that came up. "Irelands Own" and "The Farmers Journal" published essays that I wrote. Even at that time I was always looking for something different. Through "Irelands Own" I contacted a pen-pal and we exchanged letters for two or three years. I can still remember his name and address. Tom Bolger, Kilmurray Mid, Arklow, Co. Wicklow. So Tom, if you are out there, you owe me a letter for nearly fifty years!

I soaked in news and information. I read history books from cover to cover and knew the chapter before we came to it at school. I learned the capital city of every country in the world and when Joe Linnane on Radio Eireann's "Question Time" asked a question of an adult which they didn't know, I was delighted when I could answer. Even Daddy was impressed with this! I read everything I got my hands on; "The Far East", "The Messenger" "The Dandy", "The Beano", "The Irish Catholic", Election Literature, but my greatest gem of all was when I was allowed to put my name down for the new GAA paper; "The Gaelic Weekly". Now, not only could I read about all my Gods, but I had pictures of them as well. Many of these great men didn't look right to me. In my minds eye I had created a picture of how they looked and the real photo didn't look like that at all. I didn't care, - now I felt I knew the players. "The Irish Press" serialised the "Nicky Rackard Story" and Bridgie Bartley brought me the paper every day. GAA was my greatest love. In "Gaelic Weekly" I read about a man from Mooncoin and how he finally won that illusive medal. Time was almost up, the aged hurler was on his knees when he got the ball. With the last puck of the match and still on his knees the hero sent the ball over the bar. I promptly got my hurl and ball and headed out to "the field fer nint the door" to try it. On my knees, I threw up the ball and swung. I missed the ball but managed to hit myself on the head. No, if I ever found myself in that situation, I'd stand up first!

Round our area there was a tradition of lads going to work in Canada and when I was going to school, I knew lots who were in Canada. One of the newspapers covering our area was called "The Midland Chronicle", as far as I can remember.

Anyway, my families' only interest in that paper was when Paddy Fagan from Brownstown and later successful Mullingar businessman, started writing pieces for the paper from the Northern wilds of Canada. Paddy Gill and other locals were there and Fagan wrote in great detail about how they worked and how they survived. I remember he wrote once about getting a consignment of hurleys sent out and the disappointment at how easily they broke on account of the freezing temperature. I was fascinated by the tales I read and heard. I had visions that someday I might try this myself, but I wondered would I be able for it. Deep down I felt insecure and unsure of myself.

CHAPTER 7

Next!

Any digression at school was most welcome – bar one, the dentist. The school doctor would come from time to time and examine us. What he was looking for was T.B., which was still killing some of our neighbours. An educational film on tips to avoid T.B., and also one on dental care also came to the school. We didn't care what it was about. "The Pictures" were coming! From one of these picture showings, Master Lawlor, carried a scar on his forehead – something else I later slagged him for over a drink or two. The Master got up on top of the porch to put a blind over the high window and fell in the process. As far as I can remember two big boys, Ralph Kelleghan and someone else, broke his fall on the way down.

Of course we also had the inspector and the catechist, as well as the priest examining us. We were always well prepared and there never was a problem with any examination.

Then occasionally a live entertainment show would come. What excitement! They would be part of one of these travelling shows playing in Delvin, or sometimes we got a Punch'n'Judy Show. Four pence each we had to pay and our parents always made sure we had the money. A few unfortunates wouldn't have the money, but Master Lawlor discreetly ensured that everyone got to see the show.

I suffered dreadfully with toothaches as a young fellow. I had big teeth and when a cavity occurred the nerve stripped and the pain was excruciating. One day at ten to three, the Master asked me to repeat something he had just told me at the same time the tooth just lifted me out of it and I couldn't speak. Lawlor though I just wasn't paying attention, called me up and gave me four slaps. I cried all week-end with the tooth-ache. The following Tuesday evening, Daddy hopped me on the back of his motorbike and brought me down to Daly's Shop in Collinstown. Barney was a dentist and he pulled out the offending tooth. The cost should have been thirty shillings, but he did it for fifteen – still a lot of money. Daddy had a few pints in 'Bertie Rowe's' from the fifteen shilling discount! The joy of the offending tooth being gone was as good as Christmas.

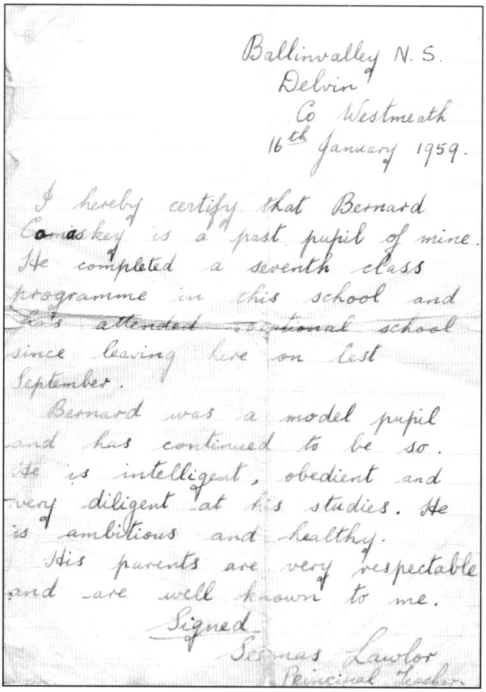
Ballinvalley N.S.
Delvin
Co Westmeath
16th January 1959.

I hereby certify that Bernard Comaskey is a past pupil of mine. He completed a seventh class programme in this school and has attended vocational school since leaving here on last September.

Bernard was a model pupil and has continued to be so. He is intelligent, obedient and very diligent at his studies. He is ambitious and healthy.

His parents are very respectable and are well known to me.

Signed
Seamus Lawlor
Principal Teacher.

School reference

Jackie Bray was the school dentist. He was a local man from Killadoran and all our parents were proud of this fact. His first visit to the school was easy, you just opened your mouth, Mr. Bray looked in, talked to his assistant and she wrote on a card. The return the following week was the problem. I never had to get a tooth out, but getting fillings, which I got loads of, was worse.

As the kids got their teeth pulled, they came out The Big Room door, to the school yard. Here it was like a skulling of cattle in Harris' – blood everywhere. A bucket of water would have been brought down from Dunne's pump. In the bucket was one chipped, white enamel mug and everyone rinsed their mouth from the same bucket, from the same mug. That was also how we got a drink every day during playtime.

Back to the "filling", Jesus, I can still feel the drill. At least the extractions had an anaesthetic, fillings didn't. Then the drill would hit a nerve, Jesus again! I got such a doing that after I left school I almost let every tooth in my head rot and only dealt with the problem as pain dictated. Once in England, I paid to be put to sleep to have one tooth pulled. Much later, I went to a dentist, Mr. Kelly, In Mullingar and told him I wanted to be put to sleep and have all my teeth extracted. However, he talked me into allowing him to save the teeth.

The Master had a wry sense of humour and I could get to him. We slagged him whenever Kerry was beaten and he took it in the perfect spirit. There was a line which most of us knew not to cross. Hurling in the playground one day, Jimmy pulled "rough" and hit the Master on the knee. The Master said nothing only turned him head over heels with a box and the game never stopped – and it made my day. "The kind of teacher I would like", was the subject given to us for a composition one day in fifth class. I watched The Master correcting the copies and I knew when he had come to mine. When he was laughing he used rub the tip of his nose with the palm of his hand. Without "crossing the line" I had written all the opposites of what he was and finished up with; "It is very important to have a teacher without a Kerry accent". I remember asking Lily Murtagh, who was a couple of classes ahead of me, how to spell "accent". She told me without hesitation. Weren't children much better at the three R's in those days?

In fourth and fifth classes we would sit doing sums, compositions etc., while the big ones of sixth and seventh stood around the wall reading and spelling, or history. I rushed to get finished my stuff, so that I could listen and I was enthralled. I was fascinated by history and Lawlor gave us a good old fashioned green version of it. I was ready to go fight for Ireland. The stories in both the Irish and English reading books were wonderful also. My all time favourite, which I still remember was "Jimín Mhaire Thadhg", from the Irish. The antics of Jimín agus Michaelín Eoin captured my imagination and at the end, when Jimín went off to be a priest; well, that is what I would do too! Two years later, when it came to my turn to do the book, I would remember every detail of it – including the questions The Master would ask.

Adventure stories gripped me; "Paul Revere's Midnight Ride! I leaned my back against the wall as I read of Paul Revere, in 1775 borrowing a horse and riding to warn Samuel Adams that the British were coming, stopping along the way, to rise up the people. I wonder do any of my class-mates remember doing that lesson? Who would have believed that one day I would stand at Paul Revere's grave in Boston, close my eyes and get the scent of old second-hand school-books in Johnstown school.

When writing a composition, we put the date first, at the top of the page. One day, sitting beside Dessie Briody he nudged me and said look "it's all fives to-day": 5-5-55. That really stuck in my memory. I remembered it on 6-6-66, 7-7-77, 8-8-88 and on the 9-9-99, I wrote Dessie a note, stating that it was now my turn to draw his attention to this unique date.

Dessie was the only one I remember to have suffered a serious injury in the playground. When any of us got the odd cut from the belt of a hurl, The Master hopped the injured boy into his car and took him to his house in Delvin. Mrs Lawlor was a nurse – a kind and gentle lady, who dressed and inspected the cut. When Dessie went down, we knew it was different. Eddie Drumm, a big lad, with not a bad drop in his body, ran into Dessie at full speed and broke his leg, when they fell.

Goodbye Johnstown

The day we got the results of the Primary Cert., as soon as my father landed into the yard with the horse and cart, Mammy went out to talk to him. He came in, looked at me and said "Yer one great gosson", putting his hand in his pocket and taking out a few coins. Nothing ever came out of his pocket without a good layer of cigarette tobacco, from putting "butts" back in his trousers pocket. When he was out of cigarettes, this mix of tobacco, fluff and dirt was rolled in newspaper and smoked with relish. From this pile, he extracted a shilling and handed it to me.

Michael O'Donnell, a real 'Dub' and my uncle through being married to my Aunt Marie, had a good job in Guinness and my Mother approached him and asked what would be my chances of getting into Guinness; in a year or two. Michael said "no problem", if I could pass the exam. He sent down that year's exam papers. I was ok with them, except for algebra and geometry. I showed the papers to The Master and he offered to take me on my own for these subjects. He got me books and set about doing those extra lessons with me.

I was thirteen and the exam would be next year. In Guinness there was night school, where you could further your education.
Then the unexpected happened. A vacancy occurred for principal in Ballinvally, the Delvin school and Master Lawlor applied to transfer. This was totally unexpected. Fr. Smith, the PP was totally against Lawlor moving, but move he did. He would take up his new position after the Christmas holidays.
Because I was studying for the Guinness exam, my Mother went and asked The Master if I could move to Delvin also. He willingly agreed, provided she could get the permission of Fr. Smith. Permission was grudgingly agreed.
The day of the Christmas Holidays 1957 was my last day in Johnstown school. It seemed such a long time ago that Mammy had brought me that first day. I looked around at the faces of the boys and girls who were my friends and whom I would miss. The Master had a bad day also. He never really wanted to leave Johnstown. He should not have gone.
Jimmy taunted me about the eejit I was to be going, and riding a bad bike four miles to be mixing with "The Spike" (slang name for a housing estate in Delvin). I didn't care what he said because after to-day, there would be no more Jimmy.
Soon afterwards, Jimmy went to a few dances, qualified as a daddy and went to England. Now though, there was nobody to carry news like that to Johnstown school!
I already had a friend in Ballinvalley, Anthony Burke. When Johnstown played Ballinavalley in the previous year's hurling championship we played on each other. We both played well but as we won easily, we were chatting even before the game was over. Every second Sunday, Anthony would come to our house, or I would visit Burkes over in Moyloroe. Mrs Burke would stuff me until I could eat no more. I loved going over there.
On my first day in Ballinvalley Anthony had told me to bring my hurl. The lads wasted no time in asking the new Master if he would train the team and of course he agreed.
I was to spend only six months at school in Ballinvalley, but I learned a lot about life and how things work in those six months.
The entrance exam was scheduled for March. I had studied well. The Master tested me on another set of papers and I satisfied him. I got on the Granard bus at Drumcree, for Dublin. I was met there, not by any of the O'Donnells,

but by Auntie Kathleen. This was on a Friday and I was to present myself at St. James' Gate next morning at 11.00am. Aunt Kathleen had me there in lots of time. There was a queue a block long and we were eventually ushered into a huge hall. Then some guy stood up an announced that only sons or daughters of employees would be allowed do the exam.

Auntie Kathleen took me back to her flat in Capel Street. I met people from home. Nanny Harris, The Hynes', The Murrays and others. They all gave me money. I went out and bought a necklace for my mother and a shaving set for my Father. Kathleen put me back on the bus on Sunday, loaded with loads of goodies and home I came again.

We were all very nationalistic at school – especially Anthony Burke and myself. The IRA border campaign was in full flight. Sean South and Fergal O'Hanlon were both shot dead and Anthony and I decided enough was enough! We formed a "Junior IRA". First just the two of us and then we "recruited". We wrote posters and put them up everywhere, urging people to join the IRA. We held secret meetings in a shed at Mooretown. We recruited too many. I can fully appreciate and identify with the present day fear of a split in the IRA because the split came in my IRA within two months of its inception and the entire organisation disintegrated! I grew out of my militant stance, but as far as I know, Anthony didn't. I hope it wasn't my fault, Anthony!

The hurling was going great. We played Johnstown in a challenge and beat them. Willie was playing against us. One of our lads pulled across his legs and when he "smirked" I hit my own man a shoulder in the chest and The Master had to intervene.

Michael O'Donnell made no contact after the Guinness exam debacle and my parents were livid – as well as Aunts Betty and Kathleen. Then Betty decided that I should be a school-teacher "or something" and she would pay for my education. After discussions with Master Lawlor it was settled that the best thing would be for me to go as a boarder to St. Finian's College, Mullingar.

In the meantime, a priest came to the school looking for vocations to the priesthood. Burke and I were the only two in seventh class, so he took special interest in both of us and it finished with him taking down our names and details. The following year, Anthony headed off to be a priest and stayed four years, I think.

Ballinvalley, Devlin, Primary Schools Hurling Champions for 1958
I am second from right, at back

One day that summer a priest from the order called at home to interview me. I was undecided, but would have gone. After talking, to me in the parlour, he asked to speak to Mammy alone. I never heard another word and years later I found out from my Mother why. The priest asked if there was any insanity in the family. Mammy, honest to a fault before a man of the cloth, trawled him through generations of family madness!

The holy man picked up his hat, excused himself and left hurriedly. We were far too mad to have a priest in the family! Mind you, this didn't prevent Sean from entering the religious, where he spent a few years and which had an awful bad effect on him. I was due to sit the entrance exam for St. Finians, we were in the semi-final of the Comortas na mBun Scoil hurling championship and I had a job for the summer. It was a lovely fine summer and all was well with the world. The Russians had launched "Sputnick" and you might say, everything was looking up!

I got a lift into Mullingar to do the Finians exam with Al and Mrs Sherwin, as Joe was doing the exam also. The exam was easy. There were fellows there who had failed the Primary Cert., and I had got the highest marks in the school for mine and then done two years more.

We beat Ballycomoyle by three points in Collinstown, in the hurling semi-final. I had scored in every match, which was my target. The final was set for early July in Cusack Park and our opponents would be Kilbeggan. I couldn't think about anything else and the excitement was unbearable. The final was played on a Tuesday evening. We were working on the bog. I quit early; when I got to the house I knew something was wrong with my Mother. She handed me a plain postcard, with the St. Finians name and crest at the top. "We regret that we are unable to offer your son a place at the college etc., etc…! Mammy just whispered; "It's not what you know, it's who you know".
She told me to tell Master Lawlor before the game. I hated her for that, because I wanted to leave it until afterwards, but I think she hoped The Master would know somebody in Cusack Park who would fix it.
We got togged out in our blue and white striped jerseys. The Master said a few words, wished us good luck and told us for "every man to do his best". We ran from the dressing room, except me. "Please Sir, I failed the exam for St. Finians". Master Lawlor came over and put his arm around my shoulders. "You don't worry about that now, you just go out there on that pitch and show everyone what you can do". I found out years later that next day he went in and went ballistic in St. Finians. He told me it was the worst row he ever had – so much so, that when it came to his son Eamon's turn, he was afraid he would be rejected also.
I ran onto the pitch and I played the best game of hurling I ever played in my life. I got the ball from the throw-in and sent it over the bar. We were easy winners and I finished up with a tally of 3-2. We were county champions! A sign of the times was that all that team, except Lorcan Sherwin, emigrated. A few of us did come back.
I couldn't wait for the "Westmeath Examiner" to come out and when it did I was devastated. In all of the previous reports I would have got a "mention". In the report on the final, my name was spelled totally incorrectly in the line-out and I wasn't even mentioned, even as a scorer. I was told afterwards that a man who wasn't at the game, wrote the match report. Since that match report a long time ago, I cannot take anybody spelling my name wrong. If so many business's only knew how often their otherwise attractive deals found its way into the waste-paper basket, or somebody with a good C.V., looking for a job, got no acknowledgement, simply for spelling Comaskey incorrectly.

I got my medal. A solid silver medal, with the Cumann Luth Cleas Gael crest to the front and engraved on the back. It came in a little blue box wrapped in cotton wool. It was to be the only hurling medal I would ever win.
I lost it in Ballinasloe.

The 'Tech'

Was it the Jesuits who said; "Give me the boy till he's seven and I'll give you the man?" Well, Master Lawlor had me until I was twice that age and I owe an enormous debt to him. I got very little additional formal education and I was "no eejit" when I left him.
Things went down hill for "The Master" after he left Johnstown. He never had the same interest in Ballinvalley. He had personal problems and separated from his family. He took a drink! I still have the tattered reference he wrote for me. When he died it was his wish to be buried in Killulagh. I wrote an "appreciation" in the "Westmeath Examiner" which concluded with these words. "The Master has paid the pupils of Johnstown the supreme compliment of choosing to have his last resting place amongst us. Welcome back, Sir. Rath De ar a anam".
My Mother and I were on the horns of a dilemma. What would I do next? I wasn't good enough for St. Finians and too mad to be a priest. Master Lawlor called to the house and said he had a college to take me. We decided against it. I had lost interest and it's probably just as well because, with the best will in the world, paying the fees would have been a big drain on Auntie Betty and put an even greater strain on my parents.
The Vocational School in Castlepollard, or "The Tech" as it was commonly known, was the answer. It was nine miles from my house and like everyone else around, we cycled to Castlepollard. There was an entrance exam and a ten pound a year scholarship for whoever got the highest marks.
I got the scholarship. When the first five pounds cheque came, my father changed it in Fays in Collinstown. I agreed that my parents would keep four pounds. With my one pound I bought a hurling ball for eleven shillings in Castlepollard and I squandered the rest of it on my brothers and on myself.
Mr. O'Loughlin was the Principal. I didn't like him. On the same day I started in The Tech, a young teacher had his first day there also. He was Kevin O'Reilly from Kerry. Mr. O'Reilly was a nice decent man, good to us brats and good for us as well. Starting off, he didn't have a natural discipline and

we repaid him by "acting up". After a year or so he ceased being a soft touch. Master O'Reilly taught us to do Irish dancing and play music. He coached us at basket-ball and essentially did his level best for us. He used read my English compositions sometimes for the class and he actually got a story I wrote published in some magazine.

Michael Curran taught woodwork and mechanical drawing. I was useless at woodwork so we were off on the wrong foot. Mr. Curran reminded me of my Father, same size, same temper! Mr. O'Loughlin taught maths and Rural Science.

I was missing an awful lot of time from school and with any new subjects I was being left behind. My mother hadn't been well and a lot of stuff was falling to me.

The following January, Anthony was born. We were all delighted with the new baby. I wrote to tell all the Aunts the good news and right on queue, the few bob and parcel presents arrived.

Daddy fell off the motor-bike twice when Anthony was born – partly as a result of winter road conditions and partly due to celebrating with the lads. He got numerous falls and how he wasn't killed is a miracle.

He used do "hackney" for his drinking buddies. The Mulvannys used have a new addition to the family every year and Billy Mulvanny would "hire" my father to take him in to see Mrs. Mulvanny and the new baby in Mullingar. Mick Nolan was another regular "Fare". One night, on the way home, late at night, they hit a cow at Cloughan. They just didn't hit a cow, when my father told it; he brought the cow a hundred yards on the handlebars of the bike! Somebody brought them both (not the cow) to Doctor Cox's house in Delvin. Nolan banged the door and eventually the Doctor stuck his head out the upstairs window. "It's four o'clock in the morning", he shouted down. "We had to wait until we fell"! came the reply.

I should mention another house I visited regularly from my earliest days in Johnstown and into adulthood. That was O'Farrells in Rickardstown. Finbarr and I started school together. Finbarr was very well off being by far the youngest of a family who were doing well. He and I never once had an argument.

The O'Farrells are some of my favourite ever people. Tom, the Father, was a quiet gentle, popular hard-working man. The Mother "Granny Farrell" came from Clare when she was nineteen and never lost her Clare accent. She was one of the well known McMahon family; patriots, Irish scholars, musicians and now famous hurlers through Seanie, Diarmuid and Alan Markam. Years ago, Seanie McMahon played on Francis O'Farrell and only at the end of the game did they realise they were playing on cousins. Previously, the older generation of O'Farrells had excelled in hurling for Rickardstown and for Westmeath.

I was very fond of old Granny O'Farrell and she of me. Little did I think that she was to be the Granny of my future wife.

In September of 1959. Willie started The Tech also. Bicycle racing was now one of our challenges and he could beat me at that as well. I was only going through the motions at school. Sometimes I wouldn't even have the school books. Mr. O'Loughlin called up to our house to see what the problem was. I don't know if he got any answers, but maybe he didn't have to ask the questions. Things were rough at home and looking back now I have no doubt but that my mother was suffering from depression - post natal or otherwise. This was a bad time for both my parents and for all of us boys.

One day Willie suddenly said to me "I'm going to go out to work". How it happened was that Billy Gilroy, a grocer in Delvin asked Pat Fox, the fruit and veg man, if he knew of any honest, hard working, mannerly young fellow to "serve his time". Pat replied; "If you could get one of the young Comaskeys, you won't do any better". Willie was home when Mr. Gilroy called, Mammy felt guilty about it, but agreed. For one pound a week, the first Comaskey was going out in the world. He was exactly fourteen.

The die was cast for me. It was mighty relief in fact. No way would I stay in school now. I told Mr. O'Loughlin the Headmaster I was leaving, to work in a pub. He tried to talk me out of it. "Those type of jobs will always be there. If you are to have any chance of making anything of yourself you have to stay here another year". I stayed another day – and whether I "made anything out of myself" or not – my money is on me!

A well known pub in Delvin had just changed hands and I persuaded my Mother to go and see the new owner and ask if he would take me on.

R.E. – or better known as Bertie Merlehan had purchased the pub from well known bookie and sportsman, Harry Barry. Harry was an excellent hurler and was on the great three in a row winning Delvin team of the early fifties. A guy by the name of Butler from Tipperary was also on that team and how he came to be playing for Delvin was when Harry put an advertisement for a barman in The Irish Press. It read "Barman Wanted; Good pay and conditions: Only good hurler need apply". Before Harry Barry, the pub was owned by Joe Clyne, who also had a butcher shop there. He would be some far out relation on my Mothers side. Joe featured heavily in the aftermath of the publication of Brinsly McNamaras; "Valley of the Squinting Windows", and the public burning of the book in Delvin. Joe was reading the book and by reliable accounts was getting a great kick out of recognising his neighbours, until he came upon a reference to himself. "The greasy butcher with his barren wife". Joe Coyne was the main instigator in the burning and the subsequent boycott of Ballinvalley school, where Brinsly McNamara's father, Master Weldon, taught.

So, the pub had a history. Harry Barry spent loads of money on it and it had a good name and decent clientele. It wasn't everybody who would be taken on to "serve their time" a short time before then you would have to pay a fee and work for nothing. A shop-boy had to come from a "respectable" family. I wasn't "good enough" for St. Finians, too mad to be a priest; so it came as some relief to me to establish that Willie and I were both respectable enough to work in Delvin shops!

Mr. Merlehan agreed to take me on to "serve my time". My Mother, proud to the last, told him that the training was much more important than money. Talk about "bidding against yourself"! He said he would give me ten shillings a week and pay for my dinner in Fays.

I was in business! I started work in 29th December 1959, at fifteen years and three months. From that day to this, I never drew a days unemployment benefit, or social welfare of any description and I never "fiddled anyone". My parents instilled in me a code of honesty, hard work and the certain belief that I would be successful and "get on". My brothers inherited this as well. Aunts Betty and Kathleen were proud women who always helped and encouraged us but above all, Mother had a vision and she was my great motivator.

From my weekly wage I gave five shillings at home and had five to spend on myself.

The following summer Sean went to Clara, to become, he thought, a Christian Brother.

CHAPTER 8

Bar Apprentice

I was nervous on my first day as a bar apprentice – terrified that I might not measure up and be sent home. I cycled the three miles back and forth, for the first few months. My Boss, Mr. Merlehan, knew nothing of the running of a bar – Mr. Merlehan knew nothing about the running of anything. The manager was a girl from Clonard called Frances Campbell. My Mother had warned me to call her Miss Campbell, but after a while, I called her Francie, like everybody else. For the year we worked together, Francie never once spoke a cross word to me and we got on great. I was eager and willing to learn the trade and in comparison to working in Mackens, the whole thing was a "doddle". The majority of the customers were good humoured and kind towards me. As well as the pub, we had petrol pumps outside, so I spent a fair bit of time, filling petrol, pumping tyres and dipping for oil. We also took in bets for a well known bookie – illegal – but I don't expect anybody to be prosecuted now. With this going on, it was only natural that I would develop an interest in horses. One day I was looking down a big field of runners in England, when I spotted this horse called "Bernie". No form – no chance!? "Couldn't be a bad one" I announced to the local experts. No one listened. I put a shilling each way on him and he won at fifty to one. I gave one pound to my Mother and bought myself a pair of shoes.

Behind the bar in Delvin, with Michael Carroll, March 1961

I had all the yard work to do; sorting bottles, keeping the stores tidy and generally keeping shape on the place. This was made more difficult and complicated by the fact that for a time, Harry Barry continued to use the dog kennels in the yard for his greyhounds.

There was a bad smell around, with the dogs and particularly as the result of the animal carcases which were brought in from farms daily and cut up in the "meat-house", for feeding to the hounds. In this same yard, we had a bottling store, where we bottled our own stout – as did most pubs at that time. First, the porter bottles had to be washed and right from the start, this was my job. Cold water, vertical brushes, on which I ran two bottles at a time up and down, before stacking upside down in large crates to dry. My hands would be numb with the cold, especially in winter time. All this work was done at speed.

Albie Leonard was the bottler, on a part time basis. They say "there is a trick in every trade" and bottling stout was no exception. The wooden barrel of Guinness was tapped and fed into a trough type contraption. The stout was totally black and flat at this stage. Out of the trough were four syphons. You had to suck on each of these siphons at the start to get the flow coming. As a pioneer and somebody who was never going to drink, I was ultra careful to spit out any stout from sucking the air from the syphon, to start the flow. Mr. Merlehan told me that part of my job was to "develop a taste" for good stout, even though I told him I was a Pioneer. I told my Mother and she said I would have to leave there if he tried to make me drink. Sitting on an up-turned beer case, you positioned the crate of upside down clean bottles on your left, with an empty crate on the right hand side. There was a valve on the syphon which the weight of the bottle opened and the stout flowed into the bottle. Four bottles filling, but you got a rhythm going, two full just as you got the next two empty bottles started. We always timed ourselves to see how long it would take to bottle a barrel. Outrageous claims would be made by various publicans and barmen – but I'd say a lot of these records were wind assisted!

Next came the "corking" of the bottles, one at a time. You pressed down on the handle of a "corker", which drove the cork into the neck of the bottle. This was dangerous enough, as sometimes a bottle would shatter and it's many a nasty cut I got on my left hand as a result. Soon the corker was replaced by the "capper" - similar principal, but not as many bottles exploded. This bottled stout then had to be left for about three weeks to mature and hopefully, there would be a "fine head" on the glass when poured.

Mr. Merlehan never once praised me for anything I did, but I was so proud to be there that I never thought about it much. I was so anxious to please, though. Soon I was nearly as good as Albie at the bottling. Mr. Merlehan asked me could I bottle on my own, "I can", I said. He never even answered but turned to Frances and told her to tell Albie we didn't need him anymore. After a few months Barry's dogs were moved to the new kennels at Martinstown and I missed the lads who worked with them. Michael Curran, Donal Davis and Nicky Grassick. There was always banter and devilment going on. I was no match for Grassick, with his merciless Dublin wit.

I got on so well with most of the customers and I knew that "brought me out of myself" a bit. The first few months I mostly worked days and cycled home afterwards. Then, one day, the Boss came to me and informed me of a new plan. There were several rooms and a kitchen over the bar, which were not being used. Mr. Merlahan said he was going to take in lodgers, for B&B. These were builders who were working at St. Mary's Convent, Southhill, just outside the town. The arrangement was that I would stay there, have my own little room, get the breakfast ready for six men every morning, Monday to Saturday. I would have a half day Thursday and every Sunday off. But the really good news was that my wages would go up from ten shillings to one pound, ten shillings, a week. Willie was still on a pound a week – the correct order of things had been restored!

There were men there from Galway, Longford and Cavan and they weren't great breakfast men – liquid suppers and all that jazz! They were easy on me and any morning I didn't get up, they got their own and never said a word. The great thing about having Sundays off was that I could go to matches – and I had money for the mineral or ice-cream. One day Joe Bray came into the bar and asked me would I play minor for Delvin. The previous year I had played for Collinstown – but it was no wonder if nobody noticed! Of course I would play for Delvin. We played Castlepollard and were beaten, but I had a lucky game and played o.k. I played with the seniors before I was 16. In the 2004 Delvin Parish Magazine a photo of a team with the caption; "Delvin Hurlers early 1960's appeared and I was in it. I had never previously seen the photo, but I think it was taken before a tournament final, which we lost in 1960 or early 1961.

Moving On

My Boss 'Bertie' Merlehan, came from what one might call "Catholic Gentry" and had had all the privileges which went with that standing. In other, or in any words, he was an important man. From the time he inherited the family estate, he was on the way down. He was, you might say, on the crest of a slump. The selling of the land and the buying of the pub, would have been one of his final "kicks". His household staff still called him "Master Bertie" though. A middle-aged bachelor, "he took a drink"! At best, I was uneasy around him and a bit scared when he came back at night, drunk. He was popular with some, who thought it was great to be drinking with him, but he was not nice to me. When my Granny died, he insisted that I come in to work immediately after the burial. When I was leaving after a year and a half, without having had a day's holidays, he gave me a pound "for luck!" instead of the holiday pay I was due. Whilst he was odd and erratic and I was afraid of him, it is important that I state that he never once laid a hand on me.

After a year Frances Campbell could take it no longer and left. My luck held when she was replaced by Michael Carroll, from Ballinock – whom I had known all my life. Michael had served his time in Dublin and knew his stuff at nineteen years of age. We got on great and I looked up to him. To add to the regard I had for him, he was playing hurling for Rickardstown. I actually played against him when Delvin played Rickardstown in a challenge. I could not have been good enough at that stage, to make the Rickardstown team. I was happy to be playing for Delvin, but nothing could replace Rickardstown as my team. Had I hung around with Rickardstown, I would have got a run before too long. Mind you, the club had a responsible attitude in minding young players and not playing them too early. This cost them the services of Petey Loughlin when, because he wasn't picked to play, he went and declared for Clonkill, resulting in a lot of bitterness.

Willie played for Rickardstown. At the age of seventeen, he played centrefield, alongside the great Jobber McGrath. One Sunday, during a match in Mullingar, Paddy Flanagan, County Secretary and great Westmeath Gael, called aside Peter Murtagh, a Rickardstown Selector. "Who is the lad playing at centrefield?" "Young Billy Comaskey, a local lad", replied Peter. "Lookit, this is off the record", said Paddy, "I just want to know who he is"? "Willie was playing so well that Paddy Flanagan, thought he was a "dark horse", brought in from outside the county. Soon he was to become just a statistic, another good hurler, slushed down the dark funnels of emigration, never to 'hurl' again. In 1981 Willie won the Thompson Open Racquet Ball tournament and he also held the golf course record for a time.

One Sunday night, cycling home with a few lads, from the pictures in Castlepollard, I went to my first dance, in Collinstown, without the permission of either parent. I thought there would be war, when I told them, but there wasn't much fuss at all. I really was flapping my wings now.

As far as I was concerned, Michael was an expert on the ways of life, he being nineteen and having worked in Dublin. I was beginning to take notice of girls, but extremely shy in that department. A lot of my same-age-buddies, would have "gone with" a girl, so the pressure really was on me. I didn't want to appear too ignorant, so I talked the talk and listened to Michael. I felt I could go through with it until I suffered a set-back one night. Michael explained that some women would French-kiss and he explained how it worked. I was so disgusted that now, as well as never going to drink, I might now never kiss a girl! However, all the lads were "goin' wud women", so I had to be seen to have me a girl.Though coming and going and sending message I got a date on a Sunday night with Betty. Betty was, and is, a grand girl – long since happily married.

On a cold frosty, night, Betty and I walked out the Ballyhealy Road. Eventually we sat down on the root of a big Beech tree.You would hear my teeth chatter a mile away – cold and nerves! I put my arm around Betty's shoulder, but at the last minute, the courage to try a kiss deserted me. It didn't matter in the least, because the primary purpose had been achieved, I was seen walking down the road with a woman.The world was wonderful place – until I heard back that Betty said I was "no good!!" I never got a second chance with Betty, but more importantly we have remained good friends.

After Betty, I made up my mind that I would, come hell or high water, kiss the next girl I "went with".That lucky girl was Bridie, a really nice girl also. This was soon followed by my first "line".This distinction fell to Laura, an older woman! Laura, a lovely young lady, was an eighteen year old Cavan girl, working in St. Mary's Convent, at Southhill.As for being "no good", well, even if I say so myself, I improved. I applied myself diligently to the task!

Two local guys, Vincent and Matty Mullen came home on holidays, from Canada.They were two of the nicest guys I had ever met, jokes, laughter, handsome, lots of money and a car. Regular customers in the bar, they befriended me and would often bring me with them to a dance.They had a different girl every dance and I dreamed that some day I could be like them! I wonder if they ever knew how much their friendship over six or eight weeks, meant to me?

Two other guys I still remember, were Tom and Paddy, off the Drogheda and Dundalk coal lorry. They were so kind, and constantly engaging in good humoured banter. They never saw anybody stuck for a lift on the road, either.

I sensed,"in the air", that my days were numbered and really, it was a relief when it came – although I didn't know I had two tougher months ahead of me.

Mr. Merlehan had a habit of offering jobs to young lads.When drinking in a pub, full of drink and importance, if he liked the barman, he offered him a better deal than where he was.When I was a year and a half there, I got moved sideways. I had been, telling my Mother I wanted to change jobs but she insisted that I should stay until I had completed two years and then I

Devlin Hurlers Early 1060's
Front L to R: Jimmy Leavy, John Comaskey, Jimmy Andrews, Kit Drumm, Joe Bray, Ciaran Carroll, Sean Leavy.
Back L to R: Michael Leavy, J. Andrews Snr., Ned Drumm, Pat Lynch, Matt Hiney, Bernie Drumm, Jim Burke, Richard Cully, Michael Wymes, Bernie Comaskey.

could move on as an "improver". Due to Bertie's "hiring", we found ourselves with more staff than customers. Well, if Bertie could hire through drink, he could also off-load through drink. One morning he announced the "good news" that he had managed to get me into The Greville Arms in Mullingar.

I saw little of my first boss, after that. Sometimes he came into The Greville, but I kept away from him. Some years later, when I was home from Canada, I met him on the street in Mullingar. He invited me in for a drink. Those days, I would drink with anybody – almost! "No thank you, Mr. Merlehan". "Call me Bertie, and come on for one". "I'm in a hurry" (and I didn't say "Bertie") "Nobody has time for a drink anymore", were the last words he spoke to me.

The Greville Arms

To-day, The Greville Arms, in the centre of Mullingar, with its excellent management and staffing, is one of my favourite places, for "getting fed", or meeting friends for coffee. Whatever pleasure I get from being there now....Well, let's say – I paid my dues!

I understood I was going there to work as a barman and so I did and so I was; BUT; everybody in the hotel was my boss and anybody could tell me to do anything. The hotel had recently been purchased by a Mr. Jessop, for around thirty thousand pounds, they said. I was absolutely astounded that anyone in all the world, could have thirty thousand pounds – actually it turned out that Mr. Jessop night not have had – but that wasn't my concern. My concern of the moment was that, when he stayed at the hotel, his shoes, his wife's shoes and all his children's shoes, were left out each morning for me to polish. Deep down, Mr. Jessop must really have cared deeply about me, because one day he told me that I should give customers their change on a wet tray and that I would get more tips! I tried it once or twice, but couldn't bring myself to do it! My wages were two pounds per week "indoors". I did get tips from some nice customers and in this regard, carrying in or out luggage was usually a lucrative chore.

The senior bar people were a Miss Houlihan from Killogrlin and a Miss Fitzpatrick. Both these ladies were very fair and kind to me – as was also a Miss Reynolds, on reception. Miss Hanley was the manageress and she persecuted me and there was no rhyme or reason to her attitude towards me. It was no use telling her why I was doing something else. One day, I was carrying a guest's suitcase down the stairs. In front of everyone in the lobby, she tore into me for only carrying one case at a time. When I got a word in, I explained that the guests had three cases and that I had carried two the first time. Her logical answer to this was; "Mr. Merlehan was asking how you were doing and I'll have to tell him how far back you've gone since you've been here"! Miss Hanley would condescend to attend some dances in "The County Hall". At the dance, a couple of senior staff would have to sit with her all night, much to their dismay.

My main persecutor was a porter called Paddy – I can't remember his surname. Paddy was a very little man – in every sense of the word. To Paddy, I was his junior assistant. Sorting bottles and things like that, I didn't mind at all. That was bar-work. It was the kitchen cleaning and in particular the lighting and stoking of the huge anthracite cooker which got to me. I'm sure there weren't many people in Paddy's life he managed to bully, so he was delighted to have me. I tried to get clarification from Miss Hanley with regard to my duties; but her response was that I was there to work and Paddy "knew what had to be done". I almost clocked him, but the lessons I learned at home and in the playground, stood me well.

Bend with the wind, but don't break. The lesson of waiting and biding my time was not lost on me. I gave Miss Hanley a weeks' notice, when she needed me most, at the start of Paddy's holidays.

In spite of all of above, I really enjoyed my two months in "The Greville". I was still judging a place, first and foremost, on how well I got fed and the hotel was "five star" in this regard. The chef decided what any of us would have for dinner and as I got on great with him, I was well looked after. Ester, the young apprentice chef, was a good sort also. Besides, we could raid the pantry – especially after dances, so really, the world was a wonderful place. As well as food, there was also girls – lots of them. Again, lots of harmless, innocent fun. Off to dances in The County Hall and carnivals all over the country. I was really chuffed when a twenty three year old waitress fancied me and we "courted" at every opportunity. I was even more "chuffed" when Miss Hanley, scolding me one day mentioned this and said the girl in question "should have more sense". I knew then what Miss Hanley needed – but that wasn't my job!

One morning whilst I was washing the toilets, who should charge in for a leak only Brendan Behan. I didn't know who he was until I went back into the bar. Brendan engaged me in chat and then asked to borrow my comb which I gave him. He combed his unruly mop and said something to the effect that he wouldn't see anything worse for the rest of the day, then the man in the mirror. Brendan then took his own comb from his pocket announced that mine was a better one and swapped combs with me. What would that comb be worth to-day! Who would believe me!?

A nice story I often tell is that of local draper, Joe Healy and my new suit. In those days you didn't go to a dance in anything other than a suit and my wardrobe had a "tired look", to put it mildly. Joe, the most eligible bachelor in town was a regular customer in the hotel bar, where he always found time to have a few pleasant words with me. One evening I told him I was "thinking of buying a new suit". Joe invited me up next day, insisted I take the best suit in the shop, took a deposit and told me to pay for it when I had the money. I try not to hold grudges, but often I will not forget a bad turn, but the absolute certainty is that I never, ever, forget a good turn and I never for-

Still proudly wearing the
Pioneer Pin

got Joe Healy or that suit. It served me well in The County Hall and much further afield, for a long time.
Both Mr. Merlehan and Miss Hanley had promised to write me a reference, at different times, but always, when I called back it wasn't done. After a month in The Greville Arms, I started answering "Bar Situations Vacant" in the daily newspapers. I got a reply from J. J. Spain, Kilcormac, Co. Offaly, I phoned up to ask if I could go for interview. "Not necessary", said Mr. Spain. "I will send you references" I volunteered. "Not necessary, Mick Casey, the D.E. Williams' rep (or "commercial traveller", as reps were then called) speaks very highly of you and he is a good judge"! Somebody was noticing me after all! Whilst in The Greville, I went home on my days off. Now, I was expanding my horizons as far away as Offaly. Life was changing fast and would never be the same again.

"Glory Spain!"

Only last week, I called to visit Mrs. Nancy Spain, in Kilcormac. Now, in her eighty sixth year, she is the same lovely woman she was forty four years ago, when I arrived on her doorstep; "the new barman". My wages were to be three pounds a week "indoor", but no money could ever equal what the Spains gave me; appreciation, warmth, stability, security and affection. It's hard to believe now that I only spent a year in Kilcormac, but in that time, I became like a member of the Spain family.
The name over the bar said "J.J. Spain and Sons"; the sons being Micháel (my

age) Tom, a couple of years younger and Seamus, whom, I think, was around ten. There were also two daughters, Bríd, a year younger than I and Ann, "the baby", six years old.

Jack Spain was a good man. He was your typical small town entrepreneur and driving force. Spain's had two pubs in the village; the Flagship and another small pub, "The Cosy Bar", which was mine to run.

I arrived in Kilcormac on a Sunday evening. Everybody was talking in the bar about "the game" – some quietly and philosophically, some loudly, some pitifully; a few hysterically. If anybody was to be believed, the fiercest, most blood-thirsty enemy in all the world had to be the hurlers of Drumcullen. I gathered that Kilcormac and Drumcullen had played that day and a good few of the players felt that an hour was too long to wait for a result!

Jack loved his GAA and worked tirelessly for Kilcomac and for Offaly. This was 1961 – great days for Offaly. Naturally, I never called Jack by his Christian name while I worked for him. At the start it was Mr. Spain and then it became "Boss". We had a great relationship. Two things I told him, which I lived to regret and which he teased me with until the day he died. One was the "never heard of them" reply that a Dublin man gave to my "Up Westmeath", when I was twelve and the other was when Westmeath got a bad beating while I worked there. In defiance to the Offaly crowd who kept jeering me that Westmeath were "no good", I retorted, "They mightn't be great, but they're good!"

In September of 1961 I, along with ninety thousand five hundred and fifty five others filled Croke Park to see Offaly bid for their first All-Ireland. It was my first All-Ireland final. I roared on Offaly till I was hoarse, but it wasn't enough and a hugely talented, exciting Down team won their second All-Ireland. On the bus home the atmosphere was – ah, you know. Jim Murtagh, after fourteen pints, stood up and said; "Lads, what about it, it was only a game of football". "Sit down, ya stupid oul shite", was greeted with a chorus of approval maybe that is why I still can't take it, when someone says "Cheer up, it's only a game"!

I played for Kilcormac and still carry a "dimple" on my left cheek acquired whilst playing against Lusmagh in Birr. Of course I was no good – no training or anything, but my hurling career was to suffer a terminal turn before I was to leave Kilcormac. The closest The Boss came to giving out to me for the entire year I was there, was in the car coming back from a match in

Tullamore. We lost, Jack's car was full and nobody was talking. Then Jack spoke to the dash-board; "Everytime Bernie got the ball, he fell!!"
As well as the pubs, Jack was also an auctioneer, an insurance agent and an Offaly County Councillor. Considering the fact that he had, a few years earlier, just about won a hard-fought battle with T.B. – he was some man and I learned many lessons from watching him in action. If ever there was a truism that "behind every successful man is a great woman", Mrs. Spain was that. As well as raising five children, who are a credit to her, she ran the bar, dealt with insurance clients and every crisis. She was one of the best I have ever seen to deal with a troublesome customer. Neither Mr. or Mrs. Spain "took a drink".
Kilcormac was regarded as a rough town due to the influx of so many Bord na Móna and Boora Power Station workers, all making good money. I never saw it to be anything of the kind. I saw more rows on any fair day in Delvin than I did in any month in Kilcormac and weren't there such characters. Bob Warren especially, springs to mind and of course my fellow countyman "The Knacker" Casey.
Micháel was at college in Ballyfin. He had no interest in the bar and he only worked when he couldn't avoid it. Ironically, he finished up managing a pub in England. "Mick" and I got on great. Never once, did he talk down to me because he was in college and I worked for them. Nevertheless, he did me an "awful turn", which really was my own fault. Micháel had had a lovely girl-friend called Bridgie ("Biddy"). Things cooled and I couldn't believe my luck when I got her. I was "head over heels"! Biddy was in boarding school and a day pupil posted her love letters to me. I had one in my pocket where she wrote that she thought she was in love with Micháel until she met me. I was walking on air and I had only thought the world was a wonderful place – until now. Micháel, myself and a few of the lads, were in the bar and Micháel said to the boys, for my benefit that he thought he would to back to Biddy, when she came home. "I don't think so", said I, producing the letter! Before the week was out, Biddy heard and her next letter broke it off, but Mick didn't get her either. My heart was broken! I did go out with her again, much later but that magic of first real love was gone. Brid, a lovely young lady, was also my girl-friend for a while.
The next door publican, Bertie Feighery "took a drink". Bertie was some character. He had been off the drink for years, but broke out a week before

I arrived. There are many funny incidents I can attribute to Bertie and the antics he performed for those around him. However, he coined a phrase at that time, which is still chanted in Offaly, when things are going good. Offaly were Leinster football champions, Spain's was full and the craic was mighty, when Jack walked in behind the bar. Bertie overcame by a feeling of well-being, jumped up on a chair, clenched fist in the air and bellowed "Glory Spain, glory Spain". It caught on and that became the everyday greeting of everyone around Kilcormac and soon it spread further afield.

May Day, May Day

I just loved working the "Cosy Bar". It wasn't too busy and Micháel, Bríd, or Mrs. Spain's niece, Frances would help me when required. Frances was great and would work on any Sunday I was at a game. Other than matches, I didn't care about time off. I had all day Tuesday off and other than that, I worked opening till closing time. Getting home wasn't easy, but I wrote every week and sent a few bob. When I did get home a businessman from home, Paddy Foley, was a Godsend. Paddy delivered newspapers and I would meet him in Tullamore. He was a most interesting and obliging man and died recently in his ninety third year. My Mother's letters were too often full of doom and gloom but I also got all the news about how things were going around Drumcree. Then one day in October 1961, I got a phone call to say that I had a new baby brother. Camillus was number six. In the course of my fathers' customary celebrating in Bartleys, he boasted that now "he had six sons to carry him out". "Ah, for Christ's sake", quipped 'Small Johnny' Bartley; "wouldn't one of them carry you out in a hand bag"!

I had come on well. We went to lots of dances after closing. Ten o'clock was closing time on Sunday nights, which was perfect for going out afterwards. I was very happy. Joe Healy's suit looked splendid on me still and I was never without a girl-friend. I had the advantage of being a pioneer. Half my buddies, or more, "took a drink" and women didn't like lads that drank! I was never going to drink – I had seen too much of it. I never went anywhere without wearing my pioneer pin.

I thought I could play poker before I went to Kilcormac, but I had a lot still to learn - and I did! There were always twenty-five card drives going on and a hard core of poker "sharks" went just to play poker. "The Mouse" Troy was the king. Younger than most of the fellows he played with; he had the per-

Working behind "The Cosy Bar" Kilcormac, Co. Offaly

fect poker-face and rarely lost. If lady luck didn't deal the cards to suit him, he was capable of helping her along by "slipping", or holding an oul Ace or picture card here or there. He was such a likable rogue. One day he announced to me that we would soon have to increase our usual "deal" from one shilling to two shillings as he was getting married the next month and the card players of Kilcormac would now "have two to keep!"

As well as The Power Station and Bord na Móna, P. H. Egan and D. E. Williams had shops, bars and grain depots in the town. Williams' had a mill which gave a significant level of employment. All in all, Kilcormac was a prosperous place. Paddy McCormack – the Westmeath version of, was in the process of building a cinema and dance hall. There was a girl's convent school, as well as a Vocational School in the town.

Many counties were represented among our bar customers and the slagging and banter, especially before and after big matches was mighty. Seamus Mortimer from Laois, was my buddy. He worked in P. H. Egans, Bar and Grocery. A very good, strong hurler, Seamus played at minor grade for both Laois and Offaly. Modest and likable, he fed me many a ball, when we played together. Our paths crossed over more than once during our lifetime and to-day, Seamus, married to a local girl, Mary Doyne, owns a supermarket in my home parish of Collinstown. As well as Seamus, I met Paddy Casey, who

then worked for D. E. Williams in Mount Bolis, three miles from Kilcormac. Paddy later ran his Uncle's pub; The Cloughan Inn, near Mullingar, where I often went to "Evening Mass", Paddy now lives in Mullingar.
I was never lonely or homesick in Kilcormac. Willie got a job in Rafters pub, Harbour Street, Tullamore, so we saw each other at least once a week. Neighbours, Nancy and Mary Reilly were also working in Tullamore, so, we had enough to form a "clique" at the dances!
Then it happened. I don't ever remember making the decision – in fact, I'm sure I never made it. It was totally against everything I proclaimed but on the 1st May 1962 at the age of seventeen and a half I "took a drink".
I got a lift to Birr with Michael, a fellow who used come into the bar and often carried us to dances. He was a few years older than I and also a non-drinker. Dooleys' Hotel had recently been re-opened and we went in "to see what it was like". I called for two club orange and the barman didn't hear me. We waited and whatever got into me; I turned to Michael and said; "I'll drink a bottle of stout, if you have one too". "Right", he said. We drank the two bottles of stout.
I came back to Kilcormac, had my tea, went down to Williams' and had a bottle of Double Diamond beer. I was savouring my next move: Seamus Mortimer "took a drink", so I walked slowly up to the counter in Egans and asked Seamus for a bottle of Phoenix.
May Day, 1962 was the first day in my now unmanageable life.

No Problem

This drink was magic. I could ask anyone out to dance. I could talk to anyone – young or old – male or female in the pub. I could dance like Fred Astaire; Lord, I could even sing, - for the first time in my life! I now looked forward to Tuesdays, my day off. On the first Tuesday of my drinking career, Seamus and I walked out the mile to Ryans' in Ballyboy, where we got "nicely", but I secured a date with Molly, the publican's daughter. This drink just had to be the most unbelievable stuff.
Mrs. Spain was up when I got back. She knew by me and I could tell she was surprised and disappointed. Typically of the wonderful kind person she is, she didn't give out to me, but she did advise me to be careful with the drink. She told me about relations of hers who had "gone to the bad" from drink and about all the young lads she had seen destroyed since she had been behind

the bar. She made me tea and I eventually went to bed. Next morning my throat was dry and I didn't eat any breakfast. No doubt, Jack knew by now, but he said nothing and the work routine went on unhindered.

The "Knacker" Casey used drive us to dances for a couple of shillings each. He knew at least one pub in every town, where you could get an after-hours drink and this became more important than the dance itself. As well as this, there were sometimes late night bar extensions when there was a carnival in a town. The drink was the highlight of most outings, including GAA matches. I had some great times drinking but an indication that something was wrong is when a seventeen or eighteen year old is continuously taking pledges, in his first year of "taking a drink".

I did not crave, need, or have a drink the next day, but I looked forward to the next session. I worried that my Mother might find out. She had often warned; "None of ye need ever come home here, if ye take a drink". Sean was to be the only one of the six who remained a life-long pioneer.

One out of every twelve drinkers either is, or will become, an alcoholic. Most peoples idea of an alcoholic is the wino on Skid Row, searching through garbage-cans. This person, in fact, only makes up two percent of alcoholics. The rest are people who go about their business and everyday lives, leading what might appear to be normal lives.

Alcoholism is an illness – a progressive disease. It gets worse, never better. Most progress through the stages of social drinking, heavy drinking and to alcoholic drinking, I was never a social drinker. I drank for effect, for what it could do to me. It is my belief that alcoholism is not acquired, but is inherited. It is in the genes and all it takes is that first drink to set it off.

I was to learn the hard way. I knew nothing, but if anyone tried to advise me, I wouldn't listen. I went through hell for the following eight years, always insisting, there was "no problem".

Next door to "The Cosy" was the bar of D. E. Williams. Another Westmeath "Blow-in", Mick Hennessy, had recently been appointed bar-manager. Mick "took a drink"! He was much older than I, didn't have a great interest in sport and we really didn't have much in common – except our native county. I was a year working for Spain's, growing up fast - ever becoming more street wise. I never took a drink in either of Spain's pubs, on or off duty.

Then, one day, Mick Hennessy was gone. My brain raced. 'What if' I could get the job of Williams's Bar Manager – one of the best jobs in Kilcormac. As if on cue, Mick Casey, walked in the door for his order. I asked him "What would be my chances of landing the job"."None, he replied, we couldn't take you from Spains. An hour later he was back;"I have been talking to Jack and something big has turned up". The something big was that Jack had been made an offer for "The Cosy Bar" and told Mick about it. Really, Kilcormac wasn't big enough for the one owner of two pubs. Jack wouldn't sell to anyone who might compete for his business, but what had happened was that Mr. Coffey, a draper had made an offer for The Cosy Bar property and it would be run as a clothes shop. Two weeks later, I pulled the door of "The Cosy" closed, for the last time.

Both Jack Spain and Mick Casey recommended me to Williams'. I thought this would be sufficient for me to get the Managers' job – although Mick did remark that I was "horrid young for it".

A man came out from Head Office to interview me. He told me of the prospects I would have with his firm, but that right now, I was too young for a Manager's job. I was offered a job in Dysart, starting in three weeks time. The wages were not very exciting, but a job was a job and I would have a couple of week's holiday at home.

I was sad leaving Kilcormac – all my new friends and especially the Spain family. I promised I would always call to see them – a promise I kept. I had thirteen pounds in the Post Office, plus my wages and holiday pay. Jack and Nancy Spain left a life-lasting impression on me. Good, decent hard working people, they raised a fine family of five children. Although Tom once got his bags packed and it took all of his Mothers' diplomatic skills, to have the penalty overruled, for going to a rugby International. It was Jack's one ambition that his sons would play hurling or football for Offaly. I suppose out of five, the law of averages would dictate that one would go wrong. That one was Seamus, the youngest boy and the fair–haired darling of both parents. Who would have thought that he would have turned out the black sheep. Seamus played soccer.

"Now She Had Two of Them"

It was great to be home. Anthony had grown so much and the new baby was a 'dote'. Not being used to the smell of nappies, I was very conscious of how the odour penetrated every corner of the house. Sean was in Clara and Fechin at eleven was probably taking most of the brunt of my father "suf-

"Taking a Drink"
Seamus Mortimer, Willie (not drinking) and Myself

fering". I never was good at being a hypocrite and wearing my pioneer pin around the house really bothered me – not to mention the guilt. On the Saturday night, Paddy Reilly and I rode the bikes the three miles to Collinstown, where he drank three bottles of stout and I had three bottles of beer. Mammy made tea when I got in and was relieved that she didn't appear to suspect anything.

I think it was the following Tuesday, I got a lift into Mullingar. I bought a V-neck slate-grey pullover with a white fleck in it, from Joe Healy. Wandering down the town, I met Mrs Crone, who told me they would give me a lift home, when Dermott finished work. I was to meet them in Butler's pub at four thirty. I duly arrived and bought them a drink and a bottle of harp for myself. The Crones took a drink. After an hour or so, I gave up "minding myself" and willingly slotted into the tempo of a serious drinking session. Around seven o'clock, shaking off the drinkers who had joined us, we headed for home. Half-way home, we decided we would have one in Cloughan. I overheard Mena tell Dermott to let me "do the buying", but I didn't care, as I had lots of money and the world was a wonderful place to be a man who "took a drink". "Going in for one" is reputed to be the biggest lie in the world and this "one" was no exception. This was the drunkest I had been.

There was this middle-aged hard chaw there, who butted into our company. Anyone who bought a drink could "butt in" as far as Crones were concerned. Eventually he picked on me, although I have no doubt but that I was far from blameless. He gave me an awful verbal lashing and I backed down, but I felt humiliated "in company". After mulling it over another bottle I said "just as well you didn't hit me because I'm as good a man to fight as any"! "Come out to the yard then he yelled", jumping up and heading out. I thought somebody would stop me but Mena said; "Go on Bernie". I unsteadily marched two paces behind my opponent.

Here I was, on the crest of history and didn't know it. The Guinness book of records is incomplete - I took part in the shortest boxing match, in the history of boxing. Three seconds, I believe. As we cleared the back door and entered the yard; in one graceful movement this hardy man, swivelled on his left foot and landed a perfect right-hand haymaker into my mouth. I came to, with Dermott kneeling over me, attempting to "stem the flow". Eventually he got me over to a water-tank, washed my face with a dirty rag, got me out the gate and into the back seat of his car. We got back to Crones, where the Granny, Mrs Reagan, made me a sardine sandwich and a mug of tea. The tea was too hot, the bread was too hard and the sardines were too salty, for a man with a dismantled mouth!

I announced that I would head home and headed off to walk the half mile. My condition was my own fault. I rarely have ever had any problem in accepting the consequences of my actions. But, I was still not eighteen. Dermot and Mena Crone were my parent's age-group and to this day I feel that they should have made some effort to prevent me from going home to my Mother in such a state. It was bad. There was a scene. Daddy wasn't there. Mammy ordered everyone in the house to bed and then tore into me. The only bit I remember was "My heart is broken" and the quote from Brindsley McNamara in "The Valley of The Squinting Windows" – "She had two of them now!" I gave lots of "back-chat", before pulling myself up the stairs to bed. I was home, but the sweater I had bought from Joe Healy didn't make it!

Malahide

The following Saturday night I went to confessions and took a six months pledge, which ran its standard term of three weeks.

I didn't feel great about the job in Dysart. A lot of people I told I was going to work there, laughed or made some derogatory remark about the size of the place – although, no doubt, it would have been big enough for a young fellow, out of the bog.

I got the paper every day and studied the "Situations Vacant" column. Lo and behold, what appeared but this hugely attractive advertisement for a barman in Malahide. "To take charge", great prospects. Five pounds indoors – "to start". I always liked the "To Start" bit because it held out the promise of fast wage increase. I went to Collinstown, phoned the number and spoke to the bar owner. I thought it was a man I was speaking to, whom I called "Mr" and "Sir". The fact that it was a woman, who didn't correct me, was probably a bad omen. I couldn't believe my good fortune when I was offered the job, there and then and I was asked to start immediately. Two days later, I was on the Granard Bus for Dublin. Auntie Kathleen met me, looked after me well, as always, and put me on a forty two bus to Malahide.

"The Claddagh Bar" was owned by an elderly lady, whose name was Mrs. Walsh. The reason I got the immediate start, without references or anything, was because nobody could stay working for her. If ever the devil was "crossways" in anyone, he was firmly entrenched in Mrs. Walsh. Her husband was the local G.P. and he did not have any input into the business.

I, along with whatever other staff came and went, lived over the pub, whilst the owner lived in a big house, past the Grand Hotel, at the end of the village. I went down to the house daily for my dinner and the housekeeper did the best she could.

I was the only experienced barman and lots of other bargain staff came and went. There were however, a couple of great part-time barmen, who came in on the nights of music or functions. It was a crazy set-up. The boss kept all the bottles of spirits up at the house and we were always short of stock. My time off was erratic or non existent. A barmaid from Rooskey arrived in early September. Mary and I made plans to go to the Roscommon Kerry all-Ireland final. We asked for the day off more than a week in advance, arranged cover, but on the Saturday the Boss announced that nobody got Sundays off. Then we got a yard-man to do the donkey work. John was out of John of Gods and it was not that the place was called after him. I often wondered what became of this unfortunate human being. John was, I would say in his late thirties. He had been brought up in "St. John of Gods" and never knew a family life. His only possession was a transistor radio, which he told me he bought from his savings out of the two shillings a week pocket money he received in the institution. Mrs. Walsh got him for little or nothing, to try him in the outside world.

One day John and I went up to the house for our dinner together. I felt confused and aggrieved to see John get a huge plate of fried chicken, whilst I got a slice of sausage roll. I was too afraid of Mrs. Walsh to say anything to her but I complained bitterly to the housekeeper. Before I left, she called me aside and whispered; "You weren't given any chicken, because it's gone bad". Enough food for breakfast and supper was supposed to be there for us in the bar kitchen, but was rarely the case. Once when we bought half a pound of rashers between us, Mrs. Walsh stole them and said a dog took them.

Like everywhere else, there were good times there also and loads of fun. One of the most wonderful things about life is the resilience of the human spirit. I never stopped being capable of having a good laugh.

The newest employee was a secretary. Nellie and I still remember her address; Lodge, Hospital, Co. Limerick. Nellie became my girl-friend and we had some very pleasant times. On a half day off, we would go into town and explore the two sides of O'Connell Street, before eating in a café and getting the bus back to Malahide. We got to know the staff of The Grand Hotel and we would get into the tail-end of dinner-dances at the hotel. There might not have been "sex, drugs and rock 'n' roll", but there was rock 'n' roll and drink - what more did any man want!

Again, some of the customers were very nice and pally with me. Some weren't. There was one man, a high ranking CIE Executive who treated me like dirt. He didn't have to pay for his drink and once when I complained to the Boss, she told me not to dare to say anything to him. It was common knowledge that the timber and roofing for the new lounge came from CIE. This man and anyone else of Mrs. Walshes choosing, could stay drinking as long as they wanted after hours and I had to remain there to serve them. I never drank during regular working time but some of the after-hours customers would buy me drink "on the quiet" and "shur" the time didn't seem long at all!

Aunt Kathleen, whom I called to when I could, was appalled at my working conditions and contacted a man she knew in the union. I was on the verge of having the place unionised when I couldn't take it any more, and left.

Nellie was instructed to put in yet another advertisement for staff. As she was giving her the wording, The Boss said that it was my job which was being advertised. Whether she was just getting at Nellie, or what, I don't know. Nellie told me immediately I was at the end of my tether anyway. Mary from Roscommon had long since left and John had been shipped back to St. John of Gods for "insubordination". I went upstairs, packed my few things and walked off the job. The one and only time in my life I did that. I had lasted ten weeks.

CHAPTER 9

Going West

I lacked confidence in many ways but I knew I was a good barman and a hard worker. Also, never once, did it occur to me to be anything other than honest, in any case, I would be too much afraid not to be. Afraid of God, mostly. Confession was becoming an awful problem (and soon to get more so!!) with "company keeping" and "impure thoughts" – not to mention finding a different priest for each new pledge. Worst of all was the "value added" fear of making a bad confession.

I wrote to Mrs. Walsh for my cards and for a reference and the bitch wrote back and asked me "where was the money from the night the money was short in the till"

There were loads of bar jobs advertised and I knew I wouldn't be idle for long. I was working again in two weeks.

I went for an interview to "The Genoa Bar", in Galway City. There, I was interviewed by Mr. Molloco. Mollocos real name was Magliacco, but the family changed it to Molloco for easier pronunciation. He, as you may well deduce, did not come from An Spidéal.

Joe Molloco, a portly Italian hired me to start the following Monday. My wages were eight pounds per week; half-day Thursday, Tuesday night off and every third Sunday. He sent me down to Mrs. Lawlor in Market Street, across the road from the offices of The Connaught Tribune, where I got 'digs' for three pounds per week. Mrs. Lawlor's son, Eddie, a middle aged divorced man, had a cobblers shop, and our room was over the shop.

Since going to school, I always had a soft spot, or "something" for Galway. Maybe it was because my Grand Father had worked there for years and spoke so highly of the people. My feelings were not misplaced. I loved Galway.

"The Genoa" was a modern, well run pub, frequented by a good cross-section of customers, including students. Close to "The Connaught Tribune" office, we were entertained by sports-writers, poets and all sorts of artistic types, as well as fishermen, businessmen and market traders. I was learning about life all the while and my new pub was an exciting environment for me. Mr. Malloco was a hard, but fair taskmaster. Standards were set high and those who didn't measure up, got short shrift. There was a very high turnover of barmen (no women were employed) and one of the reasons for this was the manager, Michael Duignan. Michael was a publicans dream manager. Honest, hardworking, totally committed to the success of the business and just loving being there. Small, middle-aged and single, Michael got trouble from his two feet and his one stomach – the hazards of a long time barman; always on his feet, eating hurriedly, not regularly and the wrong food – as well as "taking a drink"! Michael was as contrary a man as ever stood behind a counter, but was well liked and respected by the regulars, who knew he ran a "good ship".

Every new barman was treated equally by Michael. Based on his presumption, until you proved him wrong; you were "slower than the second coming of Christ", awkward, stupid, half-trained, useless and "not going to be there too long"! From the first day, I could not dislike him. There was something comical and innocent about his expression – and I was well used to small contrary men, with a bark worse than a bite!

My first Sunday evening and very busy. At the height of the rush I was washing glasses at the bar sink. (No glass-washer in those days!). Michael was stressed, as was his wont. Nobody could wash glasses faster than I was doing it. That didn't save me. Next thing I got a fair shoulder, which drove me a yard from the sink and there was Michael manning my position – the implication being that he couldn't look at me trying to do it. This off the ball incident took place directly in front of a bunch of regulars. I don't know how I thought of it, but without batting an eye-lid, I dried my hands in my white coat and said, "Ok lads, who's next... now that I have someone to wash the glasses, ye'll all get served!" Both Michael and I could hear the customers laughing as they told each other about how I handled Michael. I worked like "fork lightning", keeping out of Michael's way. I was great at figures and no matter how big the round, I had it in my head, as soon as the drinks hit the counter, whether that little incident had anything to do with it, or not, Michael never said a wrong word to me again and we became great friends and boozing buddies.

Happy Days

I was happy every day I spent in Galway. The hours were long and the work was hard, but for me, there was a vibrance and excitement in the very air of the City. I palled around with a bunch of UCG students and they excelled in sniffing out cheap and even free sources of drink. Mr. Malloco once brought me in and advised that these guys were idlers – or words to that effect and that they were bad company for me! I would say that I wasn't the best company for them either!

I got my buddy, Seamus Mortimer, a job and we shared a room at 8 Market Street, where old Mrs. Lawlor, who never stopped talking about her beloved Kinvara, looked after us in a kind and motherly fashion. Daughter Mary, a foot soldier in The Legion of Mary, quiet understandably, advised any other lodger to keep well clear of Seamus and I. A wild young buck from Kinvara, naturally, a favourite of Mrs. Lawlor's, on account of coming from the same place, shared another room and Mary always had an awful job getting him up. She would be up and down the stairs, several times, banging and banging on the door. Eventually, she would go in and shake him awake. As I said earlier Mary was middle-aged and she knew that all men were bastards – although she would never, of course, use such a word. Gerry, forever full of devilment, lay in bed and Mary became more exasperated banging on the door. Soon the door flung open as Mary stormed in. There stood Gerry; full frontal; naked! The little "vacancy" sign went up in the front window!

Seamus didn't stay long in The Genoa. He got a job in Cookes, Shantalla. We both played hurling for Rahoon, although I never did a practice or training session with the team. Imagine this. One Sunday, I stopped work at 2pm in The Genoa. Grabbed my hurley and boots and ran to Pearse Stadium in

Salthill to play a match. Surely two, maybe three miles. The game had started when I got togged out. The player taken off to let me on must have been pretty bad. I ran on, got the ball and brought it the length of the field, before losing it. Seamus said afterwards; "I thought you were going to be the best man on the field after the way you started". Weary and tired I did little else after that.

We used sometimes get after hours drink in Dohertys, but there was a great degree of control in our lives "when we worked, we worked and when we drank we drank". Race week was something else. We practically worked, flat out, around the clock. Mr. Mallocco gave every staff member an extra three pounds for the week. Well earned, I would contend! A couple of nights during race week, we would go out there after work for drink. Michael Maloney, from Athenry, had a tent there. A decent man, one time he had worked in The Genoa. By the time we got there all the other drinkers would have a very clear lead. This night I was drinking with my friends Seamus Kelly and Liam Bailey. Maloney advised us to watch a certain trouble-maker, whom he knew from Athenry. Sure enough soon The Yob, or whatever we called him at the time, approached our group. He picked on Bailey, who was drunk. "No need for that" I ventured. He ploughed towards me. I wasn't going to get caught like I did in Cloughan. I swung and connected with his jaw. Down he went, bringing a section of counter with him.

Several men came and shook my hand and told me I was a "great kid"! I was always glad that I didn't have to defend the title or that the guy never sought a rematch.

At home, Dessie and John Kiernan had "got into the Guards". I got the Garda exam papers and I really was surprised that the exam did not appear to be all that difficult. On going into Galway Garda Station, I met a friendly Garda and I told him I wanted to join the Guards. He brought me in, told me to take off my shoes and stood me up against the wall. "I'm afraid you are half an inch too short", I was informed. The kindly Garda must have seen the disappointment in my face, because as I left he said; "Don't worry, you'll probably grow that half inch yet".

In 1963, I stood in Eyre Square as President Kennedy passed, waving and smiling. I can vividly remember thinking how brown his skin was and how friendly and kind were his eyes.

Around the same time, the Pope turned me against religion. There was this lovely girl I had a dance with, a couple of times. Then, I asked her for a date. She was ever so slightly taller than I and anyone could see that she was what we might later term a "classy broad". I asked her to a dance in "The Hanger". "Tell you what", she smiled. "I will meet you there and you can take me home"! There was something special about this one. Between the bar, The Boat Club, Sea Point Ballroom and parties etc., I had no shortage of female company, but I found myself really looking forward to this date. I think "The Hanger" was on a Wednesday night, but I'm not sure. Anyway, whatever day it was, was the day The Pope died and all dances were cancelled. I never saw the girl again.

Paying The Price!

Seamus was courting a girl from home, a sparkling red head, Mary Doyne, who managed and still manages, to keep manners on him. Seamus was pining and evidently in love. Every so often, Seamus would hire out a Morris Minor and we would head for home. After whatever dance we went to and after Seamus and Mary's "bit of a court" in the car, we would head back for Galway, usually arriving as the sun came up. On one such excursion, we went to a dance in Castlepollard. If you went to a dance on your own and didn't "shift" someone, really, that dance would have to be regarded as a failure. This particular night, I had a few drinks, but not too many. The long drive, a visit home and Mortimer's detour, meant a latish arrival in "Pollard" in a sober state. A few quick ones in Murray's brought us to closing time and so to the dance.

There was this local girl, whom I had never spoken to, though we sort of knew each other. I asked her to dance. I felt in good form and we had a great jive. Playing the game meant not asking her for the next dance and see would she manoeuvre into a good position to be asked for another dance. Sure enough, I caught her watching me. A slow dance next time. The invitation and acceptance of "having a mineral" was the clincher. I asked, "was she bringing anyone to-night", and got the standard reply of "I might".

Arms around each other waists we walked well down a shop archway, nothing as yet to suggest that this was any different than all the other after dance "courts". It was. The word "Round" springs to mind.

I told Seamus on the way back to Galway only when he made some reference to it, did the possible consequence of my action hit me. It would be bad enough to be caught with an unlicensed bull on the farm, but to be one struck terror to the core. The following Saturday evening I asked Michael if it would be OK to take time after my tea to go to confession. Michael a man who never neglected his religious duties told me to go ahead. "I committed the sin of impurity, Father" (Courting would have read; "I was company keeping, Father"). "With yourself, or with another person"? "With another person, Father" "You have grievously offended The Blessed Virgin, Mary". "Yes, Father". "For your penance say five decades of the rosary and promise to avoid such occasions of sin". "Yes, Father". "Now, tell God you're sorry by saying a perfect act of contrition". "Oh my God I am heartily sorry for having offended thee and I firmly resolve by this hold grace, never more to offend thee and to amend my life!..."

It wasn't nearly as bad as I thought it was going to be. I didn't want to overload the system by taking a pledge or mentioning drink, so, to celebrate my relief, I had a bottle of stout, before I went back to work.

Eddie Lawlor was always talking about women and in order that I might benefit from his experience and knowledge, I told him. He left me convinced that I was in big trouble, but if he was in the shop and saw her parents looking for me on the doorstep, he would, "give me a hand". It was then I did a deal with God. If he saw me through this one, I would never do that again and I would pay five pounds, in instalments, into mite-boxes. I made the first payment of ten shillings and sweated from week to week. As time went slowly by, the instalments were reduced to half a crown and it's an awful thing to admit, but I have a bad debt with God on that account. Indeed, the other terms and conditions of the contract were not adhered to either.

I got three raises in wages, of a pound each time. I was there a year and the highest paid barman at eleven pounds. As Michael was only on twelve pounds, there wasn't anywhere further I could go from there and I decided it was time to move on. One day I saw an advertisement for a bar-manager in Ballinasloe and I applied. It stated that it was "Take complete control of the opening and running of a new bar". I got a phone call and the man said he would come and interview me in The Genoa. As luck would have it, he knew me from occasionally coming in and apparently I had impressed him. I told Michael and he said it would be OK to sit at a table when my interviewer came in.

If anybody ever tells you that unless a man gives you a firm handshake he's "shifty", don't believe it. This thin, slightly pale man arrived and when we shook hands, he hardly made a grip at all. I noted and sat down. He told me he was a builder, had bought and was currently "doing up" this pub to a high standard and needed someone to run it. The right man would do a good business and he would pay well. I was then getting eleven pounds and paying three pounds to Mrs. Lawlor. I knew shopboys who were working for three or four pounds a week. The wage for this job I was being interviewed for would pay twelve pounds, with free accommodation over the bar and dinner paid for in a restaurant.

I showed him my references, including the most eloquently written one, from Master Lawlor. The man sitting opposite me was a bit taken aback that I was so young for the job, even though I had stated my age in my application. There had been hundreds of applicants. I wasn't a bit overawed by my potential new boss and I found it easy to talk to him – making a good case for myself and telling him that some day I would own my own pub. I thought I had lost it on account of my age. Then I heard; "It will be ready to open in three weeks. You would need to be there for at least a week beforehand to order stock and supplies and lay it out. When could you start"? "I'll give a weeks' notice", I replied and we had another limp hand shake, but there was nothing limp about the way my head and heart was racing. In two years I was going from two pounds to twelve. My new boss was one of the most popular men around East Galway. A hard-working, self-made builder and developer, with a love of traditional Irish music, sport – especially hurling and horse racing. The man, his warm-hearted wife and so many members of their family became my friends. I am happy to state that Hubert and Mary Hardiman are still two of my most treasured friends.

Ballinasloe

My Mother was over the moon. Her eldest son was now managing a pub!

I arrived by train in Ballinasloe on 9th August 1963. A month short of my nineteenth birthday. In September Dublin beat Galway in the football All-Ireland and poor Waterford lost again to Kilkenny in the hurling decider. Worse for me, my beloved Westmeath lost the minor football All-Ireland final. I would have to "suffer" for a further thirty two years before that got rectified.

In October I bought a car on hire-purchase from Fred Kilmartin. A three year old Ford Anglia de Luxe, for three hundred and twenty five pounds, registration CI9849. In November, nobody knew it, but I cried when those warm, smiling eyes I looked into in Galway, were closed for good in Dallas. Hardimans Bar, Main Street, opened with a mighty flourish. Bar and lounge – the best in town. I just loved it and I loved the challenge and as we might say nowadays, "The Buzz". The place was constantly packed. I hired a couple of young (young, says he, at nineteen!) barmen, but we depended a lot on experienced part-time barmen. Mrs. Hardiman's Father, a fit, retired man, was a willing helper also. Hubie was always telling me to get him to do the bottles and yard work, but I didn't like asking him to do much. He was a lovely man and moderate in all his habits. (Two glasses of Guinness!) Many people remember him with affection. His name was 'Son' McHugh, but the family and myself called him "Sudda" – what his first grandchild, Marie, first called him. 'Son' was a loyal friend and the fact that he died at the same time as my father, added to the sadness.

I didn't take an hour off for the first several weeks. In the first week I couldn't even go for my dinner. Someone would bring down the plate from up town and I would wolf it into me in the store. I never called my new boss by anything other than his Christian name, Hubie, but I always called his wife Mrs. Hardiman until long after I'd left. Hubie was building The Guards Houses in Templemore, so I only saw him at week-ends. After closing he, along with his brothers, or a couple of friends insisted that I have a drink and these week-end sessions, usually incorporating keenly contested games of darts became a regular and hugely enjoyable part of my job.

People might now wonder how we were able to drink so much, in poor times. Well, drink was cheap. In Kilcormac, I sold pints for one shilling and three pence – I suppose around eight cent in to-days money. When we opened Hardimans, we were getting 1s – 8d (one and eight pence) – around ten cent, for a pint of Guinness. I was never a great Guinness lover. My drink was lager and Brandy or Vodka – or anything!

I didn't need time off from work to socialise because there was lots of time to go dancing after work. The Emerald ballroom in Ballinasloe was the usual haunt, but we travelled to dances and carnivals all over the country. Of course, after a while I was able to take nights off and with cars being scarce, I was always in big demand and the Anglia would be bulging with bodies – especially coming home. Nobody would be left without a lift. Many is the night we finished up in the ditch and it's the hand of God that nobody got killed.

It was the exciting showband era. My countyman, Joe Dolan, recorded "The Answer to Everything", which bestowed me with useful bragging rights. One night I asked Joe and Ben if they would call into the pub when they were passing through Ballinasloe. Soon afterwards at nine o'clock on a Sunday evening the bar door flew open and in comes Joe, Ben and all "The Drifters".

Showing the signs

That's the sort of The Dolans and why they are still so successful. Forty years later Joe and Ben paid me the honour of coming to visit my pub in Spain.

"The Royal", "The Dixies", "The Cadets", Cadets singer, Eileen Reid and her husband Jimmy Day are regular visitors of ours in Spain now, where they do a regular 'gig' in "Paddys Point" "The Miami", The Pacific", and many more super bands – Donie Collins – "Be my guest" all epitomised the excitement of being alive and living through the sixties. But my favourite band of all was The Capital – not so much for Butch Moore, but for the beat and for the brass. "The Capital" with The Kellys, Paul Sweeney, Don Long and especially Paddy Cole. I was a fan of Paddy then, and still am. To-day we are friends and one of my proudest moments was when "The Paddy Cole All-stars" played in my Mullingar Leisure Centre in April 1996.

I bought a new suit and Joe Healy's was demoted to working clothes. Everyone wore a suit going to dances, but there was a change coming there too. I was one of the first to wear a heavy jumper, or an Aran sweater to The Emerald Ballroom.

A car, well dressed and no great shortage of spending – money, at the age of nineteen and twenty was conducive to a plentiful supply of women, some of whom got an after dance drink, or bonus mineral in Hardiman's Bar. Two hospitals, Portiuncalla and St. Bridigs were like women factories, with the supply constantly changing. My long-term girl-friend was Bridie Finn, from Aughrim, a student nurse in St. Brigids. Bridie and I spent half our time denying and fighting over being seen "going with someone else", but it is fair to say that neither of us restricted ourselves to the joys of each other.

My Grandfather, then in his ninety-third year, was delighted that I was in Ballinasloe and he was twice as delighted when I started bringing him home the odd bottle of Poteen. Did I say that Granda took a drink? Granda had worked at the building of the church there and his local was "John Loughnane's Bar", which was now Hardimans Bar.

John Loughnane and his wife ran an ultra respectable establishment. Frequented by Bank Managers, Businessmen, professionals and at least one priest, it was not unusual for a customer to get barred for swearing or singing. Many stories about this strict pub were still fresh when I took over and this one is my favourite.

It was Sunday and under the then "Bona Fide Law" only travellers, those liv-

ing more than three miles from the pub, were entitled to be on the premises. Nobody, including John Loughnane adhered to this law. All the regulars were in the bar, whilst Mrs. Loughnane kept lookout from an upstairs bedroom window. Sometimes there would be a "false alarm", or if John wanted to get rid of a problem drinker, he would give his wife "the beck"; she would shout "Guards!" Everyone would run out the back door and down the garden. This had a dual purpose; John would empty all glasses down the sink and those chosen to get back in would all have to buy again. Word would spread amongst the regulars as to who was "expelled" and it was the duty of the chosen ones to give the slip to the unwanted.
This Sunday an undesirable had got in because of his clean looks and good suit. Turned out he was home after spending six months in England and was bad news. He spoke with an English accent and was drinking "alf 'n'alf" (a pint with half beer and half Guinness). On his third "alf 'n'alf" he became boisterous. This man was in the wrong place. "GUARDS – RAID – GUARDS"! "All out" roared John. Twenty minutes and the filtering back in was complete. The banished one knew his rights. He had left "alf 'n'alf" on the counter and he was banging on the front door, demanding to get in to finish the drink he had paid for.
Mrs. Loughnane raised the upstairs window "Go away" she said, "there isn't anybody here and nobody is getting in". The banging on the door was attracting attention up and down Main Street. "I'm not going till I get my "alf 'n'alf" he screeched. The publicans wife went and took the chamber-pot from under the bed. Leaning out the window she poured the contents, straight as a dye over the Brylcream and shiny face of the returned emigrant. "There now", said Mrs. Loughnane, "is yar "alf 'n'alf" – half of John's and half of mine!!

Darts Mad

I quickly made lots of friends. Ballinasloe cemented my feelings of being an Honorary Galwayman – especially when it comes to the Galway hurlers. I have followed them ever since – more passionately than a born Galwayman and of course, whilst I was in Ballinasloe, the footballers won the first two of the three in a row. Cyril Dunne and Sean Meade from that team were good friends and great companions to have.
But the greatest craze at that time was the game of darts. Every pub had one

or two teams and the standard was very high. Sonny Barry, and Kilkennyman, Tommy Larkin were the top players and they played for Gibbons' Bar. Any man you saw carrying his own darts in his breast pocket was good. If the darts had paper flights, then he was very, very good!

Darts is definitely a drinking mans game. The only thing which suffered as a result of my sobriety was my darts.

A good darts player has to be good at maths. You have to know what's left and what to go for with your three darts, without hesitating or changing your rhythm. For example, if I came in on one hundred and thirty four, I went for treble twenty, treble fourteen, double sixteen, but if I got a single twenty, I might switch to treble eighteen, to leave me on sixty. As soon as the dart hit the board, I and most of those guys knew what was left and how to get it. I reached the final of an individual tournament in Tom Hyne's in Aughrim, where I was beaten by Tommy Larkin.

Hubie was a keen player also and we had some fantastically enjoyable away nights at darts tournaments. We didn't have the best five players in town on our A team, but we were the luckiest. Sonny Barry, who had done well in "The News of The World" championship in England, was quoted – with some justification, as saying that; "If Hardiman's team fell into a barrel of shit, they would come out smelling like roses"! The first tournament we won was Sean Flynn's – the Bar nearest to us. Sean couldn't hide his disgust at these new upstarts, who were taking his business and rubbing salt in the wounds, by taking his annual darts competition.

Our greatest triumph was winning the "Gold-Flake Cup" which took place in Laurenctown. We got the cup, seven replicas, fifty pounds prize money, a hundred Gold Flake each and all the drink we could consume from the cup, glass, or any other vessel. My problem and therefore the teams problem, was having the correct amount of drink in me. None and I couldn't throw at all. We played a match in Mountbellew on an Ash Wednesday. We were all off the drink and the tyre around the dartboard was getting the works during the practice warm-up. Swift and decisive corrective action had to be taken. All back on the drink! Mine was a double brandy and I made the ginger ale do three of them. If I started too early, or had too much, I couldn't throw either. Timing was of the essence!

I peaked one night during a semi-final in Athlone. I knew as each dart left my hand that it would sail straight and through to any double or treble I wanted. Hubie was on before me. On the way home Seamus Fahy joked that I told Hubie to leave the winning of it for me. To win the decider, I came in on "five to do". I just loved the drama and the tension. Not a sound in the packed bar. I threw the first dart, looking for a single one and then double two. The dart lodged in treble one, leaving me with double one to finish. In order to stretch it out, I asked the marker to check if it was a single or a treble one – even though I knew well it was a treble. The marker confirmed. I threw the second dart to the exact centre of double one.

Fred Kilmatrin, used do a little bit of car-hire and I asked him about it. "If you're careful who you let them out to, there's money in it", he told me. "It's about seven pounds for a weeks' short term insurance policy – third party of course and you can easily get eighteen or twenty pounds per week. In the bar, "Gateway to The West" I had the perfect depot for a new sideline for myself. I put up a poster and put an advert in "The Connaught Tribune". The demand for my Anglia was immediate and constant. I went home and down to The Manager of the Ulster Bank in Castlepollard and borrowed the three hundred pounds to buy a second hand Morris 1000 from Fred.

This time was the high point of my Ballinasloe career. Even though I was now living the high life and with, by now, well trained bar-staff to give me time off, my wages were more than adequate to keep me in this manner. All the time, I sent home a few quid to my Mother. For a few months, during the summer of 1964 I was awash with cash, with the money coming in for the cars. I had "third party open driving" on both cars and sometimes I took a chance and didn't pay the additional seven pounds weekly premium. I would give the likely agreeable customer a couple of pounds off and tell them to say, if asked, that they had a loan of the car. All this business was taking a chance. Like I said, for a time, the money rolled and then I started to have the odd bit of damage and the repairs bill was mounting. However, the greatest damage was being done to myself and if I could see it, I couldn't do anything about it. My wonderful job in Ballinasloe, with so many of the best times of my life, was only to last for two years and was the first major casualty of my drinking.

Taking The Boat

By early 1965 I was in trouble. Too much freedom taken. Too much money being spent. Too much drink being drunk. Too many excuses.

Hubie and Mrs. Hardiman had sold their house in Killoran and moved into town. Hubie was finished in Templemore and with working "locally" he could see clearly what was going on. I and some of the lads, especially my main, boozing buddies of Joe Mulhare, Kieran Shields, Pat McManus, Pauric McGann and Sean Hogarty might go to a match on Sunday and if we "went in for one" I didn't come back to work. Other than after closing time, I didn't drink on the job, but if I met someone out town, or anywhere else and had one - that was it for the day. Hubie eventually talked to me and said my only hope was to schedule regular time off for myself and be either working or not.

The bar was making money. I was very conscious and conscientious about making profit. A penny extra on drinks in the lounge. Buying Millers ten year old whiskey cheaply, in five gallon crocks and putting it into old whiskey bottles. Getting best deals from travellers and always looking for free kegs and crates. My understudy, Pat Devine was doing well and he learned everything fast, as I delegated responsibility to him by my not being there, or too hung-over in the mornings. Pat was able to subtly let Hubie know how much he was doing – and certainly, who could blame him for that.

Mrs. Hardiman was as kind and as good to me as was Mrs. Spain before her. She would know "I wasn't too good" and make me soup. Herself and Hubie have a great relationship. She would be present at many of our social outings and always great company.

Every time the cars came back there was something wrong with them. Then, one after another, they didn't come back. I would get a phone call; which garage or which ditch. Eventually they were written off and I owed most of their original value. I got seventy pounds for the Anglia and a hundred and fifty pounds for the Morris. My friend, Sean Hogarty, who worked in a drapery shop, copied me and bought a Morris Minor, believing that he could hire it out enough to pay the H.P. instalments. My cars were out, so I hired his to drive to Joe Dolan in The County Hall, Mullingar, on a Tuesday night. No money changed hands because Sean owed me a few pounds. There were six of us in the car. Bridie and myself, Kieran Shields and Mary Donoghue, and another couple we were just giving a lift to. We had three drinks before we left Ballinasloe. There was a hill and a bridge and a fresh shower on the road, but whatever the reason, at a place called CRUSH, on the Athlone – Ballymore Road I turned over the car. We were all brought to hospital. Only the couple we were giving the lift to were detained, but Sean's Morris Minor was a right off.

Sean and I fell out over who was carrying the risk. Before I left Ballinasloe he had instigated legal proceedings against me. He never would have got anything and soon I was outside the jurisdiction. One night, nine years later, I rang his doorbell and paid him for the car; much to his astonishment and gratitude.

Relations between Hubie and myself were by now strained. He was a great and patient boss and I would never have put up with a "me" working for me. Hubie got it very hard to give out to me, but a couple of times he lost his temper on something that six months earlier he wouldn't mind.

He was a successful businessman, builder, developer and racehorse owner, so he was hardly a fool. The bar business had gone down a bit from the heady opening and it was plain that Pat and the other staff could mange without me.

One morning Hubie told me "to get to hell out of the place" and I did. I spent five days drinking round town and then came back. He asked me why did I wait five days "mouthing round town". I didn't know, but I would tell him later.

Alcoholism is a mental obsession, coupled with a physical compulsion for alcohol. I wasn't bad, or weak – I couldn't help it. I had no control. My life was unmanageable due to drink – but I didn't know that yet.

I was back working, but it wasn't the same. Raymond Chapman, whose family lived in England was going back and I said I would go with him. Joe Mulhare, from Eyrecourt said he would come to.

Hubie heard it before I told him and he was hugely relieved. The night I finished up, we had a few drinks. "How are you fixed?" he asked. "I paid off the Anglia, but I still owe The Ulster Bank and I owe you thirty pounds". "I didn't know you owed me?" "It's written in the book". Then Hubie paid me a wonderful compliment "If you weren't such an honest man, you wouldn't owe so much money" – and he pushed my brandy glass hard up against the Hennessy uptake.

Hubie made sure I had wages, holiday pay and a bit extra that night. Mulhare and I came up home for a few days but of course I didn't say a word that I was about to leave Ballinasloe. On the Sunday we went to a match. Rickardstown were playing someone in Delvin and Mulhare and I were there. We got two hurls for the pre-match puck about. Joe knew who Jobber McGrath was and manoeuvred until he was beside him. Joe ran on to a ball and picked it with panache. He threw it up to strike and Jobber just put out his hand, plucked the ball and Mulhare hit an air-pocket. Mulhare turned to Jobber and said, "Now I know why Joe Salmon said you were the best man he ever played alongside".

Willie played well and how could any of us have imagined that this would be the last year of the great Rickardstown team.

Mulhare, Chapman and myself spent another week on the beer, getting ready to go to England. I felt ashamed and for me it was sign of failure. My parents always hoped that none of us would go to England. America would have been OK but when I was growing up I would often hear in derogatory tone the term that there would be nothing for such a fellow only "to take the boat". The law of balances and counter-balances was back in play. I had had two of the best and most exciting years of my life and now I was heading for probably the worst year and a half.

On the way to the train, the morning we were leaving Ballinasloe I was coming up Main Street at seven am. The boys were with me and we had a rough night. Loads of farewell drinks, we left the girl-friends back at St. Brigids' Gate and slept in the car for a couple of hours. Hubie was getting into his car. He stopped me and called me over. "Watch your company, take care of yourself and may God be with you"! We shook hands. I can't remember how firm or otherwise the grip was, but when I took my hand back, there was a ten pound note in it.

CHAPTER 10

Paddy The Navvy

The 18th September 1965 was my twenty first birthday. I celebrated it with an unmerciful piss-up in my digs at Ravenscroft Road, Birkenhead, Cheshire. Bill, the barman at the Knights of Columbus Club, told everybody that I drank twelve pints before I went to my party. Mrs. Chapman the landlady organised the bash-up and everyone paid in an equal amount. We even had a keg on tap. The landlord and lady, their sons and daughters and all the other lodgers took a drink.

By now, I had been about five months in England and I hated every day of it and I would hate every day of the next thirteen months, until I got out of it. They say "nobody can make you feel inferior without your consent". Maybe not, but in England in the sixties, you felt them try. I would never, answer to "Paddy" – same way as I would not expect a black man to answer to "Toby" or "Boy".

When we arrived over with Raymond, his Mother, Mrs. Chapman, made us welcome and told us there was no hurry on the rent, until we started working. Ray's Father, Jack was a quiet inoffensive, hard-working man. There were four sons and two daughters. Raymond was the youngest and the most refined.

Daughters, Maura and Joan, were married nearby. Eugene was married next door. To say that Eugene "took a drink" would be to say that Wexford grows a strawberry. Eugene was a nice guy and good fun to be with. Sean and Noel lived at home. Sean was as rough a guy as you would meet. Constantly getting into fights, he knocked me out cold one night, me still not having learned the lesson from Cloughan, or that one can always back off, or run, or lie down, or something! Noel was … well, we all knew that Noel wasn't into women and that we should keep our eye on him. In another room was a pregnant in-law, with her husband of a few months. Another room was set to Harry, an Englishman, who was near retirement and had a reasonably good job. What in the name of God he was doing there, I don't know. He may have been a compulsive gambler. I'm not finished yet; in what had started off as a three bedroom terrace house, was also Joe Mullins from Meath and another Irishman called Johnny Delaney and of course my friend, Joe Mulhare. The newly married man didn't take a drink. This was a rough house, but I was as rough as any, in a rough place, in a rough era.

Mrs. Chapman was a fair woman. She was formidable, but she had to be. We got our fill to eat – even if there wasn't much variety. Liver was a great favourite of hers, but wasn't it good for us!

My first job was as a "navvy", as it paid better than bar work. I worked with Johnston Stubbs for two months, digging trenches. I would arrive home in the evening totally fatigued. Sometimes I would change the clothes, sometimes not. Almost always I would fall asleep in a chair until the dinner was ready. Other times, I wouldn't come home. Go to the pub "for one". No leaving, no dinner. Fish 'n chips in newspaper after closing time.

I was sick, sore and sorry, so I cleaned myself up and went looking for a bar job I heard was available at "The Acorn". Mulhare had landed a job at The Woodside Hotel, two days after we landed.

The Acorn was a sixpenny bus ride away. Sometimes I didn't have the sixpence and I walked. I didn't enjoy walking then!

The money was middling only and less than I was making before I left Ireland. There was however, a useful fringe benefit. It was not frowned upon to take a drink. It was customary to have a small ale with the customers. With most other staff and with the landlord, it was just for show and the sup of beer would get warm in the glass before being dumped. Not my glass; I kept it freshened up! I also had a pint glass in the cellar, just to check that nobody upstairs would get bad beer. One night I went home and left all the windows and bar door open. 'Dot' was first in next morning and saved my bacon.

I was paying Mrs. Chapman back rent, sending a few quid home and paying off The Ulster Bank, Castlepollard at nine pounds per month. I was badly broke but the Devil looks after his own – I had free drink.

Then Bridie came over from Ballinasloe for two weeks holidays. Maura kindly agreed to keep her at her house. Bridie took a drink then for the first time, but I'm sure that not even a drink could dull her disappointment at what she saw. It was a disaster. Next time I wrote and told her I heard she was going with someone else, she wrote and said she was. That called for a drink.

Michael Larkin worked on the buses. At my twenty first I asked him about the job. He was now a driver, having started six months earlier as a conductor. It sounded good to me. The day after the party, I drained out a bit and the following day I went for an interview. I got the job. I was now an employee of Birkenhead Corporation and a section of their daily commuters would soon be in my shaky hands. One of the rules was that you could not enter a pub in uniform – on or off duty. Some chance!

No Goal

I played hurling, of a manner, for a team called Shamrocks. All the lodgers, except the pregnant bride and Harry the Englishman, were on the team. It was brutal. Any opposing player, who wasn't told there were three Chapmans on the team, would definitely have won a case against the GAA for withholding vital information. There were two pioneers playing for us and you would always know them. Shaved that morning, Persil white togs and constantly testing the spring in the hurley after togging out. I had no togs and usually played in my trousers – my good ones. I spent all of the hour suffering from a hangover, not getting involved and generally practicing self-preservation. I scored a goal once, which wasn't my fault. I took up an out-half position, as a scrum developed around the twenty one yard line. Out came a perfect hand-pass. I doubled on it and blasted the roof of the net – if there had been a net. The goal was disallowed as it was deemed that the hand-pass was a throw. I never said a word to the referee about it, because when I turned round he was on the ground with five shamrock players on top of him. Rows on the pitch weren't too bad because you had space. The rows between ourselves on the last lap of the bus trip home were sort of awkward. I kept out of it, but I found it very hard to sleep.

On the bus, going to the match, we would have one pit-stop, half way. Phil would stand half way down the bus; "Lads, listen a minute, "Horses", this is a stop for a piss, not for drink. No drinking before the match; I don't want to see anyone going out on the pitch to-day, with the sign of drink". Then we stopped for a couple.

One Sunday, we arrived early and there was a curtain raiser. I was in the wrong place, at the wrong time and was conscripted to be a linesman. The simplest job there, you might think. Wrong! The line was badly marked and the flags seemed to be not in a straight line. Add to this the fact that I had had a rough night and when I looked at the line it kept moving. Ball near the line "Sweet Jesus let it stay in play"! Clash of the ash, shoulder to shoulder – or anything to anything, as far as that goes. Ball over where line was. "Line Ball". Two hairy warriors like that one on the Guinness add., with different coloured jerseys descended on me "our ball" roared both of them. "Linesman's Ball" I held my flag straight up, struggling to keep the quiver out of it. I threw in the ball. The clash of the ash. "Sweet Jesus let it stay in play"! I would say I broke the record for "Linesman's Balls" that day.

I was homesick all the time. Most of all I missed the dances. The social scene was so different in Birkenhead and Liverpool. It wasn't Liverpool's fault and I still have a grá for that city, but I didn't want to be there and I was moving in the wrong circles. The girls I met were either too hard or too soft or too stupid. Not that I would have been any catch for any category of woman, but anything I met couldn't measure up to the lovely classy girls of Westmeath, Galway or Offaly. I did have a few women, but I never had a real girl-friend while I was in England.

Mulhare and myself had moved out of Chapmans and got ourselves a flat in a house nearby. It was a costly mistake, on my stomach. At least Mrs. Chapman put food on the table. Now, if Joe or I cooked it was "the pan". Joe got fed at work and I lived on fries and beans on toast from the Bus Depot Canteen. Drinking on an empty stomach and then a feed of greasy chips before bed left me with a stomach that still shows scar tissue on X-Ray. I was drinking for a year before I smoked a cigarette but I was, by now, a heavy smoker.

Two weeks before I moved out of Chapmans, I had a bit of good fortune. It was Saturday and all the lads were looking at racing on T.V. George the Bookie was just down the road, so bets were going on by all concerned, except me. The bad news was that I had given up gambling. Where I would normally bet in units of five or ten shillings. Just to have an interest in the races, I looked at the paper and picked out three horses. The bet: 3 one shilling each way crossed doubles, 1 shilling treble, 2 shilling each way double on two of the horses. The three won, one at 9/1. You will appreciate how much that windfall meant to me when I tell you I still remember the names of two of the horses; "Robinson Crusoe II" and "Miss Togs". Shell shocked George handed me out thirty pounds. I put twenty pounds in an envelope and posted it to The Ulster Bank – the last two payments on the Morris 1000!

Recently I heard Eamon Dunphy say that a bet is only worth it if it matters whether you win or lose. How right he is. To-day I have a share in a racehorse and if he wins the National, I guarantee you it will not give me the same pleasure as did watching "Miss Togs" on T.V. bringing off my treble in 18 Ravenscroft Road!

Mulhare and I shared what we had. If one had money, we both had. He was "on the floor" in "The Woodside" and made good tips. I would arrive in with no money, when he was working. "I have no money" he would say. "You better make some", I would reply, ordering a pint. The pint would come and then, when I got near the bottom, he would try avoiding me. I would put up my hand and click my fingers. "Fuck off", he would say, with venom, out of the corner of his mouth, as he passed my table. Next I would call over one or two people I knew and ask them to sit down and have a drink. Joe then had to come over and I would order not one, but three drinks. I was then ok for the next two, because the others then had to buy. Joe drank the same amount as I did. He had a lovely sheepskin coat, which he had bought from a catalogue at work. He got into the habit of going to the pawnshop with the jacket midweek, if funds were exhausted.

One night I had a promising date. I came in from work and peeled off the uniform. Shaved and got into the bath, long time in the bath – maybe the world wasn't such a bad place after all. Winked at myself in the mirror, as I dried off. Lots of "Old Spice" and not confined to face. Clean new underpants – just in case. The suit .... the suit .... no fucking suit. Mulhare had pawned my suit!

Rock Ferry

There were two bus depots and I was based in Rock Ferry. I got a weeks training with a "clippie" (a female conductor). Our driver, a married man, was her boyfriend. I found there was a lot of that sort of thing on the buses. They were extremely nice and good to me. When Bill saw that I bought nothing in the canteen at meal-break, he realised I didn't have money and they both bought me food all week. That kindness meant a lot to me and I never saw them in a pub after that, without buying them a drink.

I had a ticket machine, carried on a strap across the shoulder and another strap with a leather money bag hanging the other side. The number of passengers and money reading was entered on a waybill at the end of each trip. All had to tally when cashing in at the office, but it was made clear to me that the conductor was expected to make enough to buy the teas, all shift, for both himself and the driver. A driver never walked up to the counter and bought teas. I regarded it as "fiddling" and I didn't like it – but that's how it was.

After training you got a mate. A driver and conductor were a crew and always worked together – barring sometimes overtime or when that crew was "spare", and either one would replace a sick or 'awol' worker. Bobby Smith was my driver. He had only recently got his drivers badge and we were each others first "mate". We got on very well. We were both cautious starting off and eased ourselves into the routine without too many problems. There were compulsory stops and request stops. If a passenger wanted to get off at a "request stop" I was supposed to ring the bell. Some drivers would show up a conductor by not stopping if they didn't get a bell, even if they could see in the mirror someone standing on the platform. If I forgot, was too busy taking fares, or didn't know the stop, I had no worry, Bobby would always look back and stop if needs be. Bobby was moderate in his habits and whilst he liked a pint, he couldn't see any sense to my drinking.

We played cards and dominoes in the canteen but soon the magnet of next door drew me. Every stationary minute I spent in "The Farmers Arms". Remember, we weren't supposed to go in a pub in uniform, but that rule was blatantly ignored. However, numerous staff were fired for drinking on the job. I don't know how I never got caught. If I was "spare" and required, the guys in the office, after calling my name on the P.A., would then send someone to the pub to get me. I gulped a mouthful of raspberry and put a fistful of cloves in my mouth before I left the pub – trying to eliminate the smell of alcohol. Soon I would be a driver and then the passengers wouldn't be able to smell my breath.

There was an acute shortage of drivers at Birkenhead Corporation. I was only there a couple of months, when I was put into driving school. These were all double-decker buses. In driving school and for the PSV test, we drove big "GUYS", with crashed gear boxes. You had to double de-clutch and if you missed a gear, you would hear the crunching in the next parish.

In January I passed my test and a few days later I was presented with my drivers badge by Joe in the office. It was a great feeling. P.S.V. DRIVER 8117. I was "cab happy". There was lots of overtime available and I worked every hour I could get. My permanent conductor assigned to me was a contrary old clippie. I didn't want working with her and I'm sure she wasn't over the moon about me either. I couldn't "take a drink" in front of her, in case she might report me. When the bus was empty, I gave her a rough "jaunt". When turning at "Acre Lane", I swung her round at such an angle that the rear skidded. It worked; she looked for a new "mate". I found out I only got her because nobody else wanted this lady for a mate. My new conductor and for the duration, was a lad my own age, by the name of Ian Bailey. He wouldn't be going into driving school because he was suspended from driving for having no insurance on his motorbike; we hit if off from the start. An only son, he lived locally with his mother, apart from in-between times whenever he met a girl with accommodation. When I was leaving, Ian took a three hundred pound watch off his arm and insisted I take it; and yet I never afterwards got a reply from the letters I wrote him. Tall blonde and handsome Bailey was mighty company. I would often have to rev the engine at stops as women lingered an extra minute on the platform. He was fit for anything and some of the stunts we got away with are now unbelievable.

Bailey "took a drink".

We drank on duty. Any conductor could make enough for tea. Ian made enough for drink. Often we would leave out a route altogether. Blank and park the bus. Keep a percentage of figures from the previous route and from the following one and fill in the figures on the route that we didn't do. You could only do this on a route, where there were lots of buses anyway and the public didn't suffer and didn't complain.

I thank God to this day that I didn't kill anyone, but I wasn't capable of seeing the danger at the time. Sometimes Bailey had to help me up into the cab. I had a few minor accidents and once I wedged an empty bus under a bridge. It wasn't my fault and witness told how an artic truck had pulled in front of me. Nevertheless, as the policeman was taking a statement from me, at the scene, (the picture appeared in the Liverpool Echo) I was afraid he might get the smell of drink off me. I kept taking a step back and we finished fifty yards from the scene!

The football specials were great overtime. I can say that John Aldridge and myself have something in common. We both got paid to watch Tranmere Rovers play!

Waste of a Life

One of my friends in the depot was Ed Houlihan, whose father came from Limerick. He had a really nice girl friend, a clippie, and I got on great with Trish. After a few months, Ed broke it off with Trish, as he planned on going to Australia. Trish was devastated and used talk to me a lot about it. One evening, we finished work together and I asked her to come for a drink. We had a most enjoyable evening – the life of the party in The Farmers Arms. I thought she was over Ed. Trish was a petite dark twenty three year old. She used too much make-up, false eye-lashes and hair lacquer – but it seemed right for her. She was good looking all right like I said, we got on great, we were friends, I didn't want to push it, but I was "interested" in her. At closing time an older guy there, offered to give us a lift home. We lived close to each other. When we got near, Trish told the guy where I lived, too quickly for my liking – as I was dropped off first and then Trish got out only a couple of blocks away. I was annoyed that she must have thought that if we got out at her place, I would take some advantage – which I never in my life did, unless it was welcomed.

In the canteen next morning, we just happened to arrive at the counter together. "I'm before you" she said. "You made bloody sure I was before you last night" I retorted. I didn't know that she went back to the office and checked out sick. I didn't know that she didn't come to work next day. I didn't know that the radio was blaring in her flat. I didn't know that she was two days dead from an overdose.

I had a letter from Willie, telling me he planned to go to Canada in the Summer of 1966. This would be my "out"; I would go too. Mulhare and I had booked two weeks holiday at home for July and after that, I hoped to make Canada, before it got too cold, round the end of October. Joe decided he would come too. There was a bit of saving to be done. The only way I could save was by putting money in an envelope, the day I got paid and send it to the bank at home. This I did. Mulhare was saving money into a savings plan at the hotel.

Christmas Day, 1965 we were hungry. The previous day, we must have been celebrating the birth of Christ, or something, because we woke up, hung-over, thirsty and not a scrap of food in the flat. Lack of food was no problem for the first half of Christmas Day, but as it came towards evening, we pounded the streets looking for a café open. Absolutely nothing. It got dark and we lay on the beds in the room, each thinking of Christmas' past. Then there was a knock on the door. It was Marco, the ten year old son of our Italian Landlady and Polish Landlord. We were invited over to their quarters. The only time ever. Bread, salads, meats galore and a big pot of tea. Don't let anybody ever tell you there isn't a God! Finished eating, then an oversized bottle of white wine was put on the table between Joe and me. The first mouthful tasted terrible. Wine is an acquired taste, which is developed over time. I acquired sufficient taste in about five minutes. Mulhare and I eyed the wine (we had been told to help ourselves) like two dogs, with one bone between them – each afraid the other might get the bigger share. The bottle emptied, we took our leave and went to bed. That was another good turn I never forgot and I sent Marco a present from Canada, the following Christmas.

During the 1990's I wrote a weekly squash column for the local papers. It developed into much more than a squash column and from the feed-back I got, I know a lot of people enjoyed it. Some of those readers may remember that in Christmas week, my last word, greeting and best wishes would be for our exiles abroad. I would be thinking of my Christmas Day in England.

One night a nineteen year old passenger and I hit it off and we both decided it would be a good idea if she overnighted with me. Mulhare was in bed, but had the good grace to pretend to be asleep. Joe left the room in the morning, for work, but was quickly back. "You are in trouble" he announced, with no little trace of glee in his voice. "There is a sentry outside" and off he went. I waited a while and then headed out for the bathroom. Directly opposite my door, back against the far wall, arms folded, was Marco. The landlady knew, and posted him there so that nobody could get out unnoticed. I got dressed. I told the girl to wait ten minutes and meet me across the road. I closed my bedroom door, gave Marco a breezy "Good morning", walked passed him, down the stairs and out. I could hear him running to give his report. Whether or not anyone said anything to the girl I don't know because by the time she was "across the road" I had ordered a pint from Mulhare, which he never got paid for. Next day, my landlady gave me a yellow card.

Holidays

I lived for July, counting every day, until Mulhare and I landed home in Ireland for our two weeks holiday. It was worth the wait. We had a great time. Having hired a Morris 1000 in Dublin, we divided our time between Westmeath, Ballinasloe and Eyrecourt. I realised afterwards how disappointed my parents must have been at how little they saw of me – but they were so pleased to see me looking so well. I was a bit bloated from the drink and they thought it was because of having a good "do". I drank with my parents now and we got on great and I never was really drunk at home. Dances almost every night, darts in Ballinasloe, women – it was just like old times. I went to pay Hubie the money I owed him, but he just pushed me away saying; "You owe me nothing". I do, Hubie!

I met a really nice girl and did a line of sorts with her, over that holiday, by mail and for a little while when I came back two and a half years later. She fell for me big time and I treated her badly. The English would have called me a "cad" and they would have been correct.

Willie had gone to Canada and was settled in the Northern Manitoba Mining Town of Thompson. There were a lot of fellows from home in that mine, including Larry Gallagher, whom I had been at school with and Johnny Deveraux. Both were shift bosses. The great Irish tradition of those out there already, looking after the newly arrived was alive and well all over Canada.

I didn't say at home that I was going; whether Willie let on or not, I don't know. Mulhare and I booked to fly from Manchester to Winnipeg on 19th October 1966. A few farewell parties and serious drinking had to be done first.

In the flat, a poor radio reception was the most important part of my life. I heard about Nelsons Pillar "going up", but it was the GAA coverage on Sundays that was the highlight and I didn't even care if Liam Campbell was the commentator. I followed the success of my neighbours, Longford with great relish and of course Joe had to celebrate when Galway secured the famous three-in-a-row.

With regard to news, I have a sort of funny, sort of embarrassing story. One morning the front of a tabloid had a photo of this young cleric, carrying a placard in Rome, with the words "Doctor Ramsey – Traitor to Protestant Britain". Apparently, Dr. Ramsey was visiting the Pope and this young fellow called Ian Paisley didn't like it. I remember, because that night I had a first (and last) date with a Northern Irish divorcee.

Joe Mulhare and Myself
home on holiday from England 1966

I read the story in the paper, feeling that it would be a good topic for to start the evening. Barely settled in the pub, I tore into the story and the bigoted protestant clergy of Northern Ireland. She was listening, so I displayed my knowledge of Irish history, up to my school days when I myself formed a junior IRA and cut out the cap and gown graduation photo of Rory O'Brady and stuck it over my bed. No, I had never debated or talked to a unionist or a Ministers' daughter – until then!

I felt confident that life would be much better when I could get out of England and so it was. The work was harder. The money was fantastic. The labels on the bottles were different – but I was the same.

With a sense of expectation, anticipation, relief and excitement, we took off from Manchester. I was so glad to be leaving England. Some of my really good friend's to-day are English and I made some friends when I worked there; so long ago now. Now I like visiting England. I go there on business or a couple of matches in the premiership every year. I stay in the best places. I am proud of my Irish accent. A lot of the time I am called "Mister" or "Sir". There is no need on my part for anyone to ever call me "Mister" or "Sir", but nobody ever calls me "Paddy" any more! Paddy is a grand name – it depends how it's used! I called my pub in Spain, "Paddy's Point"!

North of 55

It was my first time to fly. We took off from Manchester and landed in Winnipeg. The flight cost well over a hundred pounds and isn't it amazing that it can be bought for around the same to-day – forty years later? Flying in over Winnipeg, at night, I'll never forget the spectacle of the city lights dancing and glittering beneath us. For me, it felt as if this new world was putting on a fairy-light exhibition, of welcome. Joe and myself had had a few 'bevies' during the British Airways Flight and a feeling of wellbeing and optimism engulfed me, as we touched down on Canadian soil. After clearing immigration and customs we hailed a taxi and asked him to take us to the nearest cheap place to sleep for the night. He took us to the Y.M.C.A., where I crawled into bed and slept like a baby.

Next morning we caught a flight further North, to the Gateway town of The Pas (pronounced Paw). Here INCO (International Nickel Company) had a hiring office where miners were hired to work in the mining town of Thompson, three hundred miles further north and as "bush" as it gets. A decade earlier there was no Thompson. In 1957 rich deposits of nickel were discovered and the town – (now a City), developed around this rich ore-body – which is still being mined to this day.

Our Air Canada small plane landed in The Pas around mid-day and as instructed by Willie, Mulhare and I booked into The Gateway Hotel. Hiring was done from nine o'clock in the morning to give time for a medical, so we knew it would be next day before our interview. In the meantime, we spent the remainder of our first day in Canada exploring The Pas. Naturally, I had never seen anything like it – except maybe in the movies. The population was predominantly "Indian" or "Native" as it the politically correct word now.

There was a timber industry of some sorts, trading, fishing and trapping animals for fur, but the real money was generated by miners in and out to the dozens of mines which spanned North in all directions from The Pas. I could immediately tell whether miners were going in or coming out. There were two types of men going in. Those jaded, hung-over, loud-spoken hard-rock miners who had done it all before, drank the "meal stake" and were returning, and there was then the first-timers like me. "Green men" or more commonly "JIGABOOS" we were called. We were the quiet ones, with the anxious faces and the doubts in our hearts as to whether we might make it. The guys on the way out were different "Bushed", hyper, laughing and shouting, singing, blind drunk and looking for squaws. Often these met up with long lost tramp-miner friends "going up North" and there never was any question as to who bought the beer.

I minded myself that day. I was seriously worried about passing the medical. I hadn't enough money to go anywhere else. I was not in good shape. My head was blocked with catarrh, but I was really suffering with my stomach. There was a constant burning pain in my gut. It was becoming more of a delicate operation to "get the foundation down" and more importantly, to keep it there!

Next morning, Mulhare and I were two of around thirty hopefuls who hired on for INCO. Statistically only two of that thirty would remain three months. We were that days' two! We were bound for Thompson! The relief at passing the medical was immense. We were given train tickets for the eight hour journey way up into the bush. Some of those who lived there, or had been there before, wore jackets with messages of "Thompson – North of 55", or "Harrison Mining", or "P.F. Fry" or some other mining outfit they worked for.

Now was our night of freedom and celebration in The Pas. We were safe! We had a job. We were hired on the lowest rung of the ladder to work underground "shoveller", at a rate of two dollars and forty five cent per hour. I knew a few lads from home who were in Thompson, as well as my brother. I had been at school with Larry Gallagher, who had recently "made shifting" (promoted to shift-Boss), with INCO. We would be OK. They had told me in England I wouldn't like the beer in Canada. I did the best I could and like the wine from the landlady the previous Christmas; I quickly educated my pallet to acquire a taste for it. We got unmercifully drunk and boarded the CN Train in the morning with the mother of all hangovers. Somewhere between The Pas and Thompson, I vomited up blood for the first time.

The Balmoral Lodge

Willie was working afternoon shift, but in the best tradition of the settled looking after the newly arrived, there was a welcoming party to greet us at Thompson Railway Station. Charlie Darby from Delvin, whom I knew well, was there with his brother Chris. The previous year, in Thompson, Chris had married Maureen Kelleghan, whom I knew from our school-days in Johnstown. Chris was driving, but there was another car load of "welcomers" these also, whom I didn't know. The driver of the car and the two passengers were drunk, Willie had told me that he had arranged for Joe and I to stay in the same place as himself. The "Balmoral Lodge", beside the Post Office, in the centre of Thompson. The driver of the "back-up car" introduced himself to me, as Amel to be our new landlord. I just knew that Amel, Mulhare and myself would get on so well together!

After settling in – for ten minutes or so, Amel suggested we go for a beer. We headed over to "The Thompson Inn". I had to be careful with the first few, but after that I felt no pain. I met Orangeman Bob Lunny, Indians, all sorts and shapes of nationalities, a few more Irishmen, Billy Carroll from Nova Scotia, Little Tommy Gaynor from Killucan and Ron Pollock, who was the longest resident of "The Balmoral" and therefore had the one single room. Ron and I became good friends and some time after that he met an awful end. A friend of Ron's had a mobile home out at the trailer park and asked Ron to sleep in it for a few days, whilst he was out of town. On the first night, Ron after a few drinks went to bed but left a lighted cigarette somewhere. A fire started and with the smoke he became disorientated and couldn't find the door, which was locked. Neighbours could hear him banging and trying to get out, someone got an axe, but by the time they smashed the door in, it was too late for Ron.

Amel and Bob Lunny weren't speaking, so I was drinking with two separate groups. After a while, Tommy Gaynor poked me in the chest with his finger and gave me twenty dollars, "just in case you're stuck"!

At closing time we headed over to "Kens' Restaurant", where we would meet up with Willie, who finished work at midnight. Sure enough, we arrived in around the same time. He never carried much "meat" but the first thing I noticed was how thin he had become. We all eat and chatted and I gathered there was a few cases of beer back in Willies' room – so we headed over. Amel joined us. Amel "took a drink"! Along with his long-suffering German born wife, Hilda he looked after us and our friends for the few months we were there. If anyone complained about our drinking sessions, or the noise from the parties, Amel threw out the complainers.

Willies room-partner, whom I met after Kens, was Phillip Conroy, a twenty years old, big raw "gasoon" from Ballivor. Very few people are blessed to have a best friend for the guts of forty years, but I have that friendship with Philip – as I often say; It survived drink, girlfriends, wives, babies and indeed both joyous and profoundly sad days also.

This was a Friday night and although on overtime shift was optional on Saturdays, nobody was working until Monday, in honour of the new arrivals. The rooms were clean and tidy, with two single beds in each room. Naturally, Mulhare and I were room partners. Sometime, before morning, I passed out in my own bed. I woke to go to the toilet and got back into bed. Willie and Phillip had gone to sleep (theirs was the room next to ours) with the record player on and it kept repeating on one song for hours, "The Grand Old River Moy". "Many years I've been in exile – I'll have you all to know: I came from dear old Ballina in the County of Mayo ....!" I had never heard it before, but I knew all the words by the time I got up and I swear to Jesus, I never want to hear that song again.

Eventually the living surfaced. We did a walking tour of Thompson: The Post Office, Sinclair's Restaurant, The Bay Shopping Mall, Ken's again, Thompson Inn Coffee Shop, Thompson Inn Beer Parlour, Thompson Inn Cocktail Lounge, Bowling Alley (just to look!) and then we did shopping for the night at the Beer store and the Liquor store.

The liquor laws were quiet strict. Twenty one was the legal age for drinking. You could only drink beer in the Beer Parlour and shots in The Cocktail Lounge. Similarly beer could be purchased in The Beer Store and bottles of spirits in The Liquor Store. It was an offence to open a bottle, or break the seal of a case of beer, before you took it home. The town was policed, with an iron fist, by the RCMP – (Royal Canadian Mounted Police) better know as "The Mounties".

It had been my plan to arrive before the really bad weather set in and we just made it. On this Saturday, our first full day in Thompson, it started to snow. It was the 23rd October. I would see nothing only snow now, until the end of April.

There were so many people I had to have a drink with on that Saturday, that by evening, my stomach, or no other part of me, was feeling any pain. Mulhare and I were two of the last out of The Thompson Inn. Met John Gaynor (Tom's brother) Gallagher, Devereux, and lots more from my part of the world. There were about seventeen thousand at that time, in Thompson with probably one hundred of the two thousand underground miners being Irish. I think I had a drink with all of them that day!

Willie (now Billy) left, and I early days in Canada

The party was going strong. The record-player was blaring. Someone had hidden "The River Moy" for its own safety. I felt myself about to get sick, which was becoming a more frequent occurrence. I just made it to the toilet and threw up blood again. Someone called a doctor. He arrived and examined me, gave me medicine and a prescription, pointed at the bottle of Canadian Club and told me I "knew what my problem was". The doctor told me to drink lots of milk, often and to see the company doctor on Monday.

I didn't drink on Sunday. Monday was to be my first day in the job and no way was I going to risk anything by going near any doctor.

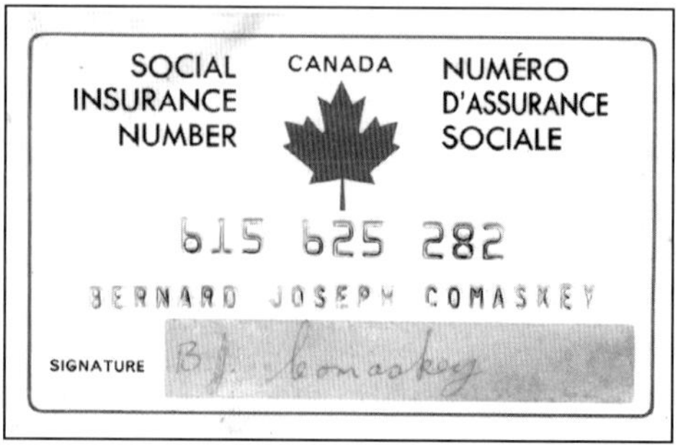

Canadian Social Insurance Card

"Give 'er Shit"

It was three miles from the centre of town to INCO'S TI shaft. I was lucky to be getting a lift – or "ride" as we would call it from now on! There were about twenty of us first timers and first of all we were lectured by the safety engineer on tips and rules – for more or less staying alive. We had been issued with a yellow hardhat, safety boots, a thick belt, miner's lamp, gloves and a pair of safety glasses. The battery of the lamp was strapped to the belt, whilst the lamp fitted into a slot on the front of the helmet. We were also given a number and a badge and a "dog-tag" with the same number. The "dog-tag" you moved to the "in" "out" board, so it was known if someone didn't come up.

The silver badge was worn, or carried in the pocket, but had to be shown at security and for picking up pay-check and other identifications.

I was now a hard rock miner, # 2927.

We waited at the head-frame for the cage to go down. Myself and two other guys were assigned to twelve hundred level. Twelve hundred feet underground, but there is no difference between four hundred or two thousand levels. One of the other guys quit on the third day, the other after getting his first pay cheque.

The cage door opened and we filed in. The cage-tender rang the bell and down we plunged into the bowls of the earth. Even men with good stomachs, I'm sure, felt the lurch, going down the first time. Now the only light to guide every man to keep himself safe and do a varied but definite hard shift, was the little lamp on his forehead. On my own, sometimes, I turned off the light, just to "see" the blackest darkness in all the world.

Every new man started as "a shoveller on the ditch". On each level, the main drift ran into the mine for a mile or more. Rail-tracks were laid along the drift, on which ran the loco which hauled the ore out to be dumped into the ore-pass. A shallow ditch, with a flow of water ran parallel to the track. As well as water which seeped through the rock, a lot of water was pumped in to stopes for sand-fill back fill. The water in the ditch always flowed back towards the station and that was one of our safety lessons. "If you get lost underground, follow the flow of water". The new men, "the green men", the "jigaboos", "the Yahoos" all started off on the most bottom rung of a long ladder, shovelling sand, rock and dirt out of the ditch. Big money underground wasn't made on basic wage. Real money was made under "incentive"

or bonus. Many good miners made more than their shift-boss with up to eighty percent bonus pay. Shovellers were not on bonus!
A miner is regarded as a skilled trade in Canada and rightly so. There are so many different jobs underground, all interdependent on each other and all executed with efficiency and speed. The bonus system made sure of that. The chute could be full of "muck" (ore) and the two men in the stope could do nothing until the motorman came with the train and pulled the chute open into his "muck-cars". The stope-crew get bonus the more they got out, but the motor crew also got bonus for the cars they dumped.
It was no place for a thin skin. In Thompson, amongst miners, a man was judged soley on his ability underground. He was a "good man" or a "Dog Fucker". "Dog Fuckers" wouldn't last long. Everyone was stressed and shouting. The shift-boss "gave shit" to the stope-leader and all the crew. The stope-leader "gave shit" to the drillers and all the crew. The driller "gave shit" to the powder man, the steel-sharpener and to the man on the tugger-hoist. Everyone "gave shit" to the shoveller on the ditch. That was me! You could be called to assist at anything – just so as you could be called a "cock-sucker"!
I was lucky with my first shift-boss. A kindly old Ukrainian by the name of John Zbitnew. In the underground lunch room he used jokingly refer to me as "my son". He minded me and brought me along gradually. Not used to the manual work, in bad shape from drink and now with a constant dull burning pain in my stomach, coupled with the worry of vomiting blood, my mind was a hell. The first two months were a probationary period and I counted the days to get beyond that period. I didn't have a drink for three weeks after I went underground.
The course, foul language used underground could not be described here. Tension, frustration, bullying, pain, despair – there were guys constantly on the edge of nervous break-downs. Every order was given with the instruction "Let's go", or "C'mon" "GIVE HER SHIT". As the shift-boss or mine-captain passed, he, at very least, asked; "Are you guys giving 'er shit? If he couldn't see what you were doing you would be asked; are you guys "fuckin' the dog again!"
INCO was a safety conscious company. Written warnings and suspensions for breaches of safety. Demonstrations of safety procedure every week. Safety slogans, first aid and mine rescue training. No matter how much safe-

ty precautions were put in place, mining – especially in those days was a dangerous game. In my first year twelve men got killed. Four of them were friends of mine.

When I was there a month Zbitnew sent me to stope-school.This was a two week course which trained me to be a driller. Now, I was a miner. My wage went up to two dollars and sixty five cent an hour, but more importantly, I was now on bonus.After working here and there for a while I was partnered with Ron Cassen. Ron was the stope leader and I was his driller.Two men worked to a stope.We mined from the bottom up, drilling off a "breast" and blasting it out at the end of the shift. Ron was easy enough to work with, although understandably, he resented my "morning sickness" and hangovers. Ron went on to be promoted to shift-boss, mine-captain and like Willie, he was appointed a Government Miners Inspector.

Each shift had a cross-shift – all four on the same bonus contract. Naturally, we got to know each other: lining each other up, slagging each other about "fucking the dog" and at week-ends, "taking a drink". John – I can't remember his surname, was my cross-shift driller. On afternoon shift, a piece of loose came off the "hanging wall" and practically cut him in two. The investigation in the stope was completed before our shift started – or maybe we skipped a shift in that stope, but I don't think so. My first job was to hose the blood from the top of the manway, where they brought John down.Then Ron and I "gave 'er shit again".

CHAPTER 11

Four Year Sentence

I liked being a driller my clean bright yellow helmet was by now scratched and nearly black from oil and grime. I didn't look like a "jigaboo" any more. We drilled "the face" with "Jack-legs" - something like a Jack-hammer, with an air-pressure leg angled on the ground. The drill was also driven on air-pressure. We had two hoses an each machine, air and water, connected to pipes which ran along the drift and up to the stope. The water ran through a hole in the centre of the drill steel, thereby washing out the hole as we drilled. It was hard, heavy work, but after a while I got the hang of it and then instead of constantly wrestling the Jack-leg, I let it do the work - learning to give the correct amount of pressure from the control on the handle. For drilling in to the roof, we used a "stoper". Similar to the Jack-leg, only it drilled straight up. This was the machine for "driving a raise", drilling holes for safety bolts or screening bad ground. When drilling with the stoper, all the water and dirt came back down on top of you. We would come up, black, soaking wet, with nothing showing only the whites of our eyes.

When I was a month or so with INCO and "taking a drink" again, I went to the doctor with my stomach. Having a good idea as to what he might tell me, I had a good session for a few days, before going to the clinic. Doctor Johnston examined me and I told him about vomiting up blood. He was very anxious to be certain that I was vomiting up blood and not "throwing it up". This is disgusting reading – but like everything else in this book – that's how it was. They sent me for tests and X-Rays and I came back in a week. The Doctor told me that the lining of my stomach was cut to hell and I had some type of ulcers. His advice was predictable; I had to quit drinking; eat little and often, drink milk (which I always hated) and take the tablets and medicine. He told me that if I did what he told me, my stomach would come ok in four years. On the day, I felt relief because now I had every reason not to drink and fear would keep me off it. That's not how it words for the alcoholic. On my next check-up, after he said there was already some improvement, I said; "Doctor, there is nothing much to do here except a bit of socialising. All my friends "take a drink", can I not even have one"? Now, Doctor Johnston was a good doctor, but he obviously knew nothing of the stinkin' thinkin' drinker's mind. "Ok, he said, but don't drink on an empty stomach. Don't drink beer; a glass of wine, or a couple of shots after a meal should be ok"! "Thanks, Doctor"! I rushed over to The Thompson Inn Coffee Shop. Ordered a steak, which I was too excited to finish and then into the Cocktail Lounge for the two permitted shots. That night I was thrown out of the Legion Hall for being a drunken nuisance.

We were all making great money and the cost of living (drink) was cheap. I never wrote to my Mother without sending a few dollars and like Aunty Kathleen and Betty had always remembered my birthday, I never forgot the younger brothers either. I paid into a savings plan with INCO and I also continued to send money home to the Bank. It was an unnatural existence though. Thousands of young men, no shortage of money, no shortage of drink - a massive shortage of women.

To safeguard against fights in The Thompson Inn they had very strict rules. Nobody could drink standing up. Only four allowed at each table and if you stopped to talk at another table, a waiter moved you on or you heard barman Bill or Cliff holler "sit down"! At that time, it and the Legion were the only two drinking places – so it wasn't a good idea to get barred! There were constant fights. I still hadn't learned why I had two ears and only one mouth. Cliff remarked to me once that he had never seen a black eye take so long to get better. What he didn't know was that it had taken a couple of relapses.

They used say about Amel that he could smell drink like a blood-hound. The bottle of Canadian Club, or the first cap off the Molsen beer, wouldn't be cracked until he'd arrive at the room door for the "party". He was a good chef and he and Hilda looked after us well, but poor Amel never eased off the drink. He would arrive at the door, sucking a cigarette and a big grin on his face. Next, he led with either of two lines; "I'm celebrating ground-hog day", or "I'm as drunk as ten barrels of shit". He was more than capable of taking care of himself – as more than one resident found out. It couldn't last and Amel and Hilda lost The Balmoral. Ron Pollock organised a petition to the owners to keep them there, but it was no use. Amel finished up doing odd jobs around town and the unfortunate Hilda worked as a shop assistant.

"Taking a Drink" - Yours Truly, Billy, and Philip Conroy (Partly hidden)

Willie was the partner of a guy called Don Riox, who had a big house in town, up at Westwood. Don and his wife Evelyn wanted four guys to room and board, so in we moved.

Willie and Phillip sharing one room; and Joe and I in the other. I reckoned it was a good move because I felt the temptation to drink would be less. Wrong! The new arrangement didn't last long. Mulhare and Conroy were kicking football in the driveway – at four o'clock on a Sunday morning. Don stuck his head out the window and told the boys to cut out the noise and get inside. Conroy turned on the cooker to make coffee. He turned a couple of extra knobs, one of which turned on the oven. In the oven was a couple of chickens, still in their plastic bags. When Evelyn got up, the cooker was sort of a mess and the boys were ordered out. Willie wasn't there, but I went too, in sympathy.

Con Lynch, a Corkman, as you may guess, was staying over in Martin Bay and there were three vacancies so we moved in there. We had the basement, which was divided into three twin-bed rooms. Jules and his wife Tony looked after us fantastically well and it was a great place to stay. Sadly, Tony died from lung cancer, just before I left.

Tragedy

Before we pulled out of Riox's, Evelyn had done me a big favour. Next door, came this really nice girl called Karen. She was the sister of the neighbour and had got a job in the INCO office. We said "Hi!" going in and out for a couple of weeks and then I asked Evelyn to put in a word for me. It worked! I had a date with a nice girl, which in a mining town like Thompson was the equivalent to having a winning lotto ticket locked in your safe. We went for a coffee one evening – I was off the drink again! I was mad about the banana cream pie in Ken's Restaurant and I eat two or three of them and several cups of coffee while Karen and I chatted easily. There was a dance in The Legion the following Saturday night and I asked her if she'd like to come. She said yes. I was over the moon. It was getting near St. Patrick's Day and I would have a date for the Irish dance. All dances were "couples only" in order to avoid fights or other forms of blackguarding. Coming up near St. Patrick's Day the hunt would really be on. It was snobbish, elitist and downright racist also; to bring a squaw to the dance, got you in, but it was really frowned on by our betters. Phillip defied convention and brought an Indian girl to the St. Patrick's Ball, but he got such "static" that at the end of the night, he sent her home in a taxi, on her own. Anyway, I was going to be the proud man, with my date on my arm on March

"Taking a Drink"
Christmas Day 1969 with Billy and Pat in Thompson

17th. The dance in The Legion on the Saturday night, I intended to be just a dry run for the big one. It turned out anything but "dry"! Had a few during the day and was "nicely" when I called for Karen. Wasn't short of guys buying me drink at the dance, so as that they might see what "the broad" was like. I got totally pissed. The dance was well finished and I was up on the stage, playing the piano with one finger. Conroy, who was there with Ann Weafer, a waitress from "Kens", came up and said "Karen wants to go". I wasn't ready. I was only half way through, "When the Saints go marching in". I said, "She can 'f'..ing well wait". She heard me – and didn't!

I finished up having to get the loan of the Cocktail Lounge's Barman's wife, to get me into the St. Patrick's night dance. In the meantime this beautiful Galway girl arrived in town and drove some of the boys over the top, just from looking at her. Her brother Mike was there, luckily enough, to mind her. I think she was a chemist, but more importantly, she actually was a 'Rose of Tralee finalist". It didn't take the usual rake of drink to make this one look good. The discussion was going on as to who might date her, when Mulhare walked over and introduced himself as the only single Galwayman in town and would she, as the Galway Rose, go to the St. Patrick's Day Ball. Brigid said yes, and every Irishman in Thompson hated Mulhare! Joe immediately called her "My Princess" and she was never again known to us by any other name. Joe only got the one date, (on account of taking a drink) but he came in the door of the Community centre with the best looking woman at the dance.

There was great preparation for the dance. Through Devereux and Gallagher, the proceeds of the dance had always been sent to St. Mary's special school in Delvin. Our green Irish Canadian Club jackets had arrived and it was not only the Irish who looked forward to the great day. Thompson would come to a standstill.

Though Thompson was a rough diamond, carved out of the Northern wilderness, I had already met many fine people there. It wasn't everyone who spent their time drinking and fighting.

Charlie Darby's room partner was a Kerryman, by the name of Mike Lucey. Charlie and he were best friends and we met often. Mike was about ten years older than me. An only son, he had been in Canada for five years and planned to go home soon. Mike was pleasant, quiet and with a lovely sense of humour. Everyone liked him. He didn't argue or fight with anybody. He just

laughed at everything. Mike and I worked on the same shift; I on twelve hundred and he on fourteen hundred, so we chatted every day in "The Dry", where we showered and changed our clothes.
All the talk was of green jackets, green beer; all getting the 17th off and things like that.
Then, on the 14th of March, Mike Lucey got killed at work.

The Easy Job
Maureen Darby was a receptionist and secretary at the clinic and therefore had first hand knowledge of my medical condition. On the night that Mike Lucey was in the morgue, a bunch of us finished up over at Mullingar man's Billy O'Callaghans' house. I was drunk – naturally. Maureen tried to talk to me about my drinking and I "took a reading on her". She also told people that if I didn't stop drinking, I "didn't have long for this world". I was very defensive and irritated by any advice but deep down I knew something was very wrong. I wanted to stop, but I couldn't and therefore I dare not admit to having any problem. One good thing was that after a session I didn't have to have a drink next day. The only cure for a bad hangover is to get drunk again, but most mornings I could be just too sick to look at drink. I worked most Saturdays on overtime and both Mulhare and I put our names down to work our holidays. In spite of the drink and serious poker games I was managing to save money by separating myself from it, through the savings fund and sending money home. I was often broke until payday, especially after playing poker all night, but I was never short of drink. As my boozing buddy, Bill Elliot and I walked unsteadily towards the Thompson Inn, broke, I would say; "He that feedeth the birds and clotheth the sheep will look after us". Sure enough, guys would buy us drink, because when we had money we spent it easily. Years later, Elliot came to visit me in Ireland and reminded me of this.
1967 was passing slowly and soon I was a year in Thompson. A few times some of us went out to The Pas for a week-end, but all that was, was a change of back-bar mirror. I was not in good shape. I got sick often, sometimes even when I hadn't drank the previous day. Most times I didn't eat breakfast and the worst time was being sick on an empty stomach. Quiet frequently I brought up blood. Now, this is the last time I will mention this, but it got worse and worse over the next three years.

I was weak and sick, and during a rough period at work, I started looking around for an easier way. Billy Ward was a cage tender and when I saw a cage-tenders job posted, I talked to Billy and decided to "bid" for the job. I had the seniority that they had to give it to me and I became a cage-tender – "a dog fuckers' job". There is pride and competition amongst miners and a man who "cannot hack it" loses respect. It is easy to transfer from, the smelter or from the refinery to underground, but never the other way round. They used to say that "the only transfer from underground was in a box". If a cage-tender never worked at mining that's ok; or if he got old, or injured – but an able-bodied miner doesn't try to get on the cage. I got loads of jeers and snide remarks and questions of "how much bonus did I make" – there wasn't bonus on the cage.

Anyway I did my job and lo and behold next thing there was a vacancy for a "top-man". A "Topman" is in charge of the cage and cage-tenders, bringing up and down men, lumber and materials. I applied and got that job. It was nice and easy. In the pub, everyone was drilling and blasting. As Paul Larson used say; "I couldn't see anyone in the pub with the smoke from blasting!" I wasn't involved in these talks now. I had no rounds to drill off and no one included me in mining talk. I went back mining.

In the summer of 1967 Willie's girlfriend, Pat Sheerin arrived in Thompson. The following year, she became my first sister-in-law.

Staying in Martin Bay was Phillip, Joe, Nick Shaw, Maurice Keogh, the recently arrived Watt Kenny, Timmy Keogh and Noel O'Sullivan form Cork. Thirty years later Noel was to become well known all over Canada, when as mine foreman he helped solve the shocking mass murder of nine miners during a bitter strike in Yellowknife. I contacted Noel after reading "The Third Suspect", the best-selling book dealing with the strike and murders.

Another drunken Christmas came and went – at least Mulhare and myself had lots to eat.

Conroy often talks about that Christmas and me singing "Rudolf The Red Nose Reindeer" into a beer can … "Rudolf with your nose so bright won't you guide my sleigh to-night?" … "Ah, go guide your own fuckin' sleigh…!"

Bushed

It turned into 1968 and I was too long there without a break. We all "blew shifts" (missing time from work). One Thursday I blew a shift and went on the beer with a guy I knew well. I can picture him clearly. Next day he went to work but I blew another one. My friend got killed that day. The awful thing for me is that I can't remember his name.

A couple of months after writing the above, I was out walking when the man's name returned to me; out of the blue. May God be good to Mike Morrow.

I was constantly fighting the battle of the booze. I could stop, but I couldn't stay stopped. Three weeks was very good for me, but a week would be the average. I got six weeks once when Doctor Johnson said we were working in opposite directions, "I am trying to cure you, and you are trying to kill you".

Conroy and Mulhare were also burned out. One day in early March, I went into The Bay and bought new working clothes. Sitting in Sinclairs, with a cup of coffee, I just couldn't contemplate going underground that day. I thought of Mike Lucey, now a year dead. I went over to the Thompson Inn and Phillip was in the coffee-shop. "I'm quitting", I said. Conroy never batted an eye-lid. "I'm coming too!" Mulhare arrived and said he was quitting also. Nobody asked, 'what was the next plan?'. Out to INCO we went and quit. They tried to talk us out of it, but no chance. I had been underground for a year and a half. Next day Con Lynch quit and said he was coming too. Bob Lunny had been fired for missing shifts and he said he was coming too. The extraordinary thing was that none of us said where we were going and nobody asked! We had about three days of "farewell parties". The only road out was a three hundred mile dirt-road to The Pas. Phillip had bought Mike Lucey's car, a 1965 Rambler. Con had a VW Beetle. There was still six feet of snow on the ground so it would have been a hazardous trip for a sober driver – but it was ok for us and we drove in our turns. We spent two nights in The Pas. If R & R stands for rest and recreation it didn't mean any such thing for five "bushed" miners, with lots of money. The two R's just meant doing it twice and The Pas didn't let us down. Next we made it to Winnipeg and from there to Saskatoon – a lovely place. We spent a week in Saskatoon – an eventful week! There was a dance on, a mile from our hotel. The agreement was that the cars were to stay parked and we would use taxis. When we were ready to roll, Phillip wouldn't come, because he was chatting up this broad. At the dance, Mulhare and I picked up two nice girls. Mine was a school-teacher and I dated her every night for the week. I told her I would come back to

Saskatoon, but when I was leaving she looked me straight in the eye and said; "You're never coming back, are you?" She was right.

Getting back to that first night. After the rest of us left, the girl Phillip met, agreed to come with him to the dance. Out to the car-park and in to the Rambler. The Rambler didn't clear the first set of lights. Conroy drove through the lights and a van ploughed into the passenger side. When the police arrived, the girl was trapped on one side and had Conroy kissing her from the driver's side. She also had a broken leg. With the impact, the trunk (boot) flew open and this is what saved Phillip. Clearly visible in the trunk were our hurleys. The cop turned out to be a Kilkennyman, lucky Phillip!

We moved on to Edmonton, where I met a lot of people from home. The Masterson family were very good to us. Even though it was sold out, Ollie Burke got us tickets for the St. Patrick's Night Dance. I'm sure it must have been a bit of an embarrassment for Ollie that we, his guests, arrived in such a drunken state. Drunk or not, Phil and I managed to take two Westmeath women, Roisín Masterson and Jean Fagan, home from the dance.

After a couple of weeks in a top class Edmonton Hotel, it was time to start thinking about work again. Con Lynch had previously worked in Manitoewadge in Northern Ontario. His brother Christy was still there and Con said he was heading back to Manitoewadge. Mulhare and I had fallen out over a waitress (he got her) so he announced he was going with Lynch. Lunny had money still, so couldn't see the point in making any decision yet. Philips brother, Tony lived in Calgary, about two hundred and fifty miles away and Phil and I decided to head for Calgary. Tony and his wife Marie made us welcome and we discovered Calgary to be a great and lively city. Statistics told us that there were five women for every man in Calgary. I don't know if that was true or not, but we did get our five.

Tony worked in a meat-packers and Philip and I got a job there too. The money wasn't a fraction of what we were used to, but we just regarded it as a working holiday. About the third week-end we went back up to Edmonton, where we had a foursome date. On the Sunday night, we were in their apartment with a case of beer and ever so cosy. Our greyhound bus was leaving for Calgary at 9.10. "May I use your phone, to see if there is a later bus", I asked the girls. "Sure, go ahead". "No sir", the lady informed me, "that is the last bus to Calgary", I hung up. "Great news, there is a bus at midnight". That was the end of the meat packing. We spent another week in Edmonton,

returning to Calgary to pick up our belongings and back to Edmonton. Now totally broke, it was time to go back to work. My "savings fund plan" money from INCO still hadn't arrived, which was probably a good thing.
The two of us went to "The Chamber of Mines" in Edmonton and we were hired for Giant Mines in Yellowknife N.W.T. The mine was paying our way up, so we were safe and secure. We had our last night on the town in Edmonton. Then a bombshell, I failed the medical; not with my stomach, but with my back. The x-ray showed that, probably due to an accident or injury, I had a bone out of place in my back. It had never bothered me (although it did in later life) and I don't know how long I had the problem, or if I had been born with it. The INCO medical did not include a back x-ray. Probability is that I sustained the injury in some car, mining, hurling or drunken incident. Conroy and I paid the hotel that morning and as we lay on the beds, smoking there was no talk. I decided I would make my way towards Manitoewadge and tell Mulhare it was alright over the waitress! It was time for Philip to go. He stood up, emptied every dollar he had in his pocket; every red cent. "I won't be needing this", he said, and walked out the door.

Joe Mulhare (centre) Philip Conroy and Myself celebrating St. Patrick's Day in Thompson, Monitoba

Manitoewadge

A few years ago Pamela and I drove along Highway 17 - "The Trans Canada Highway", from Blind River to Sioux Saint Marie. I was struck by the most incredibly beautiful scenery I had seen anywhere in the world. The Highway levels out, then twists and turns in and around, up and down mountains, with lakes and waterfalls around almost every turn. The vast array of colour, by way of the massive variety of trees and blooms along the way is magnificent. When I worked there in 1968, I didn't see any of this beauty. Manitoewadge is about forty miles off Highway 17, between Sudbury and Sioux St. Marie. Mulhare and I worked for Noranda Mining Company, "Cut and Fill" stope mining; much the same as we had done for INCO. There were some big differences, however. Manitoewadge was a copper mine. The price of copper was low and therefore there was no huge push for production. In Thompson, the mine was flat out to produce nickel to satisfy the demand created by the Vietnam War. This meant as much overtime as we wanted and really good incentives to "give 'er shit!". There was no Saturday work and no overtime in Manitoewadge and the bonus was crap. The four hundred miners were mostly old, settled men, with company houses and families. There wasn't much to do in Manitoewadge except "take a drink" – so we got on with it! It was in Manitoewadge that I first watched colour T.V. As well as the Mexico Olympics, it was there that I watched the Elvis comeback special – all in the beer parlour – naturally!

"Taking a Drink"
In Manitoewadge, Ontario – I'm on the left.

Every other week-end, or so, Mulhare and I headed for the city. The twin cities of Port Arthur and Fort William have since amalgamated into "The Lakehead" and that is where we went for "R & R". These were wild week-ends and it was on one such excursion, that I spent my first night in jail. On the Friday night, late and very drunk, Joe and I were "chatted up" by two women in the pub. We were invited back to a party. They took us to a sort of a boarding house, where "bootleg" beer was being sold at four times the normal price. Joe used always say he "liked women – but he loved drink", so we proved this assertion by concentrating on taking a drink. I woke up on a couch, with Mulhare asleep on the floor. Around 8.00 am, shakily, we pulled ourselves together and made our way back to our hotel and slept for a few hours. Luckily, we had left most of our wad of spending money in the hotel-room, before going out, the previous night.

Around lunch – time on Saturday, I tentatively started to try and "lay the foundation". After a couple of hours the dangerous period had passed and everything was remaining solidly in place. We met a few guys from work and some serious drinking ensued.

By closing time we had told them the story of the previous night. One of the guys asked us "how much we had been rolled for?" Apparently, this was a well known racket. I replied that we had feck all money going there, but Mulhare became convinced that he had more money going there than what I knew he had. "C'mon" he exclaimed to me "we're goin' to get our cock-suckin' money back". I had nothing more pressing, at the time, so off headed the two of us. Our friends hadn't had enough drink to embark on a mission such as this.

We arrived at the boarding house cum bootleggers; "bootlegging" is illegal alcohol selling. Some guy at the door told us to "fuck off" and he banged and locked the door. We weren't in favour of "fucking off". There was another way in and we could see that clearly, so, not ever so quietly, we made our way up the fire-escape and proceeded to attempt prising open the fire door, three stories up. It was sort of dark to begin with but soon we were flooded in all the light we needed – from the search beams of two police cars.

Iron bed, wire frame, no mattress. Two to a cell with Joe and I separated. Next morning, I was taken out and brought up to an office, where a plain clothes detective sat at a desk. I was surprised, in the circumstance, at how friendly this man appeared. "Your friend will plead guilty and be fined $20.00. No need to fine you both, so you plead not guilty and that will be it". Then came the breath-taking newsflash. "We are very grateful to you guys for giving us statements against this establishment. We have been trying for a long time to nab them, but victims are usually too embarrassed to press charges". Jesus Christ! "Can I read my statement again", I asked. The cop handed me a typed sheet of paper. It was like reading the first page of a book and I couldn't remember giving it – but it had my signature at the bottom. Same for Mulhare, but he sort of remembered some of what he said. The bottom line was that it was down there in black and white that we had been robbed of a total of $640.00. Jesus Christ! The court was that morning. Joe paid his $20.00 fine and then two detectives took us in a police car, back to the boarding-house, while we remained in the car. We watched them raid the joint. I had been sick in the cell; now my head pounded and I was terrified. It seemed like forever, before the two detectives returned. They dropped us back to the hotel and told us we would be summoned to appear as witnesses and would be notified through Noranda. We blew two shifts and returned to Manitoewedge on the Tuesday. This was the end of October. We both planned on coming home for Christmas and I prayed that there would be no court case before then. In November The Personnel Officer at the mine brought us into the office and told us we had a summons to attend court in Port-Arthur. I got on real well with this guy – he took a drink. "Any chance of getting it adjourned". I asked. "I will see what I can do; I know the Chief of Police well and I'll tell him Noranda needs you guys badly that week".

In early December, I got a letter from The Chief of Police that he would like both Mr. Mulhare and myself to call to his office. We almost didn't go, but were afraid not too. After a few shots of "courage", we stood at his massive desk. "I have good news for you guys", we got your money". "You what..?" Both Joe and I stood open-mouthed. "Yea, you guys sure fixed them cocksuckers". "He knew we had him, so the pimp pleaded guilty and we shut the place down. The Chief went to the safe and took out an envelope with $640.00 in it and handed it to me. "Thanks again, you guys – and bring me back a shamrock from Ireland". We stood up and shook hands. "You have the best police force in the world", I told him – and so he had!

CHAPTER 12

Coming Home

I was always a bit homesick during my first two years in Canada. I longed for the dances and the hurling and football. It was an unnatural existence for so long in a tough mining environment. There wasn't a day but that I dreamed of going home. I was warned about my health. I could stop drinking – but I couldn't stay stopped. So many mornings now, I couldn't even keep a glass of water down. Like the wounded animal, I kept thinking that things would be OK if I got back to Ireland.

Mulhare and myself were coming home for Christmas! In November, we booked and every day, I knew how many days were left. I decided I would like to visit Auntie Ann in New York on the way home. We would fly from Sioux St. Marie to New York around the 9th of December, spend a week with my relatives and then to Shannon and on to Dublin.

"The day dawned beautifully warm and fine". I remember that line from a schoolbook, but it sure as hell did not apply to the day I left Manitoewadge, a week into a Canadian December. It was Friday evening. We had spent the previous couple of days and nights, by way of a farewell party. There was this older guy called Harold, who was driving us the first leg of our journey, two hundred and fifty miles. Harold was from The Sioux and was going home for the week-end. Harold "took a drink".

We ventured forth on the Friday evening, all pissed out of our minds. There was Harold, his buddy, Mulhare and myself. We had enough drink in the car to stock a funeral wake and God alone knows how close we became to being one of those.

It was snowing when we left. Weather alerts were on T.V. and some people tried to stop us leaving. Some hours into the drive, travelling the Trans Canada Highway, we hit a blizzard, a blanket of snow, driven by gale force winds. The Whiskey and Rum only partially deadened an uneasy and worrying sense of foreboding. Eventually, Harold, blinded by snow and disoriented, drove off the Highway, down into a snowbank. The next line should read that we were found in the car the following spring, but one of the many miracles which happened in my life happened next. They say a miracle is "Something which cannot happen until it does". There had been practically no traffic on the road, due to the conditions. We could only have been a few minutes ditched, when a huge truck came along. He stopped, fifty yards past us, came back, got the car door open and got us out. The wind was so strong I fell several times. We clawed our way into the truck and were taken the remaining forty miles to "The Sioux", where we all, including the man who had just saved our lives, booked into a motel. Next morning, the driver told us how close a call we'd had. He had actually gone past us when out of the corner of his eye, through the snow, he saw a flicker of light where one of us was lighting a cigarette, and they say smoking is bad for your health!

The truck driver did not want to take anything from us, but we absolutely insisted on looking after him well.

It was the worst snowstorm for sixteen years. Flights were being cancelled. Joe and I were hours early at Sioux St. Marie Airport and we actually got off early. The previous flight, having circled New York for hours, couldn't land with the storm and returned to The Sioux to refuel. We were allowed to board and soon landed safe and sound in The Big Apple. As we were ahead of schedule, there was nobody there to meet us, so we got a taxi to my Aunt's house in Woodside, New York.

My Aunt Ann went to America when she was sixteen and returned home only once; that was in 1948. Her husband was Harold McMahon, her childhood sweetheart from home. With Ann and Harold lived my grand-Aunt Katie Walsh, a lovely regal, dignified lady – then in her ninety second year, who had never returned, but talked of Ireland all the time during my week's stay. My visit, "the link", was a momentous occasion for my kin in New York. Old neighbours from home all called round and again I was thinking that in every immigrant, no matter how well off he or she may be, there is an inbuilt little pocket of sadness.

I was "in the horrors". The ceiling of the bedroom walls wouldn't stay still and were moving in on top of me. I called Mulhare the first night and told him I was going to die. I need a doctor. "Fuck off and die" – "if you're going to die, a doctor won't save you and if not, you can wait until morning". First two days in New York I was too sick to drink, but after that, if I were careful with "the foundation". I could keep it down and keep myself going.

I never saw Aunt Ann, or any of the others again. She was no fool, probably the most sensible of that family and I don't know what she must have thought of me. She had watched helplessly whilst her older sister, Aunt Margaret, drank herself to death in New York, as did also another sister, Auntie Greta in England. Ann and I exchanged letters and cards from that visit onwards. She sent me a generous wedding present when I got married, as did also Aunt Katie.

On 18th December, Ann and Harold drove us to the airport. They were both lonesome, which I found surprising. Again, it was probable the immigrant thing at Christmas. I remember all the Irish there seeing off the lucky ones who were going home. In particular, I remember a large group of old Galway people. They were laughing and talking – all in Irish. I just thought that was lovely.

Soon the big iron bird with the shamrock, was in the air, bringing me home. Christmas 1968 would be my first Christmas at home in four years. I was still only twenty four; "If ever a man suffered!"

Dublin airport is a lovely airport to come home to at Christmas. Aer Rianta do a magnificent job in this regard, nowadays, and I presume they did it in 1968, because I remember the Ceád Míle Failte and the atmosphere. We were met by my father and Kit Lee. Kit was the local hackney man. My father was noticeably delighted to see me and me him. In a strange way, the older we got, the more time he had for us. As previously stated, he was far from being a demonstrative man. Fechin told me that a few years before he died, he tried to give Daddy a hug and it was a "disaster".

It felt great to be on Irish soil. We stopped for a few drinks in "The Warrenstown Arms" and then, near home, we called into Kieran Carroll's new pub in Crowenstown, "for a couple". I remember my Mother shaking when she hugged me. They all knew Mulhare and he was made welcome as me. Sean was working in Iralco, the new local factory. He had a motorbike and was big into music and dances. Not only that, but he was a drummer in a band. Sean was a different man. Fechin, to use my Father's words, was a "cur". Now seventeen, he wouldn't go to school and was now "taking a drink". The biggest change was in the two youngest. Anthony and Camillus were about ten and eight respectively. Everything was grand. I had just the correct amount of drink in me and later when we adjourned down to Bartley's Pub I was in excellent form and great company.

Before we parted I asked Kit Lee to drive Mammy, Anthony and Camillus and I to Mullingar next day to buy presents. Kit arrived at one o'clock. I was dying. I couldn't disappoint, so I went along. I couldn't keep down a drink in Mullingar, and came home quickly as possible and into bed until the next day. "A bad flu", my Mother said, caused by the change of climate. The cure - or foundation, stayed down next day – which was a good thing cause a house party was organised for that night. Relations and friends came from as far afield as Dublin. I rooted out and invited a girl I knew who "took a drink"

In New York with Aunt Ann and Harold, December 1968

and things like that! I had to get "The Bush" out of my system. This lady and myself were highly drunk and highly randy at the party and I suppose I made a bit of a show of myself. However, guests were there because they took a drink and lads home from Canada were expected to be a bit "haywire". I was haywire!

On Christmas Eve I put Mulhare on the train for Ballinasloe. We had a few in town, and I just about got him on the train. He wanted to stay. That night, I went to midnight mass. Standing at the rear of the church, 'drunk as a skunk'!

On St. Stephen's Night, I went to a dance in Oldcastle. I had done a pub crawl all day. In spite of this, I entered the dance hall "The Eldorado", with a baby Brandy in each trouser pocket. Then lo and behold, what did I discover but that there was a bar in the hall that night – which of course, would be a sin to waste. At some stage, I had a dance with Ann Mulligan, from Collinstown. Ann was Auntie Kathleen's step-granddaughter and a fine girl. The following week, Ann called to see Kathleen – which she did regularly as she worked in The Civil Service. "Did you see Bernie since he came home", asked Kathleen. "I had a dance with him in Oldcastle on St. Stephen's Night", replied Ann. "How does he look?" Ann's reply to this question was often quoted by Aunt Kathleen, until the day she died. "He was the best looking at the dance – and the drunkest!!"

Love

There was a dance almost every night; the pub first and then the dance. I said I wouldn't mention it again, - but I got sick every day now. Some days were worse than others and the lining of my stomach was "shredded". However, as soon as I could manage to ease the foundation into place and if it stayed there long enough to "set", I pulled through. I went down to Mulhares in Eyrecourt after Christmas. I forgot to mention that I bought an old "banger" of a Morris Minor on my arrival home. Before Christmas Kieran Carroll sold Joe and I four tickets for the Delvin Hurler's dance in Mullingar on 6th January. A week is a long time in the lives of two bushed miners and by the New Year the two girl-friends we had when we bought the tickets were long gone – maybe having counselling or therapy, or something.

On the day I was due to drive to Galway, a certain young lady's mother called and asked if I would give her daughter a lift down to visit her school-friend in Kilimor. It was the shortest journey I've ever driven. We got on great. As well as being beautiful, the girl had a sharp wit and great company. About the 3rd January, I carried her again on the return trip. On the way home in Ballinasloe, I asked her in for a drink. She couldn't refuse and had a soft drink. We were in Dick Rothwells and just made it on the stroke of closing time. The girl was a bit taken aback when I still managed two double brandies and a pint of Harp. We drove home – "neighbour's children" and I dropped her at her own house, Bartley's Bar! I had not the slightest thought of romance or dating this girl. Next night there was a dance somewhere and I asked her at closing time if she would like to come – along with the full of the car. Again, that was it, but during a dance I remembered the dinner dance tickets and I asked her would she like to come. She said yes, but I still didn't look on it as a "real date".

I only had a couple of drinks in Bartleys before we left for the dance. Then the meal and meeting loads of friends meant I was pretty sober for most of the evening. I do know, however, that I left that young girl on her own a lot of the night. Then I met Brian O'Shaughnessy, who had arrived home from Canada that day. Shaughnessys had a pub in Delvin and Brian's father, Paddy invited me back to a party in the pub, when the dance finished at 2.00 am. My date wouldn't come to the party, so I couldn't wait to drop her off in Drumcree. I got out of the car, walked her to her hall door and gave her one quick kiss. Dived into my Morris Minor to head for the party. Car wouldn't start! Back to Bartley's hall door. Rang door-bell and banged door in case bell not working. This was an emergency. The girl called her cursing brothers who pushed me and the Morris Minor up and down the road. Car wouldn't start! No party for Bernie. With her three brothers lighting candles with the curses and I throwing in a few new ones from the mines I couldn't now ask the nineteen year old publicans' daughter for a drink either. No drink for Bernie! No nothing; I walked the Irish mile home, cold, wet, thirsty and miserable and that, folks, was my first date with my wife.

Pamela, like me, is the eldest of her family and at that time was a student in Carysfort Teacher Training College. My father used kid her from the time she was a child with comments such as "Lord, you'd look "odious" well in our house. I have six sons and you can have your pick of any of them"! It might have been about five years since I had last seen her and there is a bit of a difference between a fourteen and a nineteen year old. With Pamela it was different to other girl friends of that time. Not only did I respect her, but I had such respect for her family as well. I found myself wanting to protect her and not to hurt her. It was not however, love at first sight. I couldn't believe that this girl, who could have any fellow she wanted really was that interested in me. Our love started with a flicker of fun. Soon the flicker became a flame and even though it wasn't going to be all fun, it was, nevertheless, the real thing.

Pamela's father, Johnny, "took a drink". A periodic boozer, we had a few sessions. Pamela, naturally in the circumstances, had a dread of excessive drinking. Within months I was so "smitten" that I would do anything for my new girl-friend; but it was, as if in the words of "Meatloaf", "I'll do anything – but I won't do that", when it came to stopping drinking. Pamela had no idea how much I drank, but drinking was a major problem from early on in our rela-

Bartley's Bar, Drumcree

tionship. I didn't want to be the way I was, but I couldn't admit that, because I couldn't picture my life without drink and I couldn't stop.

Like I said, the dates were casual enough for the first weeks and months. Going to dances and leaving her back in Carysfort on Sunday nights. We used also go to the pictures in Mullingar or Oldcastle. The pictures were suggested often, because it meant no drink – until we came back to Bartley's, at least. We went for drives, visited relations and friends, the odd concert and the like. For the first time I was learning to consider a girls feelings first. For the first time I was learning the difference between love and lust.

CHAPTER 13

Mining in Ireland

Before I left Canada I had written to Avoca mines in County Wicklow, applying for a job. I got an acknowledgement and was advised to call for an interview, although they didn't say that they weren't hiring at the moment. I had also heard of this new outfit who were mining lead and zinc in Silvermines, County Tipperary. All of this was great news. I had learned the mining trade well and now I hoped I could have the opportunity to practice it in my own country. A day or two after the dinner dance I asked Pamela if she would like to come for a drive down to Avoca. We left before lunch and I bought a road map in Mullingar. Really we should have driven via Dublin, but I appointed Pamela as navigator and we ventured forth in a straight line – as the crow flies to Wicklow ... and the weather wasn't great. We found ourselves well up in the Wicklow Mountains and I knew the navigator wasn't up to it when we went through "The Sally Gap" twice. The relationship was naturally at a tender stage, with not even a word of bad language being used. I stopped "Ok, let's have a look at the map". She had the map on her knee, constantly studying it and giving me directions. "Where are we and where is this road"? I asked in a gentle even tone. "This is the road we're on" she said drawing a nicely manicured nail along this blue line. At that moment I discover, beyond all doubt, that women can't read maps. "That blue line" I said struggling to keep a natural sort of tone,"That blue line is a F---ing, that blue line is a river and we are not in the river ... yet".

I made it into the Avoca office at ten to five. The guy I was sent to looked at his watch and I got the message. Anyway he told me they weren't hiring, but if I knew anything about "Sandfill" they might have something. Sandfill is where the mined out stope is back filled with sand, driven in by water. We talked for a few minutes and he was impressed enough to bring in the Mine Manager. They showed me a plan and asked me how I would go about the sandfill. It would appear that until then, Avoca had been using the "Shrinkage" system, whereby enough "muck" is pulled from the bottom, to leave room to mine from the top of the muck-pile. We had a fruitful talk about different systems, including how expensive timber was in Ireland, --- etc. The Manager said he had learned from me. I got a job. We all shook hands and I agreed to start in two weeks.

I was delighted. My future would be in my own country. Starving, Pamela and I went for a meal. I had one drink before it ("This calls for a drink!") and two afterwards and then we turned the Morris Minor to face the Wicklow Mountains again. The return trip was stress free and the navigator ran every turn and crossroads by the pilot. Somewhere high in the mountain we could look down on the twinkling lights of some town. I stopped the car. I thought of the memory of the lights of Winnipeg as I caught my first sight of Canada. It was only 2½ years but so much had happened in that time. We had a "bit of a court" in the car and moved for home. The world really was a wonderful place – after all!

I wanted to check out Silvermines and see what the score was there. The following weekend I drove down to Galway and Mulhare and myself took a drink or two and renewed some old acquaintances. On the Sunday evening we drove to Nenagh and booked into the Ormond Hotel. We got into the dinner dance, although we were no threat to the actual dinner.

The following afternoon we drove out the few miles to the Mogul Office at Silvermines. I was impressed. Although most of the mining was to be done with "Long hole Drilling" there was loads of "Jack-leg" work. It was clear that the gear and equipment was state of the art. The bonus system appeared more generous than was the case in Canada. Also there was no doubt that there would be excellent promotional opportunities for those experienced men who were in from the start. Both Mulahare and I were offered jobs on development. The money was better than Avoca and much better than we had anticipated. We could have started the next day, but we told them we would commence in a weeks time. Immediately I wrote to Avoca, thanked them and regretted that I couldn't accept their offer.

Pamela's Carysfort Graduation Ball, Shelbourne Hotel, 1969

Accommodation was provided on the mine site. What we would have called a mine-camp in Canada was euphemistically known in Silvermines as "The Hostel". It was an awful dump. Most self-respecting miners, including all the Canadians moved out and made their own arrangements in Nenagh. Mulhare and I weren't self-respecting anything so we stayed put. A Dublin catering company had the franchise for the kitchen and in comparison to what I was used to in Canada, the food was dreadful. Breakfast didn't bother me. Now, with easy access to pubs and back in the Irish social scene, I was sick every morning. A glass of orange juice would do me and even that would usually be deposited somewhere on the walk over to the "dry"

There was a good bunch of guys working there. About 400 worked underground. A few different nationalities and many counties represented. Quite a few Donegal men – who took to hard rock like a duck to water.

We had to work compulsory overtime on Saturdays when on day shift. Every second week, we worked night-shift – 8pm to 4am. Lots of work = lots of money and lots of drink. Our local was Peggy Glesson's in the village of Silvermines, where you could get a drink anytime – often even after night-shift.

Occasionally, if it was a "short-change" weekend I would go home with Mulhare to Eyrecourt, sometimes I would just stay around Nenagh or Limerick, but most weekends I drove home to Drumcree. When driving home, I would push myself to get as far as I could, before stopping for a drink. After I made the first 'pit stop' progress slowed down considerably. When I eventually would arrive in the village, I would quickly enter the Bar and order a glass of larger (not a pint, mind you). This then accounted for the smell of drink off my breath. Pamela would then come down from the kitchen. Most often her mother would "force feed" me and then I'd go home to my own house for a while. Then a wash and a change of clothes and back to Bartley's till closing time and off to the dance.

I would tell Pamela "I work very hard all week. The work is very physical and mentally stressful. It's just bed to work and work to bed. That is why you need to understand that a few drinks at the weekends is an outlet and sometimes if I have a few too many, you shouldn't be surprised". Then mid-week in Tipperary, after blowing a shift, I would tell the boys "I have this girl-friend at home who hates drink. I can't have a drink in comfort at the week-end so is it any wonder that I have a few too many during the week".

Old Friends

I repaid Chris Darby for meeting me at the train station in Thopmson, by getting him a job with Mogul and meeting him on his first day. Also, I was thrilled when I was able to do the same for Philip Conroy. Indeed there were now quite a few miners working there from around Delvin and even a Welshman with whom I worked with in Manitowadge. There was a good sense of comradeship and the best of banter. We even had a hurling team and I can always say that I played alongside the great Noel O'Dwyer!

In May my pride and excitement knew no bounds when Westmeath foot-ballers, having beaten Dublin along the way, made it to a league semi-final against Kerry. By now I had changed the Morris Minor for a sky blue VW, which I called "The Blue Bomber". I amaze myself that I can still remember the reg. no. TZD 473 and yet recently when I took my year old BMW in for a service and the girl asked me for its number, I had to go back out and look. Mulhare and I came up to Westmeath on the Saturday evening. Pamela was

staying in Dublin so we headed for "The Lake County". There was a great optimism in the air. Everybody I spoke to said Westmeath was going to win. A punter in "The Evening Press" tipped them, so it was certain now in my mind. I had waited a long time – I would have to wait another 35years.
I met Pamela in the city and after a light snack we made our way to a pub, where I had arranged to meet the Westmeath crowd. A mini-session, including fragmented singing occurred. Off to Croker in great spirits. Pamela was sitting one side of me and Mulhare the other. At this juncture just let me state that, in time, both my wife and my daughter gave up coming to matches with me. Anyway, Westmeath started brilliantly, even if they kicked five bad wides. They were all over Kerry and I was giving them every bit of encouragement with every ounce in my lungs. Mulhare made me worse "They're going to walk it. The best football I've seen. They're playing just like the Galway three in a row". Come on Westmeath! Final score: Westmeath 2-8. Kerry 2-12. Oh; another thing Pamela stopped saying to me afterwards, "It's only a game!"
My parents were delighted to have me home and even better that I was home most weekends. There was music in Bartley's on Sunday evenings, which started early for the people going home from the matches. I would take Mammy and Daddy to the pub and we would have "a few" until it was time to take Pamela back to Carysfort College in Dublin. She had to be in by ten o'clock. Pamela would delay me until the last minute at the gate, so as that I wouldn't have time to make it to the pub. Sometimes it worked and sometimes it didn't.
I had started off well at work but now a few good men didn't want to "partner" me because I was missing so much time from work and so sick in the mornings. The mine captain and later the mine manager carpeted me. "You have the knowledge, the ability and the expertise. You are an asset to Mogul, but unless you are here every day you are no good to us". I would promise; blame my ulcers etc, but in reality I got away with murder there – when so many others didn't. A couple of times I was sent home for being drunk going on night shift. Mine Captain, Jack Day filled out a report that he sent me home because I was ill and another night shift boss, Ballivor man, Jimmy Mc Cabe, spent all shift 'minding' me. I crashed "The Blue Bomber" several times, but like myself, it kept coming back for more.
One night, in Bartley's kitchen when they were all gone to bed, I proposed

to Pamela. I just couldn't believe my good fortune when she said "Yes". I promised her I would give up the drink and we agreed that we wouldn't tell anybody until we got officially engaged the following year. Pamela had just now finished College and was looking for a school. Her graduation ball took place in The Shelbourne Hotel and it was a wonderful night. I had a "few" but really didn't get a chance to drink much. The band was super and I remember the two of us running down the stairs, arms around each other to jive, when they struck up "In the Mood". At the dance I also renewed acquaintances with my friend, that great Galway footballer, Cyril Dunne. Cyril took a drink and we just managed the one that night.

Pamela had a long time plan to go to England for the months of July and August. She was going over to friends and had a summer job. I drove herself and a friend to the boat and off they went. We wrote a few times a week, but now there was nobody to watch me!

While Pamela was in England, I didn't go home as often. More time to spend in "The Zam" in Nenagh, or Killaloe, or carnivals, or my old haunts in Ballinsloe or in fact just about anywhere our fancy took us. Limerick on a Saturday night was a great favourite.

Mulhare had bought a car and was an awful bad driver, even the odd time he was in a sober state. We were on different shifts and I had just gone to bed at 4am, after coming off the Friday night shift, when in came Mulhare to the room, sloshed. A bunch of them were drinking in Gleesons and he came out for me. I just wanted to sleep and I wouldn't go. Joe tried all he knew to get me to go, but I just turned my back and pretended to be asleep. "Fuck Ya" he said and left, slamming the door. I wasn't jig-time asleep till he was back. "I need help, I crashed the car". I got up. This is what happened. Joe was on his way back into Silvermines, in a temper. At the top of the village a triangle forms, with two roads, both leading into the village. Mulhare couldn't decide which road to take – so he made no decision and somersaulted the car several times in the field, between the two roads. Joe's first car a write-off. The car was on its roof in the field, with one tyre flat. "At least you can pretend you got a blow-out" I offered by way or helpful advice. We both agreed that there was only one thing we could do at that stage, so we did it. Down to "Peggy's" and over the galvanised gate. I had a lot of catching up to do so I came with my usual late run. Peggy went to bed and her son, up for his day's work, gently steered us out, the now open, galvanised yard gate.

It was breakfast time in "The Hostel". False appetite and foundation firmly in place. Big greasy fry with loads of stringy rashers. Great feed - what are they talking about "Pigs vittles in this place". Loads of jokes now about Mulhare's Anglia. Guys diving out of his way with exaggerated terror, because they didn't know which way he'd go.
I didn't know it yet, but this was going to be a day to remember, and it still wasn't 9 o'clock. We went into a garage in Nenagh and they agreed to move the car, "before too many more seen it". Mulhare had planned on going home and had mail and clothes to pick up – so we headed off for Muckenagh, Eyrecourt. The Mulhare's were lovely people. I stayed there so often and was treated like one of the family. Mrs Mulhare was a typical Irish Mammy, couldn't do enough and all the time fussing over us.
Anyway this Saturday, we didn't spend too long there. Eat a bit of dinner and all was well. Breakfast and dinner now and the "foundation" was holding solid as a rock. We played a few games of darts in Eyrecourt, had a couple in Borrisokane and so to Nenagh. Now we were amongst our own. Mulhare was the centre of attention and everyone wanted to hear a first hand account of what happened. Ditching cars amongst thirsty miners wasn't at all unusual, but Joe's account of how it happened was! The general consensus was that Joe was lucky to be alive and we all drank to that. Day progressed to evening and evening moved into night. No sleep the previous night and there was going to be even less this night. At ten o'clock we decided we were going to the dance in Limerick. Offaly man, Jimmy Cooney said he was coming with us. Only recently have I learned that Jimmy only made it into the early eighties. I have many friends up there, who will be sussing out a good place for me to stay! We detoured round by the Hostel, to change, wash and apply the "Old Spice". The only two people in The Hostel not gone out were two Zambian mine engineering students; there for two months to do some practical mining work. Very black and very quiet, these two nice young men kept very much to themselves. They were in the T.V room when I came in. I decided it was time, in fact not a moment too soon, that these guys be shown some real Irish hospitality. We invited them to come to the dance in Limerick. They said "No thank you". The word no wasn't going to figure in this deal. We just about gave them time to turn off the television and soon the two Zambians joined the Offaly man in the back seat of "The Blue Bomber" heading forth to the treaty city. Mulhare's mood was

changing. He was missing his Anglia and it was now my fault! Had I gone for a drink in the first place and Anglia would not have finished a critical piece of tangled metal in a lonely village field. The logic of this argument failed me and the argument got too heavy, as we approached Limerick. Most I don't or didn't remember, but Cooney filled in a lot of blank spots. On the main road to Limerick, Mulhare and I got out to settle the argument. In order that we could see what we were doing, I left on the headlights. Jimmy was trying to separate us, whilst the two Zambians sat frozen in the car – as if spellbound by this demonstration of Irish hospitality. It wasn't a bell which stopped the fight. It was a siren. Two squad cars and we were all arrested. Cooney said

In 1967 Canada celebrated her 100th birthday.
As part of that celebration the Irish Canadian Club organised a 10-a-side Gaelic Football Tournament, in Thompson, Manitoba. Pictured above is the Westmeath team captioned by Billy Comaskey (Competition Winners).
Front row L to R: Vincent Conroy (Trainer), Bernie Comaskey, Pat Connell, Bill Comaskey (Captain), Jimmy McDonnell, John Ward,
Back Row L to R: Michael Cassidy, Pete Smith, Eamon Kelly, Nick Shaw and Philip Conroy.

afterwards, in his description to the boys in the pub, that at this stage the two Zambians were as "white as sheets".
I was naturally charged with drunken driving. I got the case adjourned once, but towards the end of September, I appeared in Court in Limerick. My solicitor talked a lot of rubbish on my behalf, which I wouldn't have let him, had I known in advance. I pleaded guilty and was fined £20, plus costs. In addition I was suspended from driving for a year.
When Pamela came home from England I was full of shame and remorse. She was upset. I told her she would be better off without me, but she didn't want that either. Before she came home I made the decision that I would go back to Canada. It must have been dreadful for Pamela. She had just got her first school in Clonard, Co.Meath and now the man she believed in, pulled the rug from under her feet. I swore that I would go to Canada for a year, not drink, save all my money and come home to get engaged at Christmas. We had an emotional parting. At the end of October, 3 years almost to the day that I first landed there I set out for Thompson again. Delvin man Joe Sherwin drove me from Silvermines to Shannon. I didn't tell my family I was going. The plane was delayed at Shannon and in the meantime Joe and I got so pissed that Aer Lingus wouldn't give me a drink when the plane took off.

Soab Lake

Phillip Conroy was back in Thompson also. Willie or Billy- which I could never get used to calling him, had married Pat, his childhood sweetheart. Thompson now had an airport, so I arrived in style this time. Philip and Willie met me at the airport and as always, we headed for "The Thompson Inn". Since I had left, there was now a second hotel. The Burntwood, so we divided our custom. I know I wasn't supposed to be drinking, but this was the end of October, so there wasn't much sense in stopping completely; at least, until the New Year! Most of my old buddies were still there, but Bob Grundig had been killed undergound, while I was away. I arrived back on local Election Day, so there was a buzz around town and a sup of free drink, even! I met a selection of newcomers, including Pauric Burke and George "The Doyler" Doyle. Pauric's brother Gabriel, later married Pamela's sister, so we still see each other from time to time. "The Doyler" and I became great friends. He was the wittiest and the greatest company I had ever

known. George was a larger better looking version of Noel V. Ginnity and he lived life as if it was one great, exciting, fun-filled, never ending game. He lit up a room and you never knew what he was going to do next. When Philip and I start telling "Doyler" stories it goes on for hours.
To be really accepted in our circle, you had to have done your night in jail. This is how "The Doyler" did his. George "took a drink". He was in The Thompson Inn and there was a wedding on. George met the groom in the wash-room and the groom, knowing George, invited him into the reception. Doyle is seated on the far side of the head table when the Mother of the bride spots him. She walks over and asks "Who invited you" "Stan did" pointing at the groom. "It is the prerogative of the bride's family to invite guests" "now please leave". George hesitated. "Get out" she screeched. Now everybody was looking. Dead silence. The Doyler stood up and the Mother of the bride walked back and took her seat at the head table, just behind the wedding cake. Doyler walked, straight and erect and just as he passed the wedding cake he put his fist through it, and went out licking the cream from his knuckles. Night in Thompson jail!
You could always depend on "The Doyler". Loyal and generous to a fault, I had great times with him. "Have you any money, George?" always met with, "I have all sorts of money" "Any beer at your place George?", "I have all sorts of beer". I lost so many so-called friends when I quit drinking but George remained my good friend. After I got married he came home and stayed with us a couple of times. He had the most beautiful hand writing I have ever seen and we used to exchange witty, zany letters for a few years. One night, in the middle of the night in 1981, Willie rang. I knew it was bad news. He told me "The Doyler" was on his way home for good. A week later I knelt in a seat, well in, against the wall, in Kells chapel. I am sometimes OK in these situations, but when "The Doylers" coffin was being wheeled up the aisle I just started to cry and I couldn't stop. I faced the wall hoping no one would see. Maybe part of it was for the loss of our youth and that devil-may-care life we lived with such a sense of optimism, freedom and abandon. "The Doyler" had that effect on people. Philip told me, years later, that he never said a prayer for his family or anyone else without remembering, or including "The Doyler". Another dreadfully poignant incident occurred on George's last trip. A good friend of his worked for British Airways Cargo in London. He hadn't heard of "Doylers" death and found out when the coffin

he was handling as part of his job had George's name and address attached. I didn't want to go working for INCO again and besides there was better money to be made working for mining contractors. Sixty miles out of Thompson was a developing mine called Soab Lake. Soab got its name from one of the first guys to see the place who exclaimed; this is a "Son of a Bitch" of a place - hence the letters S.O.A.B or Soab. After a few days of taking a drink in Thompson, I went out to Soab and got hired by R.F. Fry. I was "chuffed". Only good miners got hired by mining contractors. The camp was good and the food was excellent and varied. Fresh fish for starters, range of deserts, anything you wanted for breakfast; juices, coffee and snacks available around the clock. Six chefs looking after us. A far cry from "The Hostel"!

For the first week I was moved from place to place, but I was doing ok, apart from the puking and the weakness and a bit of the shakes. Then after I talked it over with Philip, he arrived and we became room-partners and partners at work. It was great. Philip was a great miner, with great hands to do anything and a great head for planning. As well, he was and still is, as strong as a horse. We worked well together, because we were on the same wavelength. If we went to town for a drink, we both did it. If we blew a shift, we generally blew it together. Philip understood that I would be sicker in the mornings and he carried me without a hint of complaint. Naturally, after a time we began to get on each others nerves and we had rows over the slightest of things, but never at work. We were driving a drill-drift. An 8_X8_ drift off the main drift. We slushed out the "Muck" with an air-slusher and we did not have to lay track. The ground was good. We were doing so well that the Captain decided to split us up. I was given a man who talked well above his ability. He couldn't drill a straight hole and I would finish up drilling off most of the round. We were always late finishing and this held up the other areas, who couldn't light up until we were all ready to go. My partner was a nice guy with a family, so I never complained about him, but I was pleased when he didn't return after Christmas.

Christmas came. I had Christmas dinner with Willie and Pat. Philip, Pauric Burke and I think, Nick Shaw were there also. I had a long phone conversation with Pamela, before I got too drunk. How that girl waited for me I'll never know. Her love letters, a couple of times a week were the highlight of my life now. As well, she sent me "The Westmeath Examminer" and Mondays "Irish Press" for the sport.

I had vowed to give up the drink on New Years Day, but Larry Gallagher was getting married on 7th January, so there was no point in stopping until after that. The seventh came and went. We had a great day, Larry was no longer single, but Bernie was still drinking.

The next working partner I got was an old Yugoslav guy by the name of Matt. Philip quit and moved back to town and Matt and I shared the room. Matt was bad with arthritis and the room constantly reeked of "Wintergreen". As he was so senior, he was the leader. Matt, due to the condition of his hands and a lifetime underground, was hardly able to drill, but we worked together for six months and got on great. He had a great miners head and was great because they listened to him upstairs. He constantly moaned until they gave us new gear. He whinged about bonus, until they gave us more than we were due. We got the best workplaces. Matt did the moaning and the slushing and I did the drilling. We made good money. One of the best bonus cheques I made underground, at that time, was $760 for two weeks work and I lost it in the Bunkhouse, playing poker – drunk.

All sorts of Drink, All sorts of Women
George "The Doyler" Doyle (centre) with another friend Gerry Cullen (left)

I was now going to give up drink after "St. Patrick's Day" and Doyler and I had two of the best looking women in town, lined up for the Irish dance. My date was the recently arrived Mary Spellman, who worked in the bank. Mary, a Galway girl, was a big step-up from having to "borrow" a barman's wife previously! We went out a few times-the four of us. Mary and I just got on great, but I told her about Pamela and Pamela in turn knew of my date for the dance – although I imagine she expected it to be a once off. Once, "The Doyler" "thumbed" "The Mounties" after the dance in The Legion and they drove the four of us home in a Police car. Nobody else would get away with that. He arrived with flowers once and made me look bad. Only the next day did I discover how he got the flowers. His neighbour was in trouble with the wife and brought her home a big bunch of flowers, which she promptly threw out the window. George swooped on them and arrived flower laden for his date - not forgetting to put one in his lapel, of course! "The Doyler" and myself were the envy of half of Thompson and I liked it that way. The girls didn't "take a drink" and there was nothing to it, except many a laugh, which this guy needed.

I was going to different doctors, hoping that maybe some of them might prescribe a magic bottle which could cure my ills. Apart from being at work, I could hardly think or function without a certain amount of drink and it was getting worse all the time. Alcoholism is a progressive disease. I now got sick every day, even when I hadn't been drinking the previous day. I was chewing all sorts of tablets and taking all sorts of prescribed and non-prescribed medicines, but nothing worked. The physical pain in my stomach varied. The mental pain in my head was now constant. I didn't want to be like this.

My Hour of Need

I bought a car and was coming into town more often and therefore blowing more shifts. Even old Matt tried to have a heart to heart talk with me. It was early April and Pamela was coming to Thompson for her summer holidays. I was, on one hand, excited by the prospect, but as against this I was still drinking and I had let her down again-big time.

I was at my lowest ebb. I didn't know what to do, or where to turn, but I knew, with all my heart, that this wasn't the real me. Deep down somewhere in my being, I knew the real me wanted to get out. I was a prisoner of alcohol. This was my "rock bottom" and if a miracle didn't happen, I was going under. Then the miracle started to happen.

My good friend and frequent boozing buddy Bill Elliot was working at Soab and we met often. We arranged to meet on Friday evening in "The Thompson Inn". When I arrived, there was this guy called Ron with Elliot. I was introduced and after holding down the "foundation" we took into a serious drinking session. I learned that Ron had been off the drink for a year until lately and that as his wife had now left him, the party would be at his place tonight. I woke up the next morning in Ron's living room floor, my head next to a book-case. I was too sick to move, but what made me stretch my hand and take a down a book? The book was "The big book" of Alcoholics Anonymous. I read the first chapter "Bills Story" lying there on the floor. Then it dawned on me! This guy Ron was an alcoholic and that's why this book was here and this is why his wife is gone. Jesus Christ! did anyone see me drinking with an alcoholic?

This was my crazy thinking. I couldn't identify with Ron, or the book and I was too proud for anyone to know I was drinking with an alcoholic. But the seed was sown. I had now come into contact with Alcoholics Anonymous. Just by chance? Coincidence? I didn't think so. The following week I picked up my copy of "The Thompson Citizen" and the first thing I noticed was an advertisement which had never been there before. It said, "If you want to drink, that's your business, it you want to stop we can help". Alcoholics Anonymous Telephone no. I tore out the advert and put it in my wallet. The next Thursday evening, payday, I came into town. First I went to "The Cocktail Lounge" to get a foundation. A "screwdriver" with two straws and loads of ice. Then I moved to the Beer-Parlour and sat drinking on my own. I didn't want to talk to anyone. I couldn't get drunk and I was sick of being sick. I went out to the lobby and phoned the number.

A friendly voice said, "Don't move, I'm coming to get you". There was a meeting on and the guy who collected me, took me there. To my surprise, I knew a few people. At the coffee break I said to a woman, "I'm surprised to see you here" to which she replied "Well I'm not one God-dammed bit surprised to see you here". I was half drunk and a nuisance really. I wouldn't have had the courage to go sober. I listened to the speakers. I learned that that only requirement for membership was a desire to stop drinking. By God, I had that in abundance. My first feelings were those of incredible relief. I wasn't bad or weak, or lacking in willpower - God knows, it was willpower alone which dragged me through the previous 8 years. They told me it was a disease, a disease for which the medical profession could do nothing, but which the sufferer could exercise a choice over. Alcoholism is an incurable disease but all I had to do to survive was to follow a simple programme; be honest and keep away from one drink, a day at a time. I noted afterwards that, that date was 24th April – my Mothers birthday. Coincidence? Maybe;

or could it be, perhaps that prayer does work? I agreed to go to another meeting the next night.

I was terrified that anybody I knew might see me going in or out of an AA meeting. John Deveraux lived in the same apartment block and in dodging him, I was ten minutes late going in to the meeting. The single greatest thing happened next. As I entered the room, who was doing the chair only an old drinking buddy of mine, Vic from Belfast. I hadn't seen him in the bar for a while and now I knew why. Vic was a barber in the Plaza. He was like me throwing darts - he couldn't cut hair until he had the correct amount of drink in him. We drank and fought. If he insulted the Pope, as was his wont, I immediately became the "Defender of the Faith" – even though neither of us was practising much of any religion. The troubles in the North of Ireland were just brewing and "The Doyler" always said Vic and I started it!

When I came into the room Vic was reading Chapter 5 of "The Big Book". He looked up, never changed his expression, but with typical northern dry wit said "What kapt ya"? and went back reading. Vic was eight months without a drink. Vic drank like I did. Anybody could tell me anything they liked, but I knew that if it worked for Vic, it would work for me. It was like coming home. I was where I belonged and I was content and happy already.

I was great material for AA because I genuinely wanted to get better. I went to meetings every chance I got. I studied and learned the programme of living. It was easy. More of life's " balances and counter-balances", I was an alcoholic from my first drink and now to balance that, I found it easy to stop from my first meeting. Whilst I was to "slip" twice before that year was out I knew that this now was the real me. From that day onwards I valued and appreciated life more for having gone through those years as a practicing alcoholic. I take nothing for granted. I love life and every day I have to live. I cherish things most people take for granted. I could be dead only for finding AA so I have lived a good many days on "borrowed time". The most important thing for me is that I never put my kids through what I would have done, had I been drinking, or that Pamela never had to live with me through drink. Having said that, it wouldn't work if I stopped drinking for Pamela, I stopped drinking for me.

The Road Back

There is an old saying that "What's in when you're sober, comes out when you're drunk". As far as I am concerned this is not true. I said and did things through drink that I would otherwise never have thought of and that was totally out of character with my nature and beliefs.

"Freedom", that is what I had now – freedom of choice. I got great satisfaction now from things like going bowling or going to a movie and not to be looking at my watch to see how much drinking time remained at The Thompson Inn. Getting a pay cheque now was so pleasantly different because I felt I had the choice of what to do with it. The first feeling I had experienced in AA was hope, which was quickly followed by a certain belief that it was going to work for me.

All was not absolutely perfect though. They say that "If you sober up a horse-thief, then what you got was a sober horse-thief". I was in piss-poor physical health. I continued to drink lots of cold milk for the stomach and I was on medication – but at least now, it had a chance of working. After a few weeks, I never again vomited up blood (I'm sorry, I know I said that twice already, I wouldn't mention that again – but it's over now). Now, I didn't have to get sick every day. For a year or so I could still get sick quite easily – usually brought on by a bout of coughing. I was a heavy smoker and I continued smoking for a further five years. As time went on, my stomach healed – very slowly. The bouts of sickness became less and less, but for the next ten years, the old tummy had to be treated with due care and attention. 'Tagamet' tablets became a Godsend and our house wasn't without a supply for a decade. For twenty years now, my stomach hasn't given me the slightest bit of bother – but the scar-tissue remains, evidence of an iron stomach, fighting to reject "The Foundations!".

INCO had gone into production with a new mine at Birchtree, six miles out of Thompson. As Pamela would soon be out, I decided to quit Soab Lake and move back into town. Larry Bell, whose father was a mine captain, was my shift-boss. Larry was a super guy, as was also a younger shift-boss over me, whose name was Bozane. Larry Bell had a degree in mine engineering, but unlike others I knew this didn't handicap him from being an excellent, common sense miner's boss. No doubt but that as we got better at the job, the shift bosses got easier to work for, applied common sense and sometimes turned a "blind eye" to short cuts. Willie had just been promoted to shift-boss and this didn't do me any harm either.

I was a stope leader in the largest stope INCO had. Eighteen men worked on each shift in the stope. Mining was becoming more mechanised. In my stope were two diesel scoop trams - the first I had seen and these could move a lot of "muck" in comparison to a small air-slusher.

One vice which I still retained was the gambling one. Boredom and fat pay cheques in a mining town is conducive to big poker games. We played regularly. Regulars included Bill Elliot and Cliff Fletcher, two great poker players and both great friends of mine and of course the inimitable Tommy Gaynor. I, mistakenly as it turned out, was under the impression that now that I wasn't drinking I would clean up at poker. It didn't always work out that way!

"Break-up" - the thawing of the snow and ice came early to Thompson in 1970 and it was an exceptionally warm Spring and Summer. Soon the long awaited July arrived and Pamela was on her way. Much to the astonishment of contrary Mine Captain, Bob Glencross, who knew me from previously, I never missed a shift at Birchtree, so when I asked for five days leave of absence in honour of Pamela's visit, they gave it to me. (Sadly Glencross was killed in a motorbike accident the following year).

Pamela was flying into Winnipeg and I was driving out the 650 miles from Thompson to meet her. George Doyle was coming with me for the trip. We would stay overnight in The Pas, and spend one night in Winnipeg and another in The Pas on the way back.

My heart full of joy, on a beautiful summer's morning, I left Thompson behind me. "The Doyler" was working at Pipe Lake, twenty miles out and just off the highway, where I was picking him up. "The Doyler" came out and I knew that something was wrong. "Bad news" he said, "I can't go". "Just got word that my father got a severe heart-attack and they are expecting the worst. I have to wait for news and go home if I have to". George and his father, who was also George, were very close. They had a wonderful relationship and used to write these crazy letters to each other.

Nobody ever knows and The Higher Power shows us that we never know. Eleven years on, when we laid "The Doyler" to rest in Kells, his father walked behind the coffin.

I was sorry George couldn't come, but nothing could dampen my happiness, so off I headed. Next stop The Pas. I booked into The Gateway Hotel, ate a big steak, walked around a bit and then headed into the beer parlour. One of the Nabess brothers (Andy and Archie were shift bosses in Thompson) was slinging beer. He knew me and thought it was a joke when I asked for a ginger ale. I met a few guys I knew and took a bit of stick over not drinking – especially when word spread that I was on the way out to collect the girl-friend.

After breakfast, next morning and after booking two rooms for the return trip, I headed south for Winnipeg. Pamela's plane was due in early afternoon. I made a few coffee stops along the way, but I was too excited to eat anything – other than the by now standard glass of cold milk. Winnipeg airport is really a small airport by to-days standard, but to us bogmen in 1970, it seemed huge. Getting there in lots of time, I savoured every moment. To this day, I am fascinated by airports. Time never seems long when I find myself waiting. I "people watch" and experience a certain "buzz" when I'm there. Now I travel by air a few times a month and I never tire of it. I think it was Willie Nelson I heard say "The nearest thing to freedom is being on the move". There is some truth in that.

It was near time for my girl to arrive. My stomach was churning a bit. I had another glass of milk. I had booked two rooms in a City Hotel. This was 1970 and this was a convent girl!

Then I was paged. "Would Mr. Comaskey pick up a courtesy phone?" The flight was delayed. Actually it wasn't delayed. Some fussy official in Toronto wasn't happy with Pamela's papers. She was on a teacher's group flight and had to visit three cities and he claimed Thompson wasn't a city. He was very wrong because Thompson had recently become a city. Pamela missed her connecting flight and would be ten hours late. I went back to the hotel for a while and watched T.V in the room. She was now due around 11pm, but I didn't bother to check flight numbers or arrivals – I just watched everybody coming through except when I ran out to put more coins in the parking meter. Eleven came and went. It had been a long day. Midnights came and went and still no future Mrs. Comaskey. At ten to one I found a pay-phone and got through to Willie's number in Thompson to see if they had heard anything. "Bernie" said Pat "Where the hell are you?" "I'm at the fucking airport for twelve hours – that's where I am". "Well, she's in since eleven and phoned here numerous times to say she couldn't find you and only five minutes ago she phoned and said she was gone to book into a hotel". Pat gave me the number of the hotel and off I set, at speed. "Jesus if ever a man suffered!" I don't know where the time went, but I remember it was near 3am when I found the hotel. The half asleep guy at reception told me "Yes, we do have a Miss Bartley staying, but visitors aren't allowed in the rooms after midnight". My tolerance threshold was low "Well, you just fucking watch me". "If you don't give me her room number I'll bang on every fucking bedroom door until I get the right one!" He gave me the number and the quickest way to get there. By the time I got there he had phoned the room. I only had to knock once. Pamela hasn't as good a memory as I have but she remembers my first words. "I caught you in your curlers!"

We now had three hotel rooms and I had to sleep in my clothes but I was happy. The world really was a wonderful place, after all.

On the drive from Winnipeg back to The Pas, there was something that just wasn't quite right. It was a long separation, nine months and there was a tension or something which surprised me. The carefree banter and easy chat wasn't there. We were both tired. Along the way, I asked, "Do you see any change in me?" I was "fishing". When she didn't take the bait I said, "I haven't had a drink for over two months". Pamela said, "Big deal, I thought you weren't going to have a drink for the year?" She didn't realise it, but she had said exactly what was good for me. I shouldn't have been looking for any praise for being normal. Then I told her that I was an alcoholic and was going to AA. I told her honestly about myself and about the disease and what I was doing about it. Pamela was only twenty-one and I'm sure all this information was a big shock to her; she listened attentively, but didn't say an awful lot about it.

Pamela arrives in Canada 1970
Photo courtesy of "The Doyler"

When we arrived at "The Gateway" in The Pas, there were quite a few guys

I knew there. Some of them were friends, others just ordinary rough miners who knew me. All were there to get a look and see what this girl that I did all the talking about was really like. This was very unnerving for Pamela. A few of the crew had been "taking a drink" and it was downright uncomfortable in the beer parlour. After staying the minimum period to pass ourselves, I announced we were going to bed. There were, at any rate, enough witnesses to see that the "Gobshite" had booked two rooms!

The 'Slip'

Back in Thompson, Pamela got a wonderfully warm welcome, both from the Irish and Canadians. It is only a myth to say that Irish hospitality is the friendliest in the world. I have never met a more open, trusting more hospitable people than North Americans – none more so than the Canadians.

Pamela was staying with Billy and Pat and I was now living with Bob and Marge Curry over on Rainbow Crescent. Bob was another Ulster Protestant, married to Marge, a Canadian Roman Catholic. Here is an interesting point; the "troubles" were now flaring in the North. In Thompson, there was an even spread of Northerners from the two traditions. Taken out of their siege environment, many of them soon realised how little separated them and that the rest of the world couldn't see any difference between a Unionist or a Nationalist. I went to parties and functions in Thompson, where the late night sing-song would include "The Sash" as well as "Kevin Barry". Granted, it must have been through drink, because I joined in.

On Pamela's first Friday night, there was a dance in The Community Centre and we were all there. Pamela was a bit overwhelmed and smothered by all the attention. Bob Glencross came over and shook hands with us saying, "I didn't believe your excuse when you looked for the time off". I had used so many excuses over the years for missing time – which reminds me of "The Doylers" most famous three-in-one excuses. He was in trouble. Five shifts blown, so in he goes with his pink card to Jess Watkinson. He needed a good one. "I was out in Winnipeg getting married". Jess stands up and shakes hands with George. "Good luck Doyle, maybe this will straighten you out. This is what you need". A couple of months later, The Doyler blew a week and arrives at Jess's desk again. Jess waits for him to speak "Wife very ill". "Sorry about that George" as he writes "excused" on the pink slip. Wasn't too long before Doyler blew again. Wife died …

At the dance we met Gary Walsh and his lovely wife, Merna. Gary was third generation Irish and a great friend to all our gang. He owned The Tasti-Burg Restaurant and he had recently become a partner in a clothes shop. He was also involved in local politics. Indeed, on the day I arrived back in Canada the elections were taking place and we were invited to Gary's party. I still had a vote and in his speech Gary thanked me for coming all the way from Ireland to vote for him. It wasn't strictly true, but it was a good line. The following year Gary was killed when his light aeroplane crashed in the bush, on his way back from Winnipeg. A year passed before the wreckage was found. Gary's body was never recovered, due to the activity of the wild animals. The wilds of Northern Canada is an unsympathetic place for man or beast.

Conroy wasn't there to meet Pamela, as he had gone into The Bush a couple of weeks back. Gallagher, Deveraux, Gaynors, Darbys, The Doyler and really, all the Irish were there. "Fiddling Red" and his outstanding band was playing. "Red" played the fiddle and I have never heard better. It was my first time to hear Orange Blossom Special when he played it. The hair stood on the back of my neck when I heard it and I have never heard it since, without thinking of "Fiddling Red", an absolute musical genius. He played at all the dances, from my first one in Thompson, but tonight was the most special. "Fiddling Red" took a drink! He was a tortured soul. On stage he expressed himself with music. I often studied his face. The concentration as he reached a difficult pitch on the fiddle, the eyes lighting up and the big smile when he hit the familiar notes and just how he fed off the wild applause of his audience. I knew, to see, the "P.J Harrison Mining Company", lamp man out at TI. He was in charge of the mining lamps and handed them out, took them in and re-charged them. With his helmet and jacket collar turned up, he rarely talked to anyone and never smiled. When I was "Topman" with INCO, I would have had some interaction with this man. I was doing this for several months before someone happened to tell me he was one and the same man – "Fiddling Red".

After the dance, I was driving Pamela home when we had a row. I didn't know what it started over, but I know how it finished. She told me, in the finish up "I don't know what I want" as she was getting out of the car. I said, "Well, if it's any help to you, I'm breaking this off".

I went back to Curry's, looked up the number of the house the party was at, rang and asked for George Doyle. "Much beer there?" "We have all sorts of drink", replied "The Doyler". "I'm on my way over". I got drunk. I just used the row as an excuse. "Cunning, baffling, powerful" - that's alcohol all right. Sometime next day George and myself went over to Billy's. Poor Pat made tea and tried to be chatty. Pamela sat there, a face like she was chewing a lemon - she had heard about the drink. Larry Gallagher arrived and said the wrong thing. He told Pamela to "Smarten up – this isn't Drumcree". The Doyler though was marvellous. He would melt an ice-berg with his charm and good humour. The three of us went down town to the Thompson Inn. George got wine for Pamela and he and I had a few. Between temper, or whatever, Pamela drank the wine like lemonade. It was the first time I noticed that she takes high steps after a few drinks – something which she still does to this day.

Etna and John Devereaux had invited us all over that evening and it was just perfect in the circumstances. I had a couple of drinks, demonstrating the point that Pamela wasn't going to tell me what to do. The truth was, though, that I hated myself for having a "slip". Previous to AA. I didn't have a choice. Now I could choose whether to drink or not and I made the wrong choice that weekend. The air was cleared anyway. Pamela and I "made up". We told each other that neither of us wanted anything or anybody else. On the Sunday night I went to an AA meeting.

It was a great time, but the Summer flew. I worked steady, but didn't work any overtime, while Pamela was there. We were invited to so many houses for "Supper", Barbecue's, and Picnic's at Paint Lake etc. It was obvious that we were in love and there were no more hic-ups during that Summer.

I have had many "close calls" underground – as would have had most of the surviving miners from that era. One such 'near thing' happened while Pamela was in Thompson. I was walking across the stope, carrying an AMEX (explosives) loader on my back. A piece of loose came down and cut the loader off my back and smashed my elbow. In hospital, they removed grit from around the elbow and stitched it up. I was on light duty for a week and could only put my left arm around Pamela. A sequel to this story is that in 1982 I developed tendon trouble in my elbow, from playing squash. I had to have an operation. The X Ray showed "something else" in there and when Joe McGrath operated he took out a piece of nickel which they missed in Thompson hospital in 1970!

CHAPTER 14

"He's Back"

All too soon I left Pamela at the airport. It was coming up to 1st September and at least, it wouldn't be long until we would be together again. I was coming home in December and she was going to tell her parents that we were getting engaged at Christmas. Life was absolutely wonderful. I threw myself into work. The yoke of alcohol was not hauling me down anymore. I attended meetings regularly. Driving home from a meeting one night, on the car radio, I heard Chris Kristofferson new song, for the first time and it really struck a chord with me. It's funny how a song will always remind us of a moment in time passed and I never hear "Sunday Morning Coming down" without thinking of that time and how blessed I am. Also, over that Summer, two songs remind both Pamela and I of the nice times, "Bridge over Troubled Waters" (our song) and "Me and Bobby Mc Gee".

I was still playing poker. I didn't "clean up" for being sober – but at least I broke even now. Two of the guys I played most regularly with was the aforementioned Bill Elliot and also Cliff Fletcher. Fletcher was a truly smashing guy, who was in Thompson before I arrived and became a good friend. Fletcher wasn't your typical miner at all. Soft spoken, well read and highly articulate, he never got in a row. He took a drink, but never blew a shift. He didn't laugh out loud but had this infectious chuckle. Highly regarded as a miner he had turned down the chance to go shifting. He just loved life, sport, reading and travel. While I was in Canada, Fletcher visited Ireland on one of his many trips. I don't know who, if anyone, he linked up with here, but to illustrate the sort of a man he was, whilst he was in Ireland, he made a point of going to a game in Croke Park. He had heard so much about the GAA and Croke Park from us that he had to see for himself.

"Fletch" was a good poker player. The last game we played we left together and he advised me "Of all the players I know, you are the unluckiest. You constantly get beaten with good hands". "You should quit playing cards". "You are unlucky and I am lucky", he said, taking a big roll of dollars out of his pocket, chuckling loudly. Fletchers luck didn't hold out. A few days later Larry Bell called me over away from the other men. Fletcher had just been killed. I went to surface and checked out sick.

The first thing I did was phone Philip. Conroy was out of town and I could have done with him. I was numb. I didn't crave a drink anymore. I didn't want a drink. I didn't need a drink, but I didn't know what to do, so I went and took a drink. If AA does nothing else, it ruins the taste of drink!! Be this as it may, I got "rotten". A lot of Fletchers friends met up and we had what I suppose you would call a "wake", over a few days.

On the Sunday night I was over at The Legion, drinking. I was throwing darts at the board – or at the tyre, to be more precise. Jess Watkinson came over and asked me for a game. It was obvious he wanted to talk to me. We started a game, but soon the talk turned to Fletcher. "I have seen too many of my friends killed here" I said. "Wait till you're around as long as I am", replied Jess. "I wont be, Jess, I'm quitting at Christmas". Jess didn't expect this and he had something to tell me. "You are making a name for yourself over at Birchtree. Evidently, Bell and Bozane had "written me up". There are plans for you. Don't quit. I'll give you all the time you want to go home, but don't quit". Eventually, just to bring the topic to a close I told him I would think about it. Elliot and I left together and got good and pissed. That was my last drink. It was around the 13th October 1970. I vividly remember every second of my first drink on 1st May 1962 but I remember nothing of my last one. Elliot too fought and won the battle of the booze.

Since that night in 1970 I have never seriously considered taking a drink. I wanted to get better. A mountain was lifted from my back and I acquired such a love and zest for life that I felt I could handle anything. From that day

Staying with us on a visit to Ireland in 1982, Bill Elliott with Ian

to this, I have never gone to bed without getting down on my knees and thanking God for that sober day. I am far from being a religious person, but even the mere physical act of getting down on my knees reminds me of how much I have to be grateful for – and I know a grateful alcoholic will never drink again.

I wrote to Silvermines to enquire if I might have a job there after Christmas. They weren't falling over themselves to get me back, because I didn't even get an acknowledgement. My years driving suspension would be up by now, so I would have no problem in that regard. I had more than a sneaking worry that Mougal might not want to rehire me. Before I quit there, Mulhare, who was now back in England, had been fired for blowing shifts and his record wasn't any worse than mine.

Time dragged. I was booked to fly home on 18th Dec, but just like that day in March 1967, I woke up around 8th December and just couldn't face going underground, so I quit and changed my flight without telling Pamela or any-

one at home. I would surprise them. I was on my way. On the flight from Toronto to Shannon, I was sitting beside a lovely young New Zealand girl, who told me she was a journalist. She
was travelling on to Dublin, as was I and then she had to make her way to Belfast to write something on the influence of the riots on young people. We were good company for each other and the time absolutely flew. After landing in Shannon, we were informed that the connecting flight to Dublin was delayed 3 hours. "To hell with this" I said. "I'm not hanging around, I'm getting off here". I walked away and then she was on my shoulder. "Can I come too?" For a second the options flashed through my mind. Nobody knew I was in Ireland. I had anything up to a week to play with. But there was Pamela. "No, you better get back on that plane". I was growing up!
I hired a car and headed for Drumcree, stopping for a coffee in one of my old haunts in Nenagh. I didn't stop till I reached Bartleys Bar in Drumcree. Pamela's mother was in the bar and I got her usual warm welcome. Sean Bartley went down to the kitchen to tell Pamela and we went into the corridor. Going through the lounge, a former boozing buddy of mine, said to his companion, just loud enough for me to hear "Jazus Christ – he's back!!
It was my first Christmas sober since I was 16. This is a good time to state three IMPORTANT CONCLUSIONS that life has taught me.
(1) The extraordinary capacity of mind and body to heal itself.
(2) The resilience of the human spirit.
(3) That there is no right or wrong way for living.

CHAPTER 15

Engaged To Be Married

Pamela didn't want to go to a dance on my first night home, but I had been looking forward to a dance for so long. I insisted and got my way. I didn't realise it yet, but the great showband era was coming to an end. All anyone talked about was Christy Maye and his Disc-a-go-go. I didn't like discos then and haven't changed my mind since. You cannot beat the bit of live music and especially with a bit of brass. I have such an admiration for my friends Joe and Ben Dolan that they were able to swim against the disco trend and leaving aside Joe's personal popularity as a singer, the "Showband Sound" is as good and as popular as it was more than forty years ago. Likewise with the "King of the Swingers", Paddy Cole.

I was happy and content, but I had to adjust in so many ways. In a way, I had to learn how to live a normal life. In fairness I found little difficulty in this, but suddenly I had all this "time" and I didn't know what to do with myself. I was lucky in so far as I had no problem being in a pub. I didn't go in unless I had a reason, but I never stopped enjoying the company of people "taking a drink" – until the "messing" starts and then "I'm outa there"! I mentioned earlier about my interest in sport and music and I cannot overstate the benefit and therapy this has been, and is, for me. With regard to work, I love the challenge of a new project. Someone said, "Find a job you enjoy and you never have to work again". I read a statistic that 90% of people are doing work that they don't like. Not me! Another advantage in my living is that I like people and am good at interacting. However, if I dislike someone, I cannot help but show it – he will know. I remember once being on a "Century Management" course run by that most affable man, Kevin Fahy. At the follow up afterwards the emphasis was on the "difficult customer". It was pointed out by Kevin, that you had to win over this client. This was really laboured. I stood up in the body of the hall and asked that "If this guy had his knife in you to such an extent that you couldn't get him, you couldn't manage him and he was doing you harm what would you do"? Kevin and the panel said that this was never the case. This was my response "Mr. Chairman, I know I cannot win by proving somebody wrong from the inside of my counter, but deep down here, maybe as far as the pit of my stomach, I reserve the right to tell somebody to "Fuck off" when it comes to that stage!" (Some applause)

I am always willing to help people, even total strangers, but I have a fearless and ruthless streak when it comes to defending my patch. The one thing I will never do is tell a lie about an "enemy" or a business opponent. It hurts even a thick skin, when people do it to me.

Pamela was teaching in a lovely school in Clonard. I soon met her principal, Sean Murray and his family and we remained good friends. Likewise, Josephine Giles, the other teacher and her husband Larry from Longwood. Pamela's first "digs" was in Donovan's Pub, great people also. This was a temporary arrangement and soon she moved in with widow, Mrs Hickey.

My second weekend home Pamela and I were approaching Drumcree, after having visited friends. It was around ten o'clock and she was to pick up her things at home and then after "céiling" there for a while, I would leave her back in Clonard.

I don't know what it started over, but next thing we were in a serious row. Then I discovered that she still hadn't told her parents we planned on getting engaged on Christmas Eve – a few days away. Mind you, if my daughter had brought home someone like me, I wouldn't blame her for not rushing to break the news! We were now parked outside Bartleys .Argument inconclusive! "I'm going up to see Brian O' Shaughnessy", I said. Brian had just then opened his own pub in Delvin. Pamela got out and, banged the car door and off I headed the three miles to Delvin. Brian was behind the bar and the only customer was a guy I had had a drunken row with in Mullingar on my previous term home. No hard feelings and we all made small talk. I had two ginger ales and headed back to Drumcree, sufficiently cooled down to make peace. Pamela was gone. She had asked her Mother to drive her to Clonard. I was livid. I didn't show it as I talked to her sister, Bernadette, but I vowed to myself that if she ever wanted to talk, she would come to me! The next evening, I drove to Clonard. Mrs. Hickey was delighted to see me, having sensed through her lodgers demeanour that all was not well. After making and giving me tea, she said "Goodnight" and made a noticeably hasty retreat to bed.

Deadly silence, whilst we both drank tea and I ate all the "Mikado" biscuits on the plate. I put down the empty cup, stood up dramatically and announced "This thing is going to be one way or the other" Pamela got up from the chair, came to face me, started to cry, threw her arms around my neck and said "What are you talking about, it was never going to be anything other than "one way"!" The reason that she had got her Mother to drive her back the previous evening was that she was convinced that when I left in a "huff" to go to Delvin it was to get drunk – same as had happened in Thompson. I am sure she must have experienced similar worries from time to time – especially in the first few years, but she never showed anything other than complete faith in me.

On Christmas Eve, the then happiest day of my life, we drove to Dublin and bought Pamela's choice of ring, a diamond solitaire in Lawrence's of Henry Street. Pamela gave me an engagement signet gold ring. What a turn around for me in such a short span of life – the ongoing merry-go-round of living. Life's balances and counter balances at its best. We came back to Kells and had a meal in The Headford Arms. I thought of "The Doyler" and the impact he had on Kells, before he came to Canada. He had a girlfriend in Kells, whose adoring Mother used to leave a tray of sandwiches and cake for them, after the dance. Eventually, the girl broke it off, on account of George's taking a drink. At a dance in Kells, "Doyler", girl-less and hungry, spotted his former girlfriend with her new beau. He left before the dance was over. He knew where the house key was hidden. He made a pot of tea, ate all on the tray and left a note, "The Doyler strikes again". A new hiding place was found for the key. I knew he had to be at my wedding.

On the happiest days of our lives, there was a shock and terrible news when

At the IFA Dance in Collinstown, just after getting engaged early January 1971 Picture taken by "Longford Leader" photographer and appeared in same paper.

we arrived in Bartleys. It took the gloss off our engagement, but that wasn't important when we were told that Pamela's Grandfather, the much loved Tom O'Farrell had had a major stroke, at his home in Rickardstown, a couple of miles from Drumcree. As mentioned previously, the O' Farrells are one of my all-time favourite families. Old Tom had married Eileen McMahon of the famous Clare clan, nearly 50 years before. They raised a family of three

girls, including Dympna, Pamela's Mother and five sons. They are a close knit supportive family, hugely successful in sport, business or anything they turned to. Great hurlers - an interesting footnote in that of the following generation, Francis O'Farrell, playing centre-forward for Westmeath hurlers played on a young new, corner to the Clare team, called Seamnie Mc Mahon! Near the end of the game, they started talking and discovered they were cousins "It was the only time I held my own" said Frances afterwards.
Dympna was naturally upset over her Daddy but it didn't stop herself or Johnny from embracing us warmly and telling us how delighted they were. We went up to my parents next and they were just so pleased. Later on, we brought them down to the pub, where they – especially Daddy, took a drink. The kitchen was full with family coming and going. The O'Farrell boys were living in Dublin and came in one's and two's as they stopped on their way to and from Rickardstown. One memory is locked clearly in my mind. The back door opened and Mickey O'Farrell walked in. He had just been to Rickardstown and he came in the door visibly upset. As soon as he saw me, he walked passed everyone, shook hands and congradulated me, as the tears rolled down his face. I never told Mickey how much the gesture, in his moment of profound grief, meant to me. Grandad O'Farrell died about three weeks later. We all went to midnight mass in Collinstown. The Choir was lovely and Fred Casey, drunk at the back of the church, was so moved by one of the hymns, that he rose on the chorus! This was home, these were my people, Pamela Bartley was going to be my wife and I was never as happy.

Back At Work

The second week in January I drove down to Silvermines, in my new two years old maroon (up Westmeath!) Ford Escort, number ILI 168. My apprehension was well founded. At the gate, the security guy, after ringing told me that "Mogul wasn't hiring". I asked him to get Pat Rafter, The Personnel Manager on the phone for me. Mr. Rafter told me that there was nothing he could do, my file said, "Not for re-hire". Herb Fredrickson, whom I knew very well from Manitowadge was the new mine manager. I knew I would be ok with Herb, with whom I was on very friendly terms with, but I was careful not to go over any heads that I didn't have to. I can't be sure of the name of the guy just above Rafter; I think it was Anderson; who would have the "say-so", but I asked if he would give me two minutes of his time. He knew me and really couldn't very well say no to "two minutes". I was through security and into his office. We shook hands and he didn't put a tooth in it. I was an "experienced top-class development miner" but Mogul wouldn't hire me because I was "no use to them working three days a week". He showed me my time-sheet, to prove that three days was my average working week. It was a short speech from him. When he was finished talking I said simply "When I was here last, my problem was drink. I am not drinking now. I need this job. If I am any use to you, giving 100% of my best, working every shift, give me a chance to show you". "Okay, you're hired". The whole thing only took two minutes.

My first day back at Silvermines was almost my last day on earth. I have not related all the near misses I had underground, but this was the scariest because it lasted the longest. Jarvis, the shift boss, for whom I had worked previously, came over to give me my "line-up". After the pleasantries he said "You are going "driving" the main drift tomorrow". This was a total surprise and a bit of a shock to me. It was the hardest and most responsible job in the mine. "Today", I have an easy job for you, on your own" went on Jarvis. We walked to a "long-hole" stope. This was like a big u-shaped pit or canyon, around the edge of which was cut a "cat-walk" into the rock. Where the cat-walk was too narrow, at the end, I was to drill off a "slash", with the jack–leg and blast whatever I drilled at the end of the shift. Jarvis told me to bring back the powder with me after lunch, as by then I would know about how many holes and the lunch room and powder room was a long way from where I was working. Jarvis went on, "When you light up, if you walk back around the stope, it's slow and you are coming back close to the blast. Do you remember when you worked on the next level, last time you were here"? "I do" I said, without giving it any more thought. "Ok, go down the nearest manway ladder and make your way to the cage on that level, when you light up". I drilled off and loaded the explosives. I don't think tape-fuses are used nowadays and that it is now all electric blasting underground. The tape-fuse was a ten foot fuse, which burned at two minutes a foot. One fuse along with the sticks of powder in each hole. The cap of the fuse was in the hole and at the outer end was a groove into which was attached the igniter cord. In this way I controlled the sequence of the shots going off. Always, outside, or earliest to "break" ones first. The igniter cord burned out at ten seconds a foot.

I lit up and started down the manway. At the bottom was a drill-drift. I couldn't remember which way to go. Every miner had a watch with the correct time, so we all lit up together and got out – only I couldn't find my way out. I panicked and got hopelessly lost, going hither and thither. I could smell burning tape fuse and there was smoke everywhere. Next I found myself in a stope, standing right beside 30 sparkling little flames, as a series of fires burned towards the explosives. I became icily calm. I was reconciled to being a goner. I thought of Pamela and I thought of my Mother. I thought of Willie getting the news in Canada – another casualty of the cursed mines – just like Mike Lucy, Cliff Fletcher and so many others. Then I saw a manway in the stope. I started down the ladder. Just as I saw track the blast went off. It blew my hat off and sucked the air out of my lungs. My lamp dangled by my side. I finished up on my knees in the ditch. The water was flowing – luckily because there was little of it and knowing me, otherwise I would probably have gone the other way. The cage was gone when I got to the station. I rang the bell and was picked up in a minute. I took off the gear and clothes, chatted to the lads, told nobody, but spent a long, long time in the shower.

Main drift miners are the most respected in the mine and now I was the one "Driving the drift" involving three men working side by side. It is a 10'x10' tunnel. All three drill with jack legs. One man, usually the leader, drills out a "cut" in the centre to allow the ground to break. The cut includes a pattern of larger holes, drilled out with a "reamer" bit. First thing though, at the start of the shift the muck-pile has to be hosed down and the ground just blasted "mucked out", with a mucking machine and transferred out, in a muck-car, pulled along the newly laid rails, by a train. Every second shift involved "laying track". Add to this daily extending of air and water pipes and you will see that not a second could be wasted. To "miss a round" was a disaster and always felt to me like having been beaten in an important match – which I suppose it was.

Partners underground generally stay working with each other and bosses are reluctant to change men around. You have to have absolute trust in your partner and he in you. I think it is a fair parallel to equate it with two cops working together in a dangerous area. Miner's lives depend on each other. Dangerous environment, dangerous equipment, dreadful pressure for results, often taking short cuts, very little slack for human error.

Donegal man, Big Jim Gallagher, or his partner John Kinehan weren't over the moon getting me. John was nice to me, but I could sense Gallagher's unhappiness, although he didn't say anything to that effect. He was just waiting for me to "fuck up", so he could tell the mine captain. "What did I just tell you?" I worked like hell and volunteered no idle talk. I moved quickly to do things, always knowing what was coming next. Gallagher was a decent, straight man. Intelligent, well informed and an avid reader, he was moderate in all his habits. The first week, he looked to see if I was in The Dry when he came in. He too stayed in The Hostel and the talk of the place was that Comaskey wasn't drinking – YET! Time moved and soon I had earned the respect of my two colleagues. Jim and I became friends, so much so that years later he called to see me a couple of times.

In good shape

I was working in my own country and earning more money on bonus in the drift, than what I had been making in Canada. During that period, stretching over five months, I missed three shifts. In my second week, the inhabitants of The Hostel were all out hurling in the evening, "Backs and forwards" I was running after this guy, as a "daisy cutter" came along the ground. He should be pulling out? I had my hurl in one hand to hook him when he pulled the other way and I got the ball in the eye. Black eye back again, two days off work. The other shift lost was when Gallagher and I went in on overtime to do some special job. It wasn't left ready for us and we came up and went home. We were suspended for a shift.

I applied for a company house in Nenagh and without any hesitation, was successful. However Pamela's hope of getting a school around Nenagh was not so successful. This was proving to be a big problem and led to much soul searching. Everything was in the melting pot, even the prospects of us both going back to Canada. Pamela had successfully interviewed for a teaching post, during her summer in Thompson. We had set a date in August for our wedding. Then, around the beginning of June, a stupid "all out" strike occurred at the mine. A guy was fired for stealing cigarettes from another workers locker. The company was probably out to "get him" – but he did steal. The union backed the worker and appealed his dismissal to the Labour Court, which ruled that the company was correct in its action, but that due to the small amount involved, it recommended that he be reinstated. The union wanted him paid for the time he was fired – Mogul said no. A bitter strike, lasting six months then ensued. The IRA took it upon themselves to make representation on behalf of the workers, by blowing up part of the Headframe. I never went back.

Uncle Paddy

I doubt is I can do justice to my Uncle Paddy, for anybody who didn't know him. A bachelor farmer, to say that he was eccentric is like saying that Michael O'Leary dabbles in aeroplanes. Paddy was as odd as two left feet, but he was also in many ways the smartest man I knew. I told a professional man once that Paddy could see around corners and he agreed. Paddy was my Mothers older brother by two years.

Unlike "the Aunties", he gave us nothing as kids. He came down every Sunday night to "céilie" in our house. Christmas, birthdays, first-communions, confirmation, holidays, weddings meant nothing to Paddy – one arm as long as the other! His theory, with regard to children, was that if you gave a child a sweet, the next time, if you didn't have a sweet – you had a terribly disappointed child!

Paddy was the straightest, most honest man in all the world. Truly, he was one of a kind and all the neighbours loved talking to him, for his knowledge, sharp brain, wit and quick turn of phrase.

I was the "Favoured Nephew" but it was only when I became an adult, that I appreciated Paddy and looked to him, among other things, as a source of entertainment. He used to annoy my Mother by stating that he would "never make a will, so as to avoid having only one praying for him and the rest cursing him!" In reality he had all his affairs in order for many years before he died. I would have a few cattle with his during my early farming days. He broke my heart, because the way we did everything was whichever way gave the most hardship. He would weigh up all the things which could go wrong and then set out to eliminate the risks. This didn't always pay dividends as envisaged. For example, my Mother who lived next door, after she moved to Graftonstown, had a young collie bitch by the name of Sally. Paddy knew animals inside out and this morning he could see that Sally was coming in heat and needed to be protected from "O'Keeffe's hoor of a dog". Sally was shut into the strongest stone shed, with enough food and water to last three days. As "O' Keeffes hoor of a dog", would "eat the door out of it", Paddy brought over a pallet of cement blocks and built them up against the door, after putting two sheets of galvanise inside them. A lot of work, but there wasn't a bark out of Sally for the three days. Paddy set about dismantling the fortress. Eventually he got to the door and opened it. "O'Keeffe's hoor of a dog" hit him in the chest – going home. Luckily Joe O'Keeffe is a vet and was able to prescribe the morning after pill!

With Pamela's Grandmother, Granny O'Farrell, on our return from Honeymoon.

Paddy had a comment to make on everything. If, for example Germany won the World Cup, he would say something like, "Would you wonder at that, when it took 34 nations to "bate" them in the last war". Some of his opinions were "strong" to put it mildly and when he wanted to be sarcastic, he had no equal. He listened to every RTE news bulletin – especially at one o'clock. One day, he was there drinking tea with my Mother when I arrived in. The main item was the amount of compensation being paid to soldiers for hearing loss. A proud Irishman, FCA stalwart and All Ireland rifle shot winner, I could see he was agitated, so I decided to "rise it". "There you are" I said, "I worked underground for five years, three drills going side by side in a confined area, no ear protection and I can hear that!" "That shows you", came the reply, "All that noise didn't harm you, and the loudest thing most of them "hoors" ever heard was a fart!!"

He had such an imaginative way with words. He loved his cattle, dogs and all of nature. He looked for signs in the weather and recorded and kept a record of the temperature every morning. We were due to dose cattle one morning, "You don't worry, I'll have them in when you arrive at ten", he told me. I arrived, started down the fields and met Paddy. The sweat was dripping from his bushy eyebrows and he was out on his feet. Normally he would easily round the bullocks into the yard, but today, they sensed something was going on. Instead of saying "I cannot get them in, he shook his weary head from side to side and informed me, "They are not in favour of it".

It was difficult to stop him talking. I was standing on the middle of the floor, waiting for him to pause, so as that I could say "Goodnight" and leave. He was filling me in on what he had learned about wild mink, from observing their habits. "I was down there fencing and I watched a big buck mink lie all evening over a rabbit-burrow, waiting for the rabbit to come out. Coming on near dark the rabbit stuck his head out and the mink got his teeth in the back of his neck and the two of them rolled around and around kicking and fighting". Trying to bring the story to its end, I asked the question, "And how did it finish?" "Oh the hoor of a red dog killed the two of them!"

Next door neighbour, Betty Kelleghan, had a much-loved, big tom cat. Tom was a bit on the "randy" side and was therefore rarely in residence. Betty was told that if she got Tom neutered, he would loose interest in kitties and become a docile, home-loving pet. The vet did the job and Tom took it badly. Next thing he was missing and Betty was out looking for him in Paddy's field, when lo and behold, up from the direction of the river Deal came the cat, walking gingerly. Betty was delighted, "I wonder where he went to" she said to Paddy. "Di ya see now", was a favourite way of Paddy's, to start what he had to say. "Di ya see now" he said to Betty, "After what you got done to the poor hoor, he went to the Deel to drown himself and I'd say yer lucky he changed his mind!"

We had a bullock, hardly able to walk, with a shoulder problem. Liam Gaffney, the vet, came to treat him twice, but there was no improvement. On Sunday morning after Killulagh mass, Jim Drumm told Paddy that Willie Loughlin knew how to cure the bullock. I was summoned with them the next day and the animal was put in the chute. Willie arrived with a valve and a bicycle pump. He punctured the hide, inserted the valve under the skin and pumped in some air. In two days the bullock was "buck lepping" round the field. The following Sunday, Paddy was sitting on the outside of the seat, waiting for mass to start. Jim Drumm got in behind him and whispered, "How is the bullock?" Paddy paused for a moment and then whispered back. "All I can say is that the brass plate is on the wrong door!!"
That was my Uncle Paddy; 1920-2003.

CHAPTER 16

Now a Married Man

I have this fantasy where I am asked the 64,000 dollar question. "On what date did Louis Armstrong die?" and I will be able to answer 6th July 1971- because it was the same day I got married. If Pamela and I stuck to our original plan, he might not have died until the 9th August. We had that date booked, photographer and reception arranged, deposit paid on honeymoon in Ostend, Willie and "The Doyler" flights booked home and nightly rows over the guest list!

I was home "on strike" and with no plan B; come to think of it, we didn't even have a plan A. I was getting married.

Then we heard Paddy O'Donnell's shop in Collinstown was for sale. The shop consisted of a bit of drapery, household goods, light hardware, and funeral undertakers, but the turnover was low. Pamela and I talked it over and went down to see Paddy. He showed us around and as we left he said, "There is nobody I would rather see with it, but it's up to the Auctioneer and whoever pays the most money will get it". I went to Castlepollard to see the Auctioneer, Mrs. Cox. She said the business would make around £8,000 so I walked across to my "old friend", the bank manager. He didn't think much of it – or maybe it was that he knew a bit about me and didn't think much of that" "If it was "Barney's (Paddy O'Donnell's brother Barney had a pub in Collinstown) that would be more like it. Optimism undermined, I went back to Mrs. Cox and put a bid of £6,000 on the place. Back home, I wrote a letter to Auntie Betty, looking for a loan. The crisp new ten shilling note, wouldn't be enough this time! Next I headed up to Graftonstown to see Uncle Paddy. I met him on the road, in his white David Brown tractor. "Paddy O'Donnell's is for sale and I'm trying to buy it" I announced. "I have £1,000 sitting idle in the bank in Delvin and you're welcome to borrow that" was his most welcome response. Next day I drove to Dublin to see Aunt Kathleen and she pledged me another £1,000, which arrived two days later. I now would be ok, even if the bank gave me the minimum. Over the next two weeks, a local man, living in Dublin commenced bidding against me. It was struck down to him at more than £10,000. As it transpired, when it came to paying, he didn't have the money, but by then I was out of the frame. Each morning I got the paper and checked both "situations vacant" and "business for sale" columns. I had gone for an interview to Tara Mines and was offered a job underground. Joe Lenehan was foreman there and I thought I might get a shift-bosses job, but at least I had a miners job, if I wanted it. However, my heart was now set on the challenge of having my own business and being my own boss. Then a shop appeared for sale in Longwood, Co.Meath and only four miles from Pamela's school. I went to look and was disappointed at how small it was – just a bungalow with a room turned into a shop. It was owned by the great Galway footballer, Mick Connaire. Pamela came to see it and wasn't too impressed either. Connaire's sold groceries, briquettes and the like and did an excellent trade in sweets and ice-cream being just across "The Green" from the national school.

I had the loans from the Aunt's and Uncle in the bank and I didn't discuss or seek permission from them to purchase anything other than "Paddy O' Donnells. Raymond Potterton was the auctioneer and he told me I could have it for £5,800. I knew that it would just be a stepping stone, but it would get us in on the property ladder, even if it was only the bottom rung. "The Shoveller on the ditch", of the business world! If I had any experience I could have got it a couple of hundred cheaper. It had to be obvious how keen I was and Patterson did his job by getting as much as he could for his client – as indeed, did he do for me when we were selling.

The deal was done. £5,800 and stock at cost. Taking possession with close of sale was set for the middle of July. I was now a shopkeeper, but more importantly, Pamela and I had a house of our very own to start our married life together.

Pamela's father had been "put off the drink" by his doctor and she was seriously worried about what might happen the day of our wedding. She had good reason to worry because when we brought Johnny to see the shop, himself and Connaire "disappeared" up to "Stoney Burkes" where they sold stuff from counters and vans, kicked a few footballs, figured out the real "arms crisis" etc. etc. … over taking a drink!

The happily engaged couple were fighting every night over the guest list. It was to be a small wedding, mostly family, but I noted that all the "outsiders" consisted of Bartley's Bar customers. I said my neighbours, Mick Forde and Paddy Reilly had to be there and the guys I worked with in Silvermines. With politicians, everything – be it funerals, meetings or weddings is transformed into votes; with publicans, it's the same thing, only that the primary purpose is to create customers for the sale of drink.

Signing the Marraige Register

One night Pamela rolled the latest wedding guest into a ball and threw it into the fire, almost in tears as she said, "I wish we could just go off somewhere and come back married". When I went home, I thought about this and didn't sleep for hours. Perhaps this could be the way to do it. There was now the additional problem that if we went ahead with the 9th August date, after taking over the shop in July, would we have to close it to get married and have a honeymoon? I had this good friend Father Larry Kearney, from Lavey, Co. Cavan, who was teaching in Kilteegan. Larry and I met the next night. "When you get your holidays, could Pamela

and I go down and have you marry us in Lavey" I asked, telling him all the reasons why. "I'll have to get the permission of the Parish Priest, Father Brady and you both will have to get letters of freedom from your Parish Priest in Collinstown (also Fr. Brady) but I can't see any problem."
The secret was kept. I asked Pamela's brother Michael, to be my best man and Pamela's friend from Clonard, Olive Stewart, was bridesmaid. We told our parents the night before and on the morning of 6th July, resplendent in my new suit and doused in holy water by my equally happy mother, I left the house where I was born and reared, for the last time where my family would have first call on me.

Mr. and Mrs.

Mrs. Tormey from Drumcree had made Pamela's wedding dress - a scaled down version, after the change of plan. I half expected that she might not turn up after all - but she did. There were just the four of us, Fr. Larry and Fr. Brady. Afterwards, we had lunch in "The Percy French" in Ballyjamesduff and soon we were heading for Donegal on our honeymoon. The weather was beautiful. It was the finest week of 1971. We booked into a hotel in Strandhill the first night. "Big Tom" was playing at a venue in the town and I wanted Pamela to go – but she wouldn't. Recently I was somewhere with my good friend,

Joe Bardon and there was a poster for "Big Tom". I said to Joe that he was playing in Strandhill on the first night of our honeymoon, but that Pamela would not go to the dance. "And did you go on your own?" asked Joe.
We spent the week along the coast, finishing up with a couple of days in Buncrana. They had a lovely warm reception for us when we arrived home to Drumcree. My parents and brothers were brought down to Bartleys, where a meal had been prepared. The neighbours came in. I was dumbstruck at how much people cared and how good they were to us. We got more wedding presents than if we had had a big wedding. Everyone was so happy that all, including Pamela's mother Dympna, took a drink. Pamela, nor I, didn't need any drink. We just held hands.

Longwood Law

"Longwood law beats the stranger", I had never heard the expression because I had never heard of Longwood until I found the shop for sale, but at that time it was a well known saying. I don't know if Longwood beat me, or even if I got an honourable draw, or even a moral victory – but I do know I didn't like Longwood and it didn't like me.
Mick Connaire gave me a list of "ones to watch" (very few) and a huge list of those
who were OK and could be trusted with "tick". The fact that 75% of the "good ones" he listed had never stood in the shop is, I suppose, neither here nor there!
I opened the shop with special offers, optimism and enthusiasm, but I was a young
upstart of a "blow-in" in a village where nearly everybody was related. To be honest, there wasn't any good reason why the locals should deal in my shop. The Dargan and Giles families had been in business for generations. They were good decent business people, who looked after their customers well. You could get six months credit in Dargan's. Pamela's brother, Sean came up to work with us for the summer. He had the grocery experience from the family business, even though he was young and at the time a boarder in St. Finians, Mullingar – before he got expelled. We were a good team. Sean was witty and cheeky and I still have to listen to him telling me that he made me what I am today! Naturally, Pamela took a great interest in the business as well and she did her turn in the shop after school.

Our next door neighbours were Bill and Mary Abbott and their family, who had a garage. Never did anybody have better friends of neighbours. They gave us every help imaginable, including sound advice when required. Across The Green lived Florrie and Mrs. Quinn. Florrie was big into horse racing and he and I became regular race goers. I understood "the politics of the business" and I supported and became involved in all local activities. I played for the team and the last hurling jersey I ever pulled over my head was a Longwood one.
I could see after a few weeks that the best hope of expansion lay in catering for the needs of young people. We started stocking fancy goods and items such as LP records and we were at least paying our way. I could see a couple of hundred students of up to Leaving Cert coming in daily to "The Tech" and swarming all over the village at lunch time. I got a brainwave and turned the little store behind the shop into a "chipper". Chips and sausages and soon we stretched to the limit to keep them dished out to the two schools. Shops "up town" were losing out and something had to be done. The street was being littered with my chip bags at lunchtime. It was disgraceful! Pressure came on Headmaster Vincent Smyth, a really nice guy – but he had to declare my shop "out of bounds" at lunchtime. My first lesson in "Longwood Law!"
Babs Dempsy had been postmistress in Longwood for forty years, when she retired in 1971. Babs was a lovely, gentle lady who gave all of her life to serving the people of the village. Closing time meant nothing. They would knock on Bab's hall door at nine o'clock at night and get the same smile and assistance as if it was three in the afternoon. Her successor could never measure up to that service. Her successor would have a difficult act to follow. Her successor was me! On the 8th December 1971, I was appointed sub-postmaster for Longwood.
This was a political appointment, everything else being equal in the world of politics – which at that time I knew little about – some people are more equal than others.
When the Post Office was advertised I along with three or four others applied for it. There was much lobbying, jockeying for position, back stabbing and bad mouthing – as one might expect in any friendly, close knit, closely related Irish village. The worst thing going for me was that I was a "blow-in" . The best thing going for me was that I was a "blow-in". Nobody asked me

what politics I was, but it was presumed that I was Fianna Fáil, as the main contender for the job was Fine Gael. "My enemy's enemy is my friend" came into play. I became a sort of an agreed candidate to stop someone else and that is how I became one of the most important people in Longwood.

The Post Office was moved from Babs premises to ours – manual exchange and all. I can still remember the phone numbers of all the "Longwood leading lights" at that time. If insanity didn't run naturally in my family, I could say that any deficit in that area, in me, could be traced directly to that manual switchboard. It had to be manned from 8am till midnight. I spent a lot of time on it, especially at night, as did also poor Pamela. The Dept of Posts and Telegraphs gave us an experienced P.O. assistant for three weeks to train me. That she was one of the unsuccessful candidates didn't help me, as her barely concealed resentment and jealousy was not conducive to "learning the trade". I hired a full time assistant and here I made a mistake. This lovely old lady Mrs. Vaughan had a niece called May Mc Laughlin, who lived with her. May worked in an office in Dublin and Mrs. Vaughan asked me to give the job to May, even though she didn't have any experience. May was a grand girl and worked to the best of her ability, but there is no short cut to experience and I paid for it in stress. However May stayed with us for a year and between us all, we survived.

Longwood brought out the worst in me. I was always a helpful, obliging sort of chap but with more than half the population "seething" because we had the Post Office, there were daily incidents where it would be pointed out to me that I was a "servant to the public". I knew what I had to do and what I didn't have to do. When it suited me, or more often, when I was driven to it I would "work to rule" – "do it by the book".

MEATH CHRONICLE

SELF–SERVICE COMES TO LONGWOOD

Opening Of Comaskey's Food Store

CONGRATULATIONS AND EVERY SUCCESS FROM

Donlon & Doyl

Building Contractors,

Clonard, Enfield, Co. Meat

"Meath Chronicle" June 1972

One postman took me on "bigtime", but it only needed a day for him to find out that he had a bit of grovelling to do.

We built on a self-service little supermarket and went with MNC – "Merchants National Co-op". Their merchandisers told me the percentage this would improve our business. Not under "Longwood Law" did it!
Nobody in their right mind would ever think of giving up the Post Office, or selling a business in which a Post Office was part of. We were there two years. One Sunday evening, Pamela, with our new baby, Olga, rushed back to

Cuir aon fhreagra chuig :-
Address any reply to :-

AN MÁISTIR POIST
The Postmaster

Do Thagairt
Your Ref.

Ár dTagairt
Our Ref.

AN ROINN POIST AGUS TELEGRAFA
Department of Posts and Telegraphs

OIFIG AN PHOIST
Post Office

Mullingar.

8/12/ 19 71

Mr. B.J.Comaskey,
Longwood.

A Chara,

I have pleasure in informing you that your appointment as Scale Payment Bun-Máistir Poist at Longwood has been approved.

It will be necessary that you proceed as early as possible with the required structural alterations in order to provide suitable and adequate accommodation for Post Office work. This will entail accommodation for ordinary P.O.Counter duties, Telephone Exchange which should be as private as possible from the public, Mail accommodation including a suitable place fof the Postman to prepare his letters and parcels for delivery etc. The Post Office will provide and fit a metal letter box in the wall of your premises, opening from the outside as in the case of wall letter boxes in rural places. We will let you see the box in due course in order that you can select a suitable place for inserting it in the wall.

It is of the utmost importance that the necessary accommodation be provided as soon as possible and if there are any difficulties you wish to discuss with me I will be available at any time. I hope to visit the area before Christmas ~~and~~ when I ~~hope to~~ shall call and see the progress you are making.

Mise, le meas,

M. JORDAN
Máistir Poist.

Letter informing me of my appointment as Postmaster in Longwood

Longwood to man the switchboard, after spending the day with our folks. We came in, I put the kettle on, turned to Pamela and said "I've had enough of this, I can't take it." Her reply surprised me a little – she always being so sensible and practical. She said simply "I can't either". Next morning I phoned Raymond Potterton and put the place up for sale. It took a long time to get out due in part to the complexities of my contract with The Dept of Posts and Telegraphs.

Our first home and shop, in Longwood, Co. Meath

When we cashed in we had a 30% return on our investment, after 2_ years. Jimmy and Camilla Giles succeeded us in Longwood Post Office. I was delighted they got it. They had been unsuccessful applicants when I was appointed. They never showed any resentment to me and we remained on friendly terms while I was there. Jimmy and Camilla had class and it showed. Tragically my next trip back to Longwood only a short time after I left was for Jimmy's funeral. Whilst adjusting a television aerial on his roof, a stay broke, throwing Jimmy to his death in the yard below. As far as I know, Camilla is still Postmistress in Longwood.

Olga and Ian Arrive

Our daughter Olga, was born on 28th January 1973. It was one of the happiest days of my life and certainly the most emotional. It was a Sunday, around 1pm. I was at home in Longwood – working of course, when I got the call from The Coombe Maternity Hospital. In fact I was just preparing to head off to the hospital, when the Matron phoned to say I was the father of a healthy 6_ lb girl. The drive up to Dublin is a "blur" – in fact even the next day was a "blur". After spending some time with Pamela, I headed back to Drumcree. When I arrived in Bartleys I was totally overcome. I just couldn't believe the feeling. I drank about 20 pots of tea and chain-smoked.

Everybody was over the moon. Olga was the first Comaskey girl from this side of the family in 50 years.
A few days later I brought the now two women in my life home. Strictly speaking, Longwood was home, but we came home to Drumcree first. As well as both families waiting for us, there was, for me, something symbolic about bringing Olga to Westmeath. Everybody said she was beautiful. To me she was both beautiful and perfect. She had one little flaw which nobody noticed and I hoped to keep quite and certainly play down. Olga was a Meath woman!!

Two new arrials – Olga and Silver in the garden at Longwood

My mother came back to Longwood with us and stayed a couple of weeks. We had been let down by a woman we employed as a housekeeper, to help look after Olga and cook the dinner. This lady's husband had had a car accident and was out of work, so we gave her a job, three months before she was needed. A week before Olga was born, the compensation for the accident arrived, so our housekeeper quit.
As well as May Mc Loughlin, we had a part-time girl working in the Post Office. She was a student called Gearldine Smith and Gearldine came to work for us full time when May left. We had part-time staff in the shop. One smashing young fellow whom I remember was Liam Murtagh and his parents, who were lovely people.

"Kickedy Cow – Kickedy Calf!"

Ian was born on 27th February 1974, just thirteen months after his sister. He might have been conceived in Co. Meath – if Posh Beckham was his mother, he would have been named "Longwood", but that doesn't count. By then, we had moved back to Drumcree and Ian was born in Mullingar – not a hint of a stain on his pedigree – a Westmeath man.
When we decided we were going to sell Longwood, obviously, we had to

plan what to do next. Both our families thought we were mad. "Imagine, giving up the Post Office, with a guaranteed cheque coming in every month." My reply was "I only have one life to live and I refuse to live any more of it in misery – if I can help it."

Feeding Ian

I wanted to buy a pub, but Pamela was against that. The "ace in the hole" was that I could always go mining in Navan. We thought we might buy a house in Collinstown, before we changed our minds again. This was all happening before we had a buyer for the premises. One day there appeared a feature in the paper on Commercial Rabbit Farming. I had actually read up on this while I was in Canada and at that time I dreamt I had a rabbit farm in Ireland. Again, now I studied the article. It looked a "good thing". Generally if something "looks too good to be true", it usually is – but I hadn't learned that lesson yet! After doing research and feasibility checks, I decided I was going to become a "Rabbit Farmer."

My father had told me more than once, that he was tired of coming home from work and having to milk cows and "burst" himself – "If ever a man suffered!" As soon as I decided the rabbit farm was a runner, I sat down with both my parents and put a plan on the table. They would give me their bit of land, for a small "consideration" and I would buy the livestock also. Further, I told them they would never again want for anything. We all kept our end of the bargain.

Enjoying a Dance

Building contractors Donlon and Doyle, from Clonard (Paddy and Joe were two great guys) had built the supermarket for me in Longwood and now I commissioned them to build a breeding and fattening rabbit farm at The Derries, Drumcree – my home place. This was completed before we left Longwood. I also bought my first brand new car – a red Ford Escort, which I registered in Mullingar, so as that it would have a Westmeath reg. - PLI350!

Pamela suggested that we should wait and see how the rabbits ("Bernie's Bunnies" she christened the enterprise) and farming at home would go before we bought or built a house. Pamela is always ultra cautious – unlike me, who often just goes on impulse or "gut feeling". I was going to say Pamela would never take a chance – until I remembered the chance she took on me!

Olga and Ian, School photo 1983

Johnny and Dympna had an old run-down cottage in the back of beyonds, a mile from Drumcree. Nobody had lived in it for years. We set about making it habitable and succeeded. We were living there when Ian was born and I have such happy memories of the nine fun-filled months we spent in Rangleborough.

Very quickly, we decided to build. The site opposite the home place was ideal and by September of 1974 we had moved into our new bungalow. I don't know if it could be termed "Bungalow Bliss", but I do know that we spent the following 17 years there as a very happy family.

Breeding Like Rabbits

I started with 100 breeding does and in a matter of months I was carrying a couple of thousand rabbits. Each doe had her own cage, as had the buck. There was one buck for every ten does and he was the one with the big grin on his face. We had two breeds; Californian white and New Zealand white. The New Zealand white was all white, whilst the Californian had black ears, nose and paws. For mating I took the doe to the buck's cage. If you did it the other way round they would fight – surely a lesson there somewhere!? I had a record card for each doe, the pregnancy of which was 31 days. Three days before she was due to litter, I would put a wooden nesting box into the cage, lined with wood shavings or clean straw. The doe would pull the fur out of herself and make a nest and her litter could be anything from 1 to 18. I would "foster out" from big litters to small, but Mammy would quickly kill the intruders, only I would fool her by shaking talcum powder on all the young. Even this didn't always work and I would often find the adopted family members dead and thrown out of the nesting box. By having 18 hours of artificial light in the shed, the doe would have 6 to 8 litters in the year. In my first year I averaged better than 50 rabbits per doe.

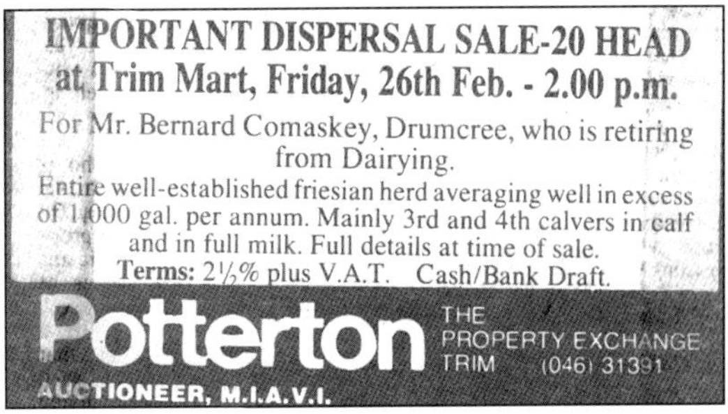
IMPORTANT DISPERSAL SALE-20 HEAD
at Trim Mart, Friday, 26th Feb. - 2.00 p.m.

For Mr. Bernard Comaskey, Drumcree, who is retiring from Dairying.

Entire well-established friesian herd averaging well in excess of 1,000 gal. per annum. Mainly 3rd and 4th calvers in calf and in full milk. Full details at time of sale.

Terms: 2½% plus V.A.T. Cash/Bank Draft.

Potterton THE PROPERTY EXCHANGE TRIM (046) 31391

AUCTIONEER, M.I.A.V.I.

Auction Notice

There was a water nipple in each cage, which was suspended 3 feet over a pit, into which the droppings fell. The manure was so rich in protein that cattle would actually eat it when it dried. I found this out by accident, but I never heard of anybody feeding it to livestock. I used to bring bags of it to Auntie Kathleen for her garden and it was little wonder that she had the best vegetables in Dublin! We fed all dry feeding in pellet form. These rabbits had the highest conversion rate known, 3 to 1: For every three pounds of meal fed, you got one pound of rabbit meat. At 6 to 8 weeks the young rabbits averaged 4_ lbs weight and were ready for killing. I sold them to an agent who exported them to France. The van came once a week or when I had 100 rabbits – which was every week.

This was my peak and I was just starting to make money when the oil crisis hit. The first feed I bought was £48 a ton and I was getting 12 pence a pound, live weight for the rabbits. Soon I was paying £96 a ton for feed – exactly double and most I ever got was 16 pence. All other costs went up as well. I had a fantastic well managed business but I was now loosing money and I stayed losing it for six months, when I could see the writing on the wall. Ego! People were coming from all over the country to view my rabbit farm. People with kids on Sundays annoying the rabbits, but great for my ego. Ego is the principle cause of business failure and I never again made that mistake. From that day on, after giving a project a fair chance, if I then believed it wasn't going to work, I cut my losses and killed it stone dead.

Two years of long hours at the rabbits and we lost money. I never use the word failure, because there is no such thing, provided you use the experience learned. "You haven't failed until you stop trying!" A lot of life is like the rabbit pit. There was no smell from the droppings, as it built up and we left it alone as long as we could, but as soon as you drove a shovel into it, the ammonia laden stench would drive you from the shed. Everyone has a rabbit-pit and the secret is not to drive a shovel into it!

One happy family

As the rabbits were doing to me – well, doing to me what rabbits do best, the cows were beginning to look after me. My father had been milking four cows and sending the milk to Westmeath Co-op via that most amicable gentleman and Daddy's great friend Jack Naughton, from Mullingar. There was one Shorthorn and two half baldface Herfords and "a hoor of a black kicker"! My father had once tied the hind legs of the kicker so that she wouldn't spill the bucket of milk. In his own words, everything was grand until he was taking the last "strigeen". Next thing he knew he "was in the manger, wearing the bucket on his head, with the black hoor in his lap!!"

I think the national yield per cow, at that time was around 400 gallons. My four cows were probably half that, including what the "black hoor" spilt. The Friesen cow was only now becoming popular in our area. I kept buying cows, one at a time, but I was nervous of buying Friesians yet, as mine were being out-wintered and I considered the Friesians less able for hardship than the Shorthorns and black hoors. After a year I was milking twelve cows by hand. When the last of the rabbits was gone, as well as the pits and the smell, I redesigned the shed for the cows and bought a bucket-plant milking machine from Joe McGovern in Castlepollard. The cows, in the words of Uncle Paddy, "weren't in favour of it" for a day or two, but soon they were "happy campers" with the new set up – and so was I. By the third year I had installed a pipe-line milking parlour and was milking up to 30 cows.

A bit of naivety is a great thing to have if you want to do something. A real farmer would never have taken on to do what I did, but I knew no better. I set about reclaiming all the bog and it worked. All our land was terrible – just bog – but the black bog half proved to be very fertile and grew excellent grass when it was re-seeded. The biggest problem was "poaching" in wet weather, which meant a short grazing season. I fed a ton of nuts per cow but from 1978 onwards I averaged over 1,000 gallons per cow – by now all Friesians, of course. I had a wonderful agricultural adviser in Limerick man, Dan Martin, whom I am still happy to meet from time to time on the streets of Mullingar – where both our boots are now clean!

Going to a wedding

In 1976 I attended the first E.E.C 100 hour agricultural course for young farmers, in Castlepollard. This was of immense benefit to me and I was an eager student. That I "knew nothing" meant I had no preconceived ideas or hang-ups, so I learned well. Following on from this, was formed the "Dairymis" group with 18 farmers having their milk yields recorded. The other 17 were on good land and yet mine were the highest yields per cow of the 18 participants. I don't know how high yields have gone nowadays, but one thing I learned in the seventies was that almost every Friesen was a 1,000 gallon cow. The rest was down to feeding and management.

By the mid 1980's I knew I had progressed as far as I could in farming. We bought a couple of bits of land, but I was still milking cows on limited acreage around the house. Land was too dear and interest rates too high. I borrowed money at more than 20% and I don't know what you would need to do to service that. We were not in financial difficulties, due to Pamela's salary going into the farm, but we always had too much money borrowed. Always something else to be done, always another cow to be bought. Farming is the worst business in the world, because it is the only business where the producer has no say over what he must get for his product. There is also such a slow and small return on what is a huge investment of capital.

I could see the face of farming changing once again and when they made the milk quota a saleable commodity, I decided I was going to take my money and run.

In 1988 I sold my 26,000 gallon quota for a pound and five pence per gallon. On 26th February 1988 I loaded twenty of my best cows and took them to Trim Mart for a special sale. All those cows were individuals to me and every cow I owned had a name. Even, Olga and Ian knew many of them by their names. Thelma, Rosy, Annette, Nan .... Many of them I had reared from calves. Unlike Ted Walsh I didn't "ride any of their mothers", but I certainly played with their mothers tits!.

I have done many different types of work in my time and when I move on, that's it. The cows weren't a job. I looked after them well and they looked after me well in return.

For 18 years now, I have a recurring dream, maybe once or twice a year. In the dream, I have forgotten to milk the cows, or I forgot to look at heifers sick to calve, or I forgot to put the dry-cow-penicillin in cows I dried off, or I'm just ready to milk when I remember I have no milk tank, because I sold it!

Where is Freud when you need him!

CHAPTER 17

Tempus Fugit

For a time after we left Longwood, Pamela drove the 20 miles to her school in Clonard. Then she was approached and offered a post in St. Mary's special school at Southhill, Delvin. She remained there for two years, until a vacancy occurred in Crowenstown N.S, Delvin. Her first day at school in Crowenstown coincided with Olga's first day at school and Pamela was her teacher, as she was also to Ian a year later. In class, they wanted to be the same as everybody else. They would tell Pamela stories from home, "Please Miss, my Daddy said to my Mammy ...!" etc. In the mornings they would ask me for money for something at school. "Daddy can I please have two shillings because the teacher said we have to bring money to school for ..." Then off they went in the car with their Mother, holding the coins in their little hands, until they could march up to Pamela's desk and hand over the money.

Pamela loved teaching, loved Crowenstown and they loved her in return; as shown by the numbers of past pupils who seek her out and by the send-off she got from the teachers, parents and pupils when she gave up teaching in 2002. It is not surprising that we encouraged our kids to play sport. They both have a range of community games medals and Olga represented her school to win a county table-tennis title. Now, though, every Christmas, or whenever the mood takes her, Olga will declare that I must have been the worst parent ever known, in the history of parenting because I made her come to every hurling and football game, made her sit beside me, made her have to listen to me, whilst all the people in front of us turned round to look at me! Ian played hurling, rugby, soccer and squash up to Leinster Premier League. In 2004 he won the Elche Squash Open in Spain.

From the time we moved back home I found myself involved in everything. I was secretary of Collinstown I.F.A. Secretary of the Fine Gael Branch and later chairman of the Mullingar Branch. I served on The County Executive of Community Games as well as local level. I was on committees of both Midland Squash and Leinster Squash Leagues and much more! I go to meetings and I can't keep my mouth shut. Any meeting I'm going to, the last thing Pamela says as I go out the back door is, "Don't come back here with another bloody job! I come home late and maybe cold, so she now moves to her own side of the bed as I get in. "Wakey, wakey if you want to hear the good news! "Guess who's the new Chairman of the whatever" ... If anyone really wishes to know the reply, I'll tell you privately!

From 1973 until 1982 I never missed a milking, so I really used to look forward to the cows being dry from mid-November until the end of January. Nevertheless Pamela and I always enjoyed a good social life. She would pick out concerts and we would go, usually to Dublin and very often with friends. We liked to go dancing and this we did quite frequently. I would go to card-plays – especially during the period in which the cows were dry. The Zoo was a regular family outing and often we would head off to Galway or the like for the day. Of course the real downer for the kids was that we had to come home to milk. I never missed any hurling match in Croke Park and rarely a football game either - except for the period when Kerry and Dublin totally dominated the sport.

But there was some little void in my life and in 1981 I found it. Squash! I was 37 and at the age when some leading heart specialists claim you should be giving it up, even if you have been playing it all your life. I do very little in moderation and I loved squash from the first ball I hit. I won a competition after two months playing and then I was really hooked. At the peak of squash, there were hundreds of members playing in Mullingar. My highest ranking was to reach number 14 on the club ladder. I represented Mullingar for years in Midland Squash League and a few times in the Leinster League.

I played until I was 57 and enjoyed it as much after 20 years as when Michael Fallon played that first ball back to me.

In 1976 my father retired from Westmeath County Council. He wasn't in the best of health. After being off work a while, we could all see a change in him. He seemed to be brooding and depressed and incredibly touchy. Now he didn't see his buddies any more and he had nothing only the pub. He complained of a constant pain in his back and looking back now I believe that his physical deterioration, coupled with the loss of his lifelong routine contributed to his mental state. Camillus, then in his early teens, had to keep out of his way, because father would stick in him at every opportunity. Mother was gravely worried. She talked to their GP and he came to see Daddy. Then the doctor came over to me and said, "Your father is seriously depressed and will have to go into St. Loman's Hospital for a few weeks or so, will you bring him in?" "Cant you give him something" I asked. "No, he needs to go in first." "Ok". It was the hardest thing I have ever had to do, because he didn't want to go. "Don't do this to me in front of The Harris's" he pleaded. My heart nearly broke, because there was nothing I could do and I had never before, gone against him. Séan came with me and we got him in, but not settled. I said to Séan coming back, "Today is the worst day of my life" – and so it was until 7th July 1998 when Camillus' and Maura's daughter, the lovely Cara got killed in a freak motor accident.

Mullingar Squash Men's D. from left: Tom Gallagher, Shay O'Rourke Front: Bernie Comaskey (capt.) and Johnny Tynan

One of my greatest friends, Pamela's Uncle, Colm O'Farrell, used to always say "Nothing is ever as bad as it first seems" and so it was with my fathers stay in St. Lomans Hospital. He was only there for three weeks, when he came home a new man. Mind you, he still had to see Johnny Harris to tell him that they said in the hospital that they "didn't know why he was there". He was on a mild dose of anti-depressants for a while and that was it. His

chest,"doul brathin" bothered him a lot. He went to the pub and listened to the céile music but he didn't play "d'oul tambourine" any more. I sat and talked to him almost every day and I learned more about "d'oul people longo" than I ever knew before then. Once again my mother had to be the patient nurse and once again, she wasn't found wanting. She fretted and worried about him. On his last trip into hospital, three weeks before he died, his GP told her "Don't be worrying - you think he's going to die. He's not.
Maybe that brass plate was on the wrong door also.
On the third Sunday in September 1984 Kerry beat Dublin in the All-Ireland Football Final. I didn't care. My father would have cared less but he did care and he got his wish when that morning his six sons carried him shoulder high from the church and gently laid him under the green sod of Killulagh.
His suffering was over.

The Turfman from Drumcree

The straightest road to success is to make the best use of your own resources - what you have. One day, in 1981, I read in "the Farmer's Journal" about a new invention for cutting turf. If turf was a resource – and it was, well then, I was a sitting on a resource. The new machine, called a Herbst Difco Turfcutter was the start of what became known as "The Sausage Turf".
Along with Colm O'Farrell, we went to a demonstration of this machine, on a bog down in Roscommon - we were both impressed. The cutter was rear mounted on the tractor, a chain-like contraption, pulled up peat from about a metre down in the bog. The tractor, driving forward in a crawler gear, left rows of turf, as the machine mixed what the chain brought up, compressed it and drove it out under pressure, through a pipe-like outfit.
The turf –cutter hadn't yet gone into production, but in theory, at least where I lived, this was a money churning machine. I ordered one there and then. The following March, I got the fifth one to come off the assembly line.
In doing so I transformed our road, "The Bog Road" back to the old days when "it was blocked with traffic, going to the bog".
I had about 20 acres of red bog, which I had drained, levelled and re-claimed, along with the rest of the land. It was of very limited use as agricultural land and I reckoned it was ideal for cutting turf on. It grew very little grass, so I sprayed it with Gromoxone and soon it looked like the perfect bog for this revolutionary new invention. The machine cost £6,900, but in addition, it

wasn't every tractor would be suitable to operate it.There had to be a slow crawler gear and the correct r.p.m (rev per minute). In addition, of course, it had to be able to stay up in the bog, which meant wide front wheels and double wheels on the back. I bought a brand new Zeteor for the job. Now I had borrowings of £20,000 on my turf enterprise, before I cut a sod and this was at a time when interest rates were at an all time high.As it turned out, only for Colm, I would have gone both mad and broke.

Colm O'Farell, as well as being Pamela's uncle, a great friend and neighbour was also a mechanical genius. He started off shortly after he and Lila got married, by buying a tractor for £25 and doing hire work for farms. Eventually, he had forty men working as a machinery contractor, with work-contracts with Westmeath County Council, the E.S.B and the then P and T. He made tractors out of scrap and good men out of misfits. Colm had a wonderful way with people and got the most out of employees, some of whom would not have got a job anywhere else. Both Colm and Lila died at an early age, from the cursed cancer. I think of them often.

I started cutting on our own bog first. Naturally there was going to be problems, because, it is true to say that "The less you do, the less mistakes you make".The chain was coming in contact with birch and sallys, saplings which had been turned during the levelling, which slowed down the work. Especially, though the machine was defective.The manufacturers learned as they went along, but I was one of their unwilling guinea pigs. I spent a great deal of time on the road to Ballintubber for spare or new parts. Often, I would only be back in action when I would hear that heart-sinking 'clatter-clatter-bang-bang', coming from the back of the tractor. Colm was kept busy welding and modifying the cutter. It is fair to say that he drastically improved on the "Herbst".

We managed to cut around twelve acres of the twenty.This was adjacent to the road and another slight problem was the numbers of people who came to see the cutting in action. Many of these were people I knew, who expected me to stop and talk to them. I could not afford to stop the tractor.

Next I negotiated with William Smyth, to rent bog from him in Drumcree Bog.There was a 60 acre span and the deal was that I could cut as much of this as possible. Subsequently, I managed to leave about 30 acres of top quality turf, on the spread.

Somebody once said "Find a job you enjoy doing and you will never have to work again". I enjoy a challenge and I got immense satisfaction from leaving acres of rows of black, shiny turf in my wake. I put in unbelievable hours. Turf-cutting would be a short season. Depreciation on machinery was drastic and that coupled with high interest rates meant that I was a "driven man". Most mornings, I started milking the cows at 6 am. Pamela would have a huge "fry-up" ready for me before she went to school and I would be on the bog by 9 o'clock. I stayed all day on the bog - "on the ball" you might say. I would arrive home and eat my dinner to the accompaniment of the 9pm news. Then I would go milk the cows, have a shower or sometimes the luxury of a radox bath and fall into bed.

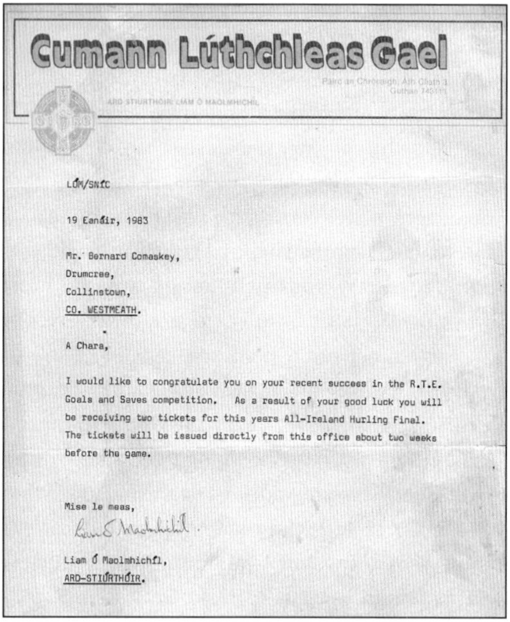

Cumann Lúthchleas Gael

ARD STIURTHOIR: LIAM Ó MAOLMHICHIL

LÓM/SNÍC

19 Eanáir, 1983

Mr. Bernard Comaskey,
Drumcree,
Collinstown,
CO. WESTMEATH.

A Chara,

I would like to congratulate you on your recent success in the R.T.E. Goals and Saves competition. As a result of your good luck you will be receiving two tickets for this years All-Ireland Hurling Final. The tickets will be issued directly from this office about two weeks before the game.

Mise le meas,

Liam Ó Maolmhichíl,
ARD-STIÚRTHÓIR.

Keeping an eye on the ball

I was in agony with my elbow as previously mentioned, whether it was from the squash or working the levers of the turf cutter, I developed inflammation of the tendon, this spread to the tissue, the muscle and then to the bone. Because I neglected looking after it, in the finish up, I could only button my shirt with difficulty. But I couldn't stop working. A few times I went into Mullingar and got a cortisone injection from my squash partner, Surgeon Peter Magill, before his clinic started.

By the time I was finished cutting in Smyth's Bog there was a new, unexpected problem in my own bog. The reason I cut turf there, in the first place, was because it wouldn't grow good grass. Now, as soon as I had it covered in turf it grew grass like hell – talk about Murphy's Law. I hired about twenty young lads at £1 an hour, to "toss" the turf out of the grass. This had the

TURF AUCTION

1982

Drumcree Bog, on Tuesday, 29th June at 8 p.m. 10 acres of dry turf on the spread to be sold in suitable lots. Per instructions Mr. B. Comaskey.
Terms: Cash plus 5%.

Turf Auction 1982

equivalent effect of spreading three bags of nitrogen on good land – the grass grew like magic. When the turf was 75% dry, the grass was winning, so it was imperative to get it off the bog. Tom McCormack allowed me the use of his disused sand-pit. I get two specially made transport turf boxes, which could be tipped from the tractor. Again, I employed the young lads to fill the turf into the boxes. I had two tractors and one box was being filled, while I was away tipping the other one. I drove to the top of the pit backed in and tipped the load over the brim, when the pile of turf filled up, I reversed in on the turf and tipped it from the top all the time. There was a huge high face from the front and this enabled the turf to dry fast.

I then hit on a plan to sell this lot. I advertised the turf thus "Bring and fill your own bags of turf for 50 pence a bag". The first pit was on the side of the road, easy access for car, truck or tractor. It went like hot-cakes. The rule was that you had to have one leg on the ground "just like a fair shoulder". I never counted the bags people were bringing out but I got paid for 17,000 bags of turf and there wasn't as much as a "clod" left in the pit.

Female Charm – Part One
Majorca 1985

We then decided to sell the 30 acres on Smyths Bog "on the spread". It was divided into lots and Murtagh Brothers auctioned it off on fine Monday evening. Every sod was sold. It was a good pay-day.

The following year, 1983 I cut more on Drumcree Bog, didn't cut any on my own bog and sold it all "off the spread". Colm had a lot of bog he could cut on also. This was his type of work, more than mine. After doing it for two years, I sold the machinery to Colm and swore that the only sod of turf I would ever handle again, would be from the turf bucket to the fire.

For the next ten years Colm cut a lot of turf. We exchanged a lot of yarns and funny stories over the turf. I had introduced Colm to "Murphy" – as in "Murphy's Law" and forever after, when something would go wrong, Colm would tell me "Murphy was at it".

Female Charm - Part Two, Olga Lanzarote 1986

My own bog, on which I cut all that turf, I later sold to the Department of Forestry. The fact that it had been drained and levelled ensured that I got the very best price for it "Making the best use of your resources". After the turf, I rented a bit more land and settled back to the easier life of milking cows, twice a day, seven days a week. Having to have the operation on my elbow meant that I had to get in a relief-milker. This was one if the best things that could have happened and I continued to use Tom frequently thereafter. Nothing much changed until 1988, when again I made a big move and made another chapter in the story of life.

Back to Canada Again

The seventies and eighties were very happy years, a time of real hard work, fuelled by it seemed, a bottomless pit of energy. There was a never-ending list of farm improvements required and we always had too much money borrowed. I say "we" like the guy who explained to his wife that the maid was pregnant and was "blaming us". I borrowed the money - Pamela would always be inclined to say "can't it wait until such 'n' such is paid for" but I was driven to push on all the time. Never once though, did Pamela complain that so much of her teacher's salary was propping up the farming. I was in part a kept man. I would reassure Pamela by saying "no matter what, the money is all in the ground", when it came to pay-back time she saw that I was right.

I had meetings and the like a couple of nights a week. My good friend and neighbour, Mick Forde and I went to a hurling match nearly every Sunday. We never missed a championship game in Croke Park or in Cusack Park, Mullingar.

Pamela and I enjoyed a good social life. We went to loads of plays, concerts and musicals. Paddy Cole and his band in the Harcourt Hotel on Sunday nights was a great favourite of mine. Our favourite night out was to go dancing with Colm and Lila. Colm was a wonderful, graceful dancer – as indeed was Lila too. They were great company with Colm's stories, wit and banter. Shortly before Colm died we went to visit him, making small talk, Pamela mentioned that she had to go for an operation on her foot. Instantly the twinkle came into Colm's eye and he exclaimed "Ah that's great, Alannaah, for I always knew there was something wrong with your feet". Colm and Lila, along with Pamela's brother, Michael – who died from cancer also, two months before Colm, at the age of 49, frequently glide through my mind. Both Pamela and I started playing squash in the winter of 1981. It was one of the best and most enjoyable decisions we have ever made.

At the Zoo

But, above all, those years were about our children, Olga and Ian. We were blessed that my mother lived across the road and we had an on the spot babysitter and an all-embracing extended family love for the kids. A mile down the road then was the other granny and over in Rickardstown was Granny O'Farrell – all such an incredible environment for our children.

We used often go to the Zoo and one day Olga was interviewed for Ian Dempsey's radio programme. I think she was about six "would you like to play a request for anyone?" she was asked "Yes please; I want a request for my three grannies". The producer was in stitches as Olga was then asked "Have you really three grannies and how come – because most little girls have two grannies?". "I have three grannies, granny up the road, granny down the road, and granny across the road".

First Communion and Conformation came and went, all big important days in the life of a child and for the family. Friendships were created, not only amongst the children, but with the parents as well. I cannot speak too highly of the Community Games movement and indeed local sports days' organiser's.

We had a few lovely family holidays abroad – usually for a week at Halloween, when the cows would be near enough dried. It was as a sequel to one of their holidays that one of the many coincidences in my life occurred. In 1983 we spent a week in Majorca, where we make friends with the Gleesson family from Offaly. Eileen, like Pamela, was a teacher and Billy, like me, a farmer; and our kids were around the same age. We vowed to meet after coming home, but other than the Christmas cards and a couple of phone calls it didn't happen.

In September 1984 the All-Ireland hurling Final was held in Thurles. Centenary Year – a once off and the whole country wanted to be in Thurles. A fortnight before the match, my squash friend Seamus McGown, announced that he had a ticket for me, which was coming from his brother in America. We headed off to Thurles, where 65,000 people had crowded into Semple Stadium. The guy sitting on the other side of me had got his ticket sent back from America also. Who had the ticket been sent back to - Billy Gleeson!

Four Generations (1988)
Back: Pamela and her Mother, Granny Bartley,
Front: Olga with Granny O'Farrell

For a few years, in the early

farming days, I did part-time bar-work for Sean and Rita Kirwan, of the Kirwan Arms, Athboy. I worked the dinner-dances and late night extensions. I was never afraid of work. I think it is fair to say that if I can take things slow now – I have paid my dues: even though I have said it already, I am sure some of you are wondering if I ever got any urge "to take a drink?". The answer is no.

Crowenstown was a wonderful National School to start our children in the most formative years of their lives. Rena Drumm, the Principal and the other teachers, as well as Pamela, did such a superb job, that the lucky pupils and their parents will always be indebted to them.

Olga, Ian and Myself

After National School, Olga wanted to go nowhere else other than the Community College – the former 'Tech' in Castlepollard, where I had gone for a while. Many of her other friends were entering there, so it was agreed. Olga did well and got a good Leaving Cert, she then went off to do computers in Dundalk, which was a mistake. It was years later she went back studying, having drifted out of college at that stage.

I felt that Boarding School would be best for Ian – so he was turfed off to St. Finians College in Mullingar. Sitting beside him was John Drumm, who had also started National school the same day and they sat beside each other all through National and now Secondary School. They are still buddies.

When I sold the cows and the milk quota in 1988, I wasn't sure what I would do next. I was leaning at first towards buying another bit of land and doing "drystock" and maybe supplementing it with something else. I still had some well-bred heifers coming on and I also felt that it might be a good idea to breed and calve Friesian heifers for sale.

Then another coincidence; I got two letters the same week from Canada.

Garreth Fitzgerald signs the visitors book at Squash Centre, on the right is Paul McGrath T.D.

One was from Pamela's brother, Pat, who, along with his wife Joan and family lives in Blind River, near Sudsbury, Ontario. The other letter was from a Canadian couple, Pete and Eunice Petkebicus. I had been best man at Pete and Eunice's wedding 17 years earlier and even though they had visited us once in Ireland we hadn't heard from them for years. Both letters mentioned the unprecedented boom in Canadian mining. The Government had made it economical to mine out small mines and there was massive money to be made by experienced hard-rock miners. I started to fantasise about going back for a while. Eventually, I made my case to Pamela. I wanted to go out in April and have Pamela and the kids come out for the summer, when school finishes and then we would all come back the 1st September. Quite frankly, I was surprised when Pamela agreed.

It really was a crazy plan, I went into a dangerous mine, where I had a few really close shaves. The fact that I had a wife and two children, who would be 'lost' should anything have happened to me and that I didn't have to do it made it a questionable call. However, "If you don't live life on the edge, you're taking up too much room". So, in April 1988 I went back mining in Canada. There were the expected rumours that our marriage was in trouble, that I had run off with a 'young one' or that I was in big trouble with the banks. As with the ones who were counting their fingers in 1971, when we went off and got married. Wrong again folks!

Pat Bartley was working as a Mechanical Foreman with "Mining Core" mining contractors in a mine at Duberville out of Wawa, Northern Ontoria. I went up to visit Pete and Eunice in Marathon, checked out what was available and compared it with the offer from Pat's Company. The first week in April Pat and I went into The Bush.

The camp was the best ever, five chefs and staff looking after us, even sham-

poo supplied free. I spent nothing; I mean nothing, for the next eleven weeks. I was part of a small development crew, brought in to rehabilitate the mine. The mining company was mining away and Mining Core was brought in to do work that the union would never have permitted the company workers to do. The ground was bad. At first I timbered 'raises' (vertical tunnels). Each of us was good at what we were doing. There were many different types of work to be done and the last and biggest job was putting in a steel shaft.
This was the most difficult, the hardest, most stressful job I had ever undertook, but I was determined to see it through. The contract was a three month contract, two weeks working and one week off, ten hour shifts. I didn't want the time off so I worked right through; listen to this, I worked 77 ten hour shifts, back to back and we finished the job ahead of schedule. I came out of the bush after eleven weeks, with twenty thousand pounds in my pocket. This was serious money in 1988.
I have given enough mining detail in previous chapters, so I'm going to leave it alone this time, with one exception. We were working off a platform in the shaft, when Dake, the foreman, shook his light down to stop the machines "You guys be careful down there; two guys just went down the shaft over at…." (the neighbouring mine, two miles away, whose name I cannot remember). Of course the two men were killed instantly, doing the same job as our crew. What had happened was that in lowering the platform they opened parallel chains instead of diagonal and the platform just heeled over. It was at least 17 years since I worked in Canada, so I wouldn't know either of them, I thought. Wrong. One was John Kennedy from Nova Scotia, a boozing buddy from Thompson and the guy whose driving licence Philip Conroy had lost nearly 20 years before. Small world, small sad world sometimes. When the job finished I was the longest serving member of the Mining Core crew. This shows the toll it took on nerves. Even my shift boss and friend, Eddie, quit before the contract was complete. "They are tough men in Westmeath".
After coming out of the bush ,I was well and truly bushed. I could not stay still and my brain was racing. I went back down to Blind River and stayed with Pat and Joan until Pamela, Olga and Ian arrived out a week or so later. There in Blind River, we rented a cabin on the edge of a lake, complete with boat, and Pat gave us a car. The weather was beautiful and we had nearly two months of the most wonderful holiday imaginable. It was just heaven. The

down side was that after the straight 77 shifts my nerves were a bit shot, which would be par for the course for any miner, doing even a lot less, under those conditions. I was very moody and very difficult to put up with, even for a long time after coming home and until I was well immersed in my next project. Once again, Pamela carried the can without a word of complaint or reproach.

The holiday had everything - weather, family, friends, the lake and fishing, barbeques and music in the evening, when Pat and his friends would sit around and entertain us with their guitars. Pamela and I drove up to Thunder Bay for a Mickey Gilley concert, Mickey is a first cousin of Gerry Lee Lewis and a superb musician in his own right. At the end of August Pamela and the kids booked a plane for home. I had decided to fly up to Thompson to see Billy, Pat, Brenda and David. I was really glad that I did. Willie and I hadn't spent much time together in years. We "bonded" again and I enjoyed a wonderful week there and also met many old friends, including Tommy Gaynor and Billy Elliot. Willie was by now a mines inspector. One day he was doing a safety inspection of INCO where I once worked. He asked if I would like to accompany him on his rounds and I jumped at the opportunity. INCO decked me in out new gear (nothing was too good for a brother of the Inspector!) and down we went. Down to 1400 where Mike Lacey got killed, more than 20 years before. I thought of all the guys who were maimed and paralyzed, had nervous breakdowns and committed suicide. I thought of my friends who had been killed and I dwelt on the gamble I took for eleven weeks in Wawa. We come to surface and as always, the daylight blinded me as I exited the cage. I turned to Willie and said "next time I go underground it will be just 6 ft".

We were brought in and I was introduced to the mine manager. I think I may have said already how he asked me to go and have a few beers and think about a job with INCO. I told him, truthfully, that the last time I stood on that carpet, that the man in his chair told me that if I didn't stop having a few beers, I wouldn't have a job. Funny old world!

Next I was back home in my own country again. I got back in time to see my favourite hurling team, Galway, win their second All-Ireland in a row. I was restless and impatient, because I didn't know what I was going to do next. I needed a new challenge.

CHAPTER 18

Back in Business

While in Canada, I studied their coffee – shop style, restaurants and road stops. I became convinced that a well run one in Ireland would give me a good return. On my return to Ireland, having the time on my hands, I decided to learn something about the fast-food business. We used occasionally call into Double D's Restaurant in Mullingar after the pictures and also Ian raved about their chips, so I used call and buy him a fix on the way into visiting him in St. Finians.

I asked Veronica, who worked in Double D's to introduce me to the boss, Seamus Daly. As it turned out, I met his son Anthony and he welcomed me in to work a few evenings a week, so as that I might learn the business. This was very decent of the Daly Family and was in keeping with the sort of people they were.

Then, I saw on a property page of the paper that there was this little house for sale in the centre of Clonmellon. It was perfect and we bought it without much fuss. There wouldn't be any trouble getting Planning Permission, as the building was in the dead centre (dead centre was definitely an accurate description of the place) of the village, opposite the Post Office and between a house which used to be a forge and the other one' which used to be a pub. Wrong! The woman on one side, without chick or child to bother her, objected and then the other people joined in. As mentioned previously, it turned out fine in the end, but it wasn't good for a bushed miner at the time. I was back enjoying my squash over the winter of 1998/89. The club was doing badly and in the spring of 1989 there were all sorts of rumours about its future. It wasn't being well run and in fact, accounts showed that the bar was even losing money.

I didn't want the place to close – which it would have and once again, my brains clicked into gear, churning around the possibilities and potential of the centre. One night, I said to Pamela "I think we should buy the squash centre". At first I got a very negative response, but after I talked facts and figures, she became, at most, lukewarm. On checking it out, I found that membership stood at 170, which included juniors and short-term memberships – not exactly a money-spinning racket – if you will pardon the pun!

One evening, I mentioned to my friend, Hugh Kiernan, that I was thinking of buying the centre. Hugh looked at me and said twice "You must be mad". Anyway, when he realised that I was serious, whether mad or not, Hugh said he would talk to Paul McGrath, who was friendly with the four owner-directors. By the end of the week, Pamela had become totally supportive and when McGrath reported back that the owners were "mad to sell", the die was cast. It didn't take long to negotiate a price – around £80,000, I think. Both Kiernan and McGrath, acting as honest brokers, were a huge help. This was all done in secret and before the news would break, I phoned committee chairman,

CONGRATULATIONS

The Squash Centre in Mullingar was recently purchased by Bernie and Pamela Comaskey and we offer them belated congratulations and good luck in their enterprise.

Bernie has always been associated with hurling on the local scene and was a member of the Ballinvalley N.S. team which brought the Comortas na mBun Scol title to Delvin back in 1968. Pamela is on the staff of Crowenstown N.S. and their son, Ian, has been a valued member of local underage teams for the past few years.

Permission for takeaway in Clonmellon

Planning permission has been granted to Bernard J. Comaskey, Drumcree, Collinstown, for a coffee shop and take away at Main Street, Clonmellon. Details appear in the latest list of Co. Manager's Orders, supplied at this week's meeting of Westmeath Co. Council.

Permission Granted

Seamus McGowan and Pamela and I met himself and his wife, Ann. Seamus was 100% supportive, as he could see that this was probably the only hope of securing the future of the club. We sat on it for another week and then I told Seamus that, as he was chairman of the club he could announce the take over at the following "Saturday Nights" tournament presentation, which he did. I did not attend the function. McGowan called a members meeting for the following Monday night. The plan was that Pamela and I would give them an hour's start and then I would address the meeting and explain my plans for the future of the centre.

Olga and Ian – growing up

When Pamela and I arrived at the agreed time, Hugh came out and asked us to wait a little longer downstairs. Both of us were members and would be entitled to be there from the start of the meeting, if we wanted to. Now, we could hear what was going on inside and I couldn't believe some of the comments; 95% were so supportive and complimentary to Pamela and I, but I cringed for Pamela at some of the "Ah yea, but what about's". These were guys who liked their squash, knew the club would probably be wound up if I didn't buy and yet the begrudgery was spewing out of their mouths. Eventually Paddy Leavy said "I think this is the best thing ever to happen to the club, but whether it is or not, Bernie Comaskey now owns the centre and he can turn it into a cattle-shed if he wants, so some of ye who like to hear yourselves talk, should quit your nonsense". Then Pamela and I were ushered in and we got a standing ovation. On my way to the top of the room, I looked to see if the "ah yea, but what abouts" were clapping. They weren't, and I remembered! In my few words I said that I would restore the club to its former glory and would then improve on that. For the benefit of the begrudgers, I finished up by say-

ing "that if I were a German or English investor, they would be outside cutting ribbons and breaking bottles of champagne against the wall. Finally, I said "If anyone thinks that their £50 membership gives them the same voice as my £80,000 investment it was time to think again". They got the message!
We were now 'borrowed to the hilt' and I think we didn't pay a grocery bill in Bartleys for the next six months. Then, we sold the place in Clonmellon and that relieved the strain. Four squash courts, a sauna and an upstairs club bar and viewing area, was the extent of the centre. The first thing we did was roll up our sleeves and wash the place from top to bottom. A few cans of paint and the transformation was amazing. I started writing the squash and leisure notes in the local newspapers which was great P.R.O and free advertising – although I did a fair bit of paid advertising as well, in recognition of this. We took over on 9th June 1989. To "get them in" we did a low price summer special, by mid November, we had almost 400 paid up adult members and this had increased to 600 before we built on the gyms and function room. The gyms pushed the membership into four figures, where it remained until we sold the premises to Mick and Eileen Lynn in 2000, for more than five times what we paid for it.

Opening Night at the new
Mullingar Squash and Leisure Centre

We started things like aerobics, in which the hugely popular Maggie Crowely was a great asset, first with step-aerobics and the like; as well as courses and dancing classes, meant that every night, as well as squash, there was something going on at the Squash and Leisure Centre.

Along with Joe Bardon, I went to the World Cup in America in 1994. In "Denim & Diamonds" in New York, I discovered "Line Dancing". I bought every video I could get my hands on; brought them home and transferred to suitable tapes here and we were first in Ireland with Line Dancing. Soon every venue was claiming to be first – including the Greville Arms which started four months after us. From the video, two of our gym instructors learned line-dancing and became 'teachers'. Usually they had only mastered one class ahead of their pupils.We had a very profitable 6 months.Two classes of 80 @ £3 each, two nights a week.We ran monthly graded squash tournaments, with a 'Party Night' for the presentation of prizes. There were many memorable social nights, with music provided by the O'Farrell Brothers.

Without the hard work of the various committees, the success of the club would not have been. I am indebted to those members and also to loyal staff like Kathleen Maguire who worked 8 years for us and who for a decade helped to make us the most popular and successful squash club in Ireland during our time there.

The New Millennium

One night in 1991, Pamela left around ten o'clock to drive home.We were still living in Drumcree – twelve miles from Mullingar. She was ten minutes gone when I received a phone call from Finbarr O'Farrell "Bad news, Bernie, we just found Johnny (Pamela's father) dead in the field". He had gone to count the cattle and when his car was seen in the same place for a long time, they went to look for him. On her way home Pamela would pass the field. I ran to my car, hoping to catch her on the road. I didn't make it and she had just been told, when I arrived on the scene. She was inconsolable. Dympna was brought there by "her rock" Colm. Poor Dympna would soon lose her mother and inside a few short years, she would lose Colm, another brother Fechin, sister Ita and son Michael. Johnny was 68.

Through the nineties I retained my interest in farming, I would have a few cattle, running along with my uncle Paddy's. In 1995 I, along with the entire county of Westmeath, experienced unprecedented joy, when we won the All-Ireland Minor Football crown. The Ber (it should be "Bear") Murtagh nearly killed me at the final whistle, as we danced around the stand.Anything up to 10,000 people turned out in Mullingar for the homecoming. For the

Pamela and I survey the fruits of our labour outside the vastly extended Mullingar Squash & Leisure Centre.

first time in my lifetime, my county could celebrate and for the first time I didn't feel like a gate-crasher at someone else's party!

Pamela loves the sun and by the late eighties, we could afford to go abroad twice a year. Usually Olga and Ian came too, but sometimes we just took off for a week on our own. Pamela wanted us to buy a holiday home in the sun somewhere. Over nearly thirty years we had been everywhere we wanted to see, by way of sun holidays. For a long time I wasn't in favour of buying property abroad, as I felt it would restrict us to that place. Eventually though, I relented and we began to look at options abroad. On a Sunday in 1998, Pamela asked me to go to a property exhibition in Tullamore; as usual I had a hurling match to go to. I was excused and Olga went in my place. The two women came home full of enthusiasm and I agreed to travel to Spain for a three day inspection trip.

I went on the trip, not expecting to buy anything, but I found myself being hugely impressed with the area outside Torrevieja, which was hugely underdeveloped. We bought a house, from plans, at La Zenia, near Torrevieja and about 30 miles from Alicante. At that time, La Zenia was just a crossroads on Caratera 332, at the turn-off for Villa Martin Golf Course. Today, there is a round about, where the crossroads was. Its official name is La Zenia Roundabout, but it is commonly known as "Paddys Point Roundabout" in deference to "Paddys Point Irish Pub", which we opened there in 1999 and is now probably the best known pub in Spain. There is no doubt but that the fact that Pamela and I decided to open the pub there, has contributed more than somewhat to the vast development of that particular area. We made friends with some other couples on that fateful inspection trip. On the last night we decided that we had to meet up when we went out there. There was no Irish Bar, even in Torrevija and no natural meeting place for us around La Zenia. "What this place needs is an Irish Pub", I said, and that is how the seed of 'Paddy's Point' was sown.

All Dressed Up

After coming home from the trip, Pamela and I talked about opening a pub out there. She was really enthusiastic about it, which in a way is surprising as buying a pub in Ireland had always been a no-no for her. A couple of weeks later I went back out on my own to check out possible locations for a bar. Initially I was going to go for a site in Torrevieja itself. I came home with that idea, but I was uneasy about the commercials I was shown – that is why I came home to think about it. I spoke to a few business friends and toyed with the idea of bringing in one or two partners for the venture. However, I quickly ruled this out. I don't like partnerships and anything I have ever done, I've done it on my own. Two weeks later I went back again and talked to more agents and developers. I was learning the lie of the land all the time and soon I realised that where our house in La Zenia was going to be, was right in the centre of where the biggest development on the Costa Blanca was taking

Together Again
At the Johnstown School Reunion with our mother
Yours Truly, Billy, Seán, Fechin, Anthony and Camillus

place. For £80,000 I bought a 110m^2 commercial unit, with not even the walls plastered and this became the famous 'Paddy's Point'. Three years later we extended by purchasing the adjoining unit for five times what I paid for the original. 'Paddy's Point' is worth a lot of money today.

Leaving the Club

In 1988 Ian came into the business as Gym Manager. He had qualified as a fitness instructor, deep tissue masseur and sports injury therapist. A year in Denmark working with Olympic athletes and a year in America made him ideal for the job. We opened a sports injury clinic at the centre and Ian was 'flat out'. He suffered a bit with his wrists from all the work and then one day, a couple of years later, he woke up and decided that he "couldn't face putting his hands on another body" and that was the end of that.

1999, and I was spending more time in Spain, setting up and opening Paddy's Point. Ian, backed up by his mother wanted to be "full boss" in Mullingar, by way of being Manager with full control. In the circumstances, I wanted this plan to work so I agreed to give him a year. I said " Don't tell me, show me".

Ian was out of his depth and did not do a good job. He just delegated and the problems were compounded by the fact that he became involved in an American style diner, down town.
As aforementioned, I put the place up for sale and pulled the door after me for the last time in May 2000. Ian learned from his mistakes and even if he wasn't my son, I would say that he is now one of the most successful and shrewdest business men I know today. Naturally, I had mixed emotions moving away from the club. We had owned it for eleven years and for ten of those, I gave the centre 60 to 70 hours a week. Great, great memories and an intense sense of pride for what we left, as against what we bought in 1989. In 1997, I was presented with the Westmeath Enterprise Award for Leisure and Tourism by Minister Mary O'Rourke T.D.
We had a high standard of squash at the top. I think that Brian Lalor, our number one player, was and is, the most naturally gifted player I have ever seen. Brian played for Ireland u19, without having received any coaching whatsoever. He is also one of the most unassuming and obliging guys you could have in any club. His good honour and sharp wit meant great craic on tournament nights. On the ladies side, Geraldine Walsh and Mary Sharry

The newly opened Paddy's Point

swapped the number one spot over the years. Both were very competitive, especially Geraldine and they gave a good account of themselves in tournaments and in Leinster Premier League. But it is in the monthly club tournaments and the party nights of the Mullingar Squash Club that gave us the greatest entertainment. I often went home, very late, very tired, with a pain in my face from the laughing.

There was a core of great club members and great characters. It is dangerous to start naming names as deserving people get left out. These were the backbone of Mullingar Squash Club.

Players from all over Ireland looked forward to the Mullingar Squash Open in January each year. So much so, that it was difficult to get playing in it. The hardest job for our committee was deciding who to leave out. 90% of the 100, or so – who would be graded into five sections, would be for players who played the previous year. Then, for the 10% of new places, a number of

Winter in the Sun - Spain

criteria applied; geographical spread; did he or she apply and not get in last year? Anybody who played and didn't 'stick around' (spend a bit of money round the bar) didn't 'get in' again.

A group used come from Coventry, organised by Alf Cavanagh and Greer Sloane would bring 30 from Belfast. Greer was in Telecom and many, but not all, were from that club. Two of the Belfast group were R.U.C. men and I would have been far better off if I hadn't known this. I worried so much, because if it were known, where would you get two softer targets, at the height of the troubles in Northern Ireland? The boys were also breaching their own strict regulations, but believe me, they felt it was well worth it for the 'ball' they had in Mullingar. A great contingent of squash players and characters. Mick O'Reilly, Sean Kavanagh, Meave O'Callaghan, Una Duignan, Paddy and Rosemary Geaney, Marie Blair and Jackie Russell spring to mind.

Hector hung out with us as one of our first customers

Many other great memories. Italia 90, the atmosphere as good as being there. Marion Brunton hanging out of the fire-escape in her green, white and gold, after we beat Romania. The staff – none better anywhere.

In November 2004 we organised a squash reunion; players from all over Ireland turned up. The boys from the north were down. A few came from England. The players were there in force. There was a great turn out from Mullingar and just for one night it was like "a night at the open", once again.

Up and Running

On the 19th March 1999, we loaded the last few items into a 40ft container, in Navan and sent it on its way to Spain. On board was the required bar furniture, all the timber, bar memorabilia, the Paddy's Point wooden shopfront sign, cash registers – in fact everything required for the making of an

Irish Pub. Carpenter Ronnie Coogan, from Navan, was the man in charge and if ever there was a right man for the job – Ronnie was it. He had done the bar for Michael in Drumcree and also Everette's in Navan, which was about the same size as the proposed 'Paddy's Point'. Ronnie was to have two helpers, my friend Joe Bardon and yours truly.

Two days after seeing off the container, Joe, Ronnie and myself loaded up the second-hand, left-hand-drive, Honda Prelude Automatic, with Ronnie's tools and then we barely made room for ourselves, and so we headed for Rosslare on the first leg of our journey to the new world. The long sailing to Cherbourg didn't seen long at all. We were all in great form, with loads of slagging; included was a few characters we meet on board. Joe and Ronnie get on great, even though they would appear to have nothing in common. Joe, who doesn't drink, was taking time off from his job as a psychiatric nurse in Saint Lomans Hospital, Mullingar. Ronnie started as he intended to continue, by taking a drink. It was a magnificent drive through France and over the Pyrenees into Spain. We stopped when we felt like it, although I regretted afterwards that we didn't stretch the drive into four days instead of taking it in three, especially, because when we arrived in La Zenia, the place wasn't ready for us and patience isn't one of Ronnie's strong points. I had engaged a Spanish builder to install the toilets, plaster the walls and put in the floor. I had given them a week longer than when the work should be finished, but it still took a further week from when we arrived before Ronnie could spring into action. Also when the container arrived, we didn't have anywhere to put it and I was lucky to be given a nearby unit, for storage, from Antonio

Mickey Harte and John O'Mahony with Ian outside Paddy's Point

Mass, the man I bought my commercial from. Anyway, we had a week with little to do, except for Ronnie to take a drink. Five weeks later, through Ronnie's genius, what had started off as something resembling a shed, was transformed into a decent, authentic Irish Pub. At this stage, I came home for a week for R&R – rest and recreation.

On my return, I was joined by an alleged Bar-Manager, my friend, retired bank-official, Oliver Carey. I don't know how we survived those early months and I'll never forget Oliver for sticking with it when he could have walked away. Never enough staff, never enough change in the bank; they couldn't understand what we needed all the coins for. Everywhere else they ran a 'tab' and therefore, didn't require so much of a float. We were 'in trouble' with many customers because we couldn't do 'tabs' and didn't do food. We were the first real pub and we had to plough our own furrow. Material and supplies were not delivered on time. We never had enough glasses. We were an official Guinness pub but even so, were badly let down by the calibre of people working for them out there. Maeve McNulty, the Guinness Coordinator in Spain did her best, but down the line those who were supposed to carry out the terms of my contract, didn't. As soon as I worked out a plan B, I cut them loose and did it my way. Oliver suggested that we promote Yolanda to Manager and this was a good idea. Yolanda was Manager for two years, followed by Ian for a short time. Assistant Manager, Rory Lee from Ballaghadreen replaced Ian as Manager. In 2003, I gave Rory complete responsibility for the running of the Bar.

Chatting with the "Prince of Galway Hurling" John Connally, in Paddy's Point

If we hand-picked 90% of the customers of 'Paddy's Point' you couldn't get nicer people. As a result of owning Spain's most popular Irish Pub, I have met so many wonderful people out there – including a lot of famous people. I would not take the liberty of naming all of them, but people who wouldn't have minded are some of my sporting hero's. Hurlers like the Connelly

Mullingar Musicians playing in Paddy's Point
L to R: Frank Darby, Noel Battle, Bart McCabe and David (from Liverpool).

Brothers from Galway, Vinny Holden from Dublin, Tomas Mulcahy and Ray Cummins from Cork, Pat Heffernan from Limerick, Frank Larkin and Frank Burke from Galway. Michael Carruth (Boxer), Footballers Kevin Walsh, Olly Brady, my friend Joe Kernan and of course the one and only Sean Purcell. There are many more, as well as top English soccer stars. We are on first name terms with many celebrities from the world of T.V. and entertainment. One Sunday morning, shortly after we opened, the late Joe Lynch, along with a lady, was served by Yolonda, outside on the terrace. I made a beeline for him, after I recognised him. Joking I started to sing "The Whistling Gypsy". He looked at me and indicated that he only spoke French or German. I knew it was Joe Lynch and I learned an important lesson. If people want their privacy, they are entitled to it and forever more, I would be careful to respect those who were there and might not wish to be recognised, or have it known that they were there.

We have a seven-a-side soccer team representing Paddy's Point and one Thursday evening, John O'Mahony and Micky Harte 'guested' together on the same team for us. As I mentioned already, we carry all sports and we have live music every night. Right now, the famous Eileen Reid & Jimmy Day do two gigs a week.

Paddy's Point was by far, the most successful venture I ever had. Many people say it was a courageous move and a big choice. It wasn't. I got in for relatively small money and I was certain that it would work. Of course I could never have dreamed that it would turn out to be seccess that it is. This did not happen by chance. You can only make a first impression once. We have excellent staff, trained to care about and look after our customers. The business was built on a personal basis by Pamela and I, and our dedicated staff have adapted that manner.

If staff are very good, I treat them better than anybody else and if they are no good I get rid of that person without delay. If I have someone who is incompetent than I am incompetent.

Ian is doing so well in the property department that I doubt if he will ever go back inside a bar counter. Some day I probably will sell "Paddy's Point", which by the way, I registered as a trade name in Europe. We regularly get "soundings" and tempting offers. Rory, Marie, Jackie, Ciara, Emmett, Barry, Alan, Oliver, Alan, Lynda, Rita and others are now years with us and that counts a lot with me. I would be reluctant to off-load, without considering how that might affect each and every one of our loyal and much appreciated team.

Winning and Walking

After the joy of Westmeath winning the All-Ireland Minor Football in 1995, I said I didn't care if we never won another match. I lied! I wanted more and in 1999 I thought all my birthdays had come together, when we beat Kerry in the U-21 All-Ireland.

The game was played in Limerick and a star-studded Kerry team were hot favourites. To beat Kerry in an All-Ireland football final makes it that bit more special – which of course is a tribute to Kerry. That day in Limerick, I was close behind where one of Kerry's greatest footballers came in and sat down. He had a couple of nephews playing on the team. It's funny that I remember him so distinctly from the 1999 game. Little could I have imagined the impact this man would have on Westmeath and by extension, on me. That man was Páidí O'Sé.

I am often asked by Westmeath "Hurling men" how come I have put so much into football in the county, when I came from a hurling area. I cannot understand the question. It doesn't have to be either or. My love is for the Westmeath jersey. Hurling is my first love and of course I passionately support the hurlers, but above all, I want Westmeath to win. If I haven't said it earlier, I'll say it now: In my opinion, one of the greatest gifts for an Irishman, is to come from a county which has a realistic chance of winning a provincial title in either hurling or football. We had a great hurling team in the mid 1980's. In 1986 Kilkenny beat us by only two points in a League quarter-final after Michael Cosgrove again in my opinion – had a perfectly brilliant goal disallowed.

Author and Sports Journalist Gerry Buckley (r) found lots to discuss with Armagh Football Manager Joe Kernan and his wife Patricia over a jar in Paddy's Point.

In 2002 I wrote a humorous letter to the Westmeath Examiner, before we were due to play Meath in the 'Leinster Football Championship'. I wrote an 'Open Letter to God', asking why I had been waiting 50 years to see my county play in a Leinster final.

The match against Meath was a draw. Our star player Dessie Dolan, one of the greatest players ever to play the game, after scoring 1 – 7, missed a close-in free, which would have won us the match, with the last kick of the game. We lost the re-play, but who is to say that my letter to God had nothing to do with getting to, and winning, our first Leinster Title in 2004? Dessie Dolan showed his strength of character and resolve, by putting that massive disappointment of "the miss" behind him and adding a Leinster Senior Medal. Along with John Keane, Dessie got an All-Star in 2004.

I was in Paddy's Point, in Spain, when we beat Offaly by a point in the first round. We went mad. There was some dispute that one of our points was "wide", but Offaly gaels will know what I mean, when I say that they are the

God and Meath

Dear God,

I often heard that there are no agnostics in the trenches on the eve of battle and here I am, Lord, living proof of it. You, Almighty, who once had your Pope bless the Spanish Armada, before it took on the English, can you, in your mercy, give Westmeath any bit of an oul' edge, against our mortal enemy on June 1st. God, do you remember, I wrote to you last year in a 'bit of a state' before the Meath match. Christ, it's worse this year. I swear to Jesus (that being your good self) that I cannot take e another Meath beating. A hundred years of f-f-footballing f-f-frustration and I have been around for half of it!

I beseeched you for the 10% luck factor last year and it wasn't worth a 'tinker's curse'...

Sorry God, speaking of cursing, I am sorry for last year and I wish to atone. I am beside myself with remorse over my language (which of course is the sign of a limited vocabulary) but you know that it would have tested the patience of even one of your saints. 'Love thy neighbour' you said; pray for those who persecute a calumniate you, Christ Almighty there has to be a limit? Did you ever stop to listen to the Meath shower? I wouldn't mind so much, only for we, in Westmeath, have shown them a degree of Christian love, in the biblical sense. In fact, many of them have been successfully integrated into our community, where they behave like ordinary people, until the f-f-fortnight before the f-f-football match. Now, what about a Garda who smiles at every MH car, which drives through his village? What about "quickish" Masses on Sunday of a Meath game? What about young Westmeath lads coming home from certain schools talking like Colm O'Rourke? What about that swagger? What about the sin of pride? " The meek shall inherit the earth' my a-a-arm. These Meath b-b-ballplayers need to be taught a lesson in humility and we, your most humble of servants, are just the one to do it for you? God, I know you had a bad oul' year yourself, what with staff problems and all that jazz. But did your Westmeath clerics cause you any grief? Not on your life! Safe pairs of hands in my county (no pun intended). Now, how about payback time for Westmeath?

Lord, you just have to help us! It's even bleaker-looking than last year, without David Mitchell. Mitchell is to us what Saint Peter is to you – only the very, very good get past either of them. Which reminds me again. Sorry about the bad language in Portlaoise – I wasn't myself – excited and stressed – just like now!

Heavenly Father, if you are to be our saviour in our hour of need, the hour is here and the need is now. God, I have a foolproof plan whereby you can help us win, without anyone being any of the wiser. The '10% luck factor' didn't work last year, but this year's formula is inspired. Just listen to this? The law of averages! The f-f-footballing law of averages! One of (sorry I'm getting excited) nature's laws. If something falls one way for a hundred years, surely to Jesus (that being your good self) nobody can consider it abnormal for it to fall the other way one year? Who would question it? And to give them their due these Meath men are not whingers of moaners when the thing does go against them.

Merciful God, if I promise you anything in return, you might not believe me after how I let you down over the 'language' last year. Worse, I still owe you that fiver over the 'false alarm' in 1962. Lord, I know no one is in a stronger position to tell me to 'go to hell' than yourself, but this time I promise you, in front of all these witnesses, that if Westmeath reach the Leinster final, I will walk from Mullingar to Croke Park to atone for my past sins. Do we have a deal or what? Let's pray together!

Your potentially devout disciple,
Bernie Comaskey,
Paddy's Point,
Le Zania,
Spain.

(From Westmeath Examiner 24th May 2003)

last ones who should complain about getting the benefit of a dodgy score! My "joymeter" reached an all-time high when we beat Dublin by two points in the next round. Through misty eyes, I remember Armagh Manager, my friend, Joe Kernan coming down and giving me a big hug and saying "I have to go ... I have a bit more work to do on my team!" Wexford in the semi-final and I was nervous. I was afraid of a "banana skin" . That was the least enjoyable match I ever sat through, because I was afraid, but we got there, after some nervous moments. The previous match I didn't think we would beat Dublin; now I knew absolutely; we were going to win the Leinster.

Now, I had to think about the walk. I was surprised at how many people remembered my promise, "you may get the walking shoes out", was regularly being directed at me. I walked most days, especially in Spain, but that was a big difference – 4 to 6 miles, as against 50 plus. Anyway, I decided I was definitely going to do the walk. As a Director of the Football Supporters Group, we felt that if I were doing it anyway, we should turn it into a fundraiser. As it turned out, "the Walk" raised €12,700 for the team. I didn't take a cent of expenses and in fact I paid in the full price of €500 to have "Paddy's Point" and "Comaskey Properties" named on my t-shirts.

With Westmeath football star Derek Heavin before the start of my walk.

The Leinster Final against our old friends from Laois was fixed for 18th July. In Spain, we are friendly with Sean O'Rourke of RTE News. Sean got wind of the walk and he interviewed me on "News at One". I was genuinely taken aback at the massive reaction to the story. I suppose it was a story with a difference. Westmeath hadn't reached the final for 55 years and here was this guy, waiting that long, who was going to walk 55 miles to the match – because he promised God! I got great support, from a number of people. Mick O'Shea and myself drove the route and planned the walk. Seamus and Eileen Fagan (Seamus was Chairman of our group) Eileen McLoughlin, Leo Dowling,

Bernie Hynes, Chris Forde, Mick Price, accompanied me on bits of the walk and the value of their contribution and in collecting money was invaluable. County Chairman, Seamus O'Faolain gave an inspirational little speech. John Cochrane, Manager of the Greville Arms organised a great send off. But one guy, especially, I will always associate, not only with the walk, but in winning the Leinster, is Gerry Buckley. Gerry was Secretary of our group. An Accountant who turned his back on that profession, so as that he could become what he wanted to be; a sports writer and journalist, Gerry is the most informed and professional sports fanatic I know. (Did you know that the word 'fan' comes from fanatic?) Gerry's boyish enthusiasm is contagious and like I said, it contributed enormously to the walk and to the victory.

A proud mother sits in the Mayor's chair in Thompson, Canada

"The Walk" turned out to be one of the most uplifting and enjoyable experiences I have ever had. The excitement, goodwill and support was tremendous. Nobody charged for anything. Chiropodist, Joan O'Neill, physiotherapist, Jeanette McDonald, looked after my feet, muscles and limbs. Joe Bracken fed us in Kinnegad. Free accommodation in The Wells Hotel, Enfield; more food and warm hospitality in 'Mother Hubards'; and a special mention has to be made of how we were wined and dined and looked after by The West County Hotel, Chapelezoid. Westmeath singer Ronan Leonard, drove up and provided musical entertainment as I reached the hotel.

The Greville Arms Hotel in Mullingar gave me a great send off when I set forth at lunch-time on Friday 16th July, as well as local radio coverage, the

extremely lovely Johanne Cantwell, Sports Reporter with TV3 was there with her camera-crew. That day, I walked the 25 miles to Enfield, stopping at every watering hole, to drink water and coffee; every step of it was a thrill. I was decked-out and carrying my Westmeath Flag and all the cars were beeping and people shouting encouragement along the way. Local radio stations carried reports of my progress and interviews with me.
Arriving in Enfield, I had a slight problem with a calf-muscle. Jeanette did a wonderful job on me, leaving me right as rain for the next day. Mick O'Shea, who drove his car most of the way, was back-up from Mullingar.

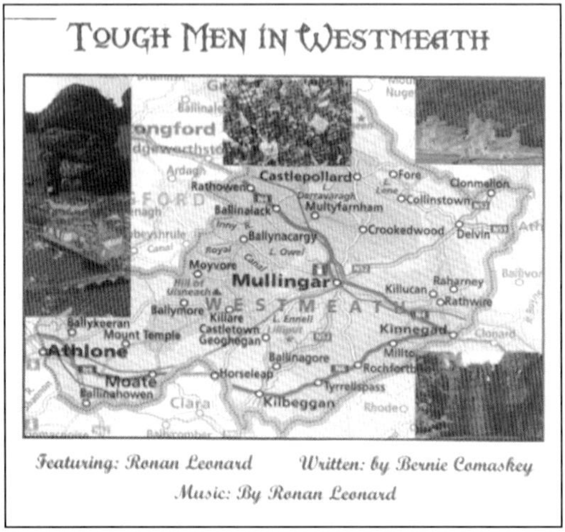

On the TV News, we watched the coverage of the walk leaving Mullingar. Saturday morning, after a good breakfast, I set out to walk another 25 miles, which would take me to Chapelezoid. Leo arrived at the start and stayed all day, walking a surprising amount of the way with me. Eileen, Bernie and Chris joined us later in the day. As walking on the motorway is not allowed, we used the old road through Kilcock, Lexlip, Lucan and down by the Strawberry Beds. In Lucan I took a wrong turn and walked half a mile the wrong road. Mick and Leo came after me and wanted me to get in the car to reverse the error, but I wouldn't – I walked back.
Around 7.30 I arrived in the West County Hotel to another great reception. Manager, Aine Grogan couldn't do enough for us. I also discovered a duty-manager there, who had worked for me in Paddy's Point; Sandi, from Scotland, who since then came back to Spain to manage one of our pubs.
A good meal, a hot bath and I slept like a top. I should have mentioned earlier that Pamela was in Spain for all of this. At first, she was glad to be away – as she reckoned I would be certified and locked up, but as time went on she appreciated how the adventure had captivated the county and further

afield and she missed not being home. After breakfast on the Sunday morning, I went to mass in the nearby church. Read the papers and soon it was time to set off on the last five miles of the trip. Again, I got a great send off and reception at Croke Park. I presented a t-shirt to George Delaney outside Croker. For forty years George was the face of the GAA at every match at headquarters, until his retirement in 2005. I also meet George in Paddy's Point. I hope he writes the book we talked about.

One of our own
Joe Dolan visits Paddy's Point

Nothing ever runs without some hitch and my biggest disappointment was that through misunderstandings, my family were not there to meet me and also failed to link up with me after the game. Before and during the game I had kids coming and asking me to sign their programme. At half-time I was talking to Joe Kernan and a brother and sister came up and asked for an autograph – mine!

We were leading by a point in injury time, when Laois equalised, was it going to be the same old story? Would we lose the replay?

Six days later, the history books will show that Westmeath made history by winning its first ever provincial title. "The greatest day ever in Croke Park" wrote Eamonn Sweeney, in the "Sunday Independent". Before the match I met Colm O'Rourke and I said; "Colm, my greatest wish on this earth is for you to have to eat your words" – he having given Westmeath no chance in any of their games. "Won't I be very happy if I have to do that" he replied and true to his word, next morning appeared a beautiful piece by him which read, in part "I was wrong about Westmeath, no braver, more committed or no more worthy winners have ever been Leinster Champions".

Páidí O'Sé, in his post-match interview exclaimed; "They are tough men in Westmeath". Gerry Buckley immediately adopted this catch phrase – or war cry would be more like it. Soon it caught on – just like "Glory Spain" some 33 years earlier.

In April of 2005, I wrote the words of a song called "Tough Men in Westmeath". Well known Westmeath man Ronan Leonard, put music to it and subsequently recorded it. It is a good 'catchy' tune and is not strictly a football song – it is a Westmeath song.

Seated beside my boyhood hero Willie Rackard, at the Texaco Sports Awards in Dublin

Just as I was coming to the end of writing this book, I was invited by the editor of 'The Westmeath Examiner' newspaper to become a weekly columnist with the paper. This is yet another new challenge for me. I relish the prospects and no job offer has ever given me more satisfaction or even delight. I am happy that I have never lost my boyish enthusiasm for a new adventure. Who knows, maybe my next book will be; "The Best of Bernie"!

Looking Forward - Looking Back

I have been asked by many people why I have written this book. There is no single answer, but there are a number of reasons. Whilst I was never ashamed of being poor; nevertheless I was conscious of our humble standing as children, and, like most parents, I wanted it to be better for my own children, and I vowed that it would be. Now they will know and appreciate how it came about.

Another vitally important motive is that it will show someone who has hit rock bottom from drink that they don't have to stay down there. My story may give an alcoholic the first thing an alcoholic needs – HOPE. Hope and belief in a better, happier life – without booze.

Without the throwaway remarks of two friends this book might not have happened. A couple of years back I met schoolteacher, academic and sports buff, Tom Hunt, on the street and we stopped to talk.

"You know" said Tom, "I envy you; with all the adventures you've had, and all the different thing you've done; and here am I, still doing the same job.

I replied "Tom, when you're not educated – you have to think."

"You should write a book', Tom advised, and every time I met him afterwards he asked:

"Did you start the book yet?"

Then one day I was having a coffee with my aforementioned friend, sports journalist and writer, Gerry Buckley, and in the course of conversation I said I would write my story someday.

After all these years
Philip Conroy, Billy and Myself in Bartlerys, Drumcree

"Someday?!" exclaimed Gerry. "Do it now".
"How do I go about?" I asked.
"Horse into it!"
So I bought a bunch of copybooks before I came home, and started horsin'! The final reason is that I like to write. Yes, I do believe that there is a book in everybody. There is a book in me; how I have succeeded in getting it out is for others to judge.

Dancing with "Me Mammy" on her 80th Birthday

"Yesterday is gone, forget it: Tomorrow didn't come, don't worry; Today is here, get busy!" Today is the only day we can live and the future is only an option. I value every day. I do not work hard now. I have, at last, learned to delegate and not to feel guilty, when not being 'flat out'. Having said that, I never waste a day, because that day is too precious and will never come again.
Sometimes we say "Life is not fair". Sometimes I am glad it's not fair, because if it was, I should be dead. God has been very good to me and I have everything I could ever have wished for. Looking back, there is very little I would wish to change. "What doesn't kill you makes you stronger" and in this regard I have been strengthened by the tough times in my life. My parents were good people, doing the best they knew how, at the time. We are not trained to be parents and I too, made mistakes in this department. Very often, I was too strict when it came to depriving Olga and

Ian of some pleasure that wouldn't have done a bit of harm. Of course, there are some things that I would do differently. Wasn't it George Bernard Shaw who said "It's a pity that youth is wasted on the young", but I wouldn't change much.

I would hate if any financial success made me in any way, selfish or arrogant. A good deed – a really good deed, is only a good deed if nobody knows about it. I do the odd good deed. The one thing that I would love to change about myself, is that I wish I could sing. I love music. I can play a bit on the accordion or with a finger on the piano. I have a beat and I dance well, but I can't sing. It is a wonderful gift for anyone to sing – even to be able to join in on a sing-song.

I value my friends. I have held friends from anywhere I have ever been. I can ignore people who do things to me or who don't like me. There are people, whom it is better for me not to speak to, but I won't wish anybody ill and I don't hate anybody. I read a saying somewhere which says, "It is impossible to hate, if you know the other mans story".

Sometimes I fear for the future of society, with the difference between right and wrong becoming more blurred, especially when it comes to the training of children. Children need the security of rules and if parents, or now even teachers, cannot say no to them, they won't know how to cope with the "no", when it does come.

The church doesn't talk about sin anymore and police don't even think of prosecuting for things that once were regarded as serious enough offences. Respect for authority has diminished. As against the above, there are more young people doing good, caring work than ever before.

I hope to be around for a long time yet. Maybe, there will be Book No. 2 in years to come! The most important thing in my life is the same thing in both my past and my future: that is my children, Olga and Ian. The only absolute, unconditional love in the entire world is a parent for their child. "You can only be as happy as your saddest child". Whatever else I did, or whatever my contribution was, I got my son and daughter right. They are good, caring, popular, hard-working solid citizens. As with so much else, most of the credit for this must go to their mother.

"If ever a man suffered"! Presuming that you have read the book thus far, looking for suffering; well then, I have fooled you, because I never suffered at all!

In this year of 2005, it is now around 36 years since my first date with Pamela. Since then she has been my rock – the foundation on which I have built my life. We have our ups and downs, but she is still here putting up with all my moods and crazy ideas.
I'll tell you one last thing – If ever a woman suffered!

The End

New Year's Eve 2005
Ringing in another Happy New Year in Paddy's Point, of course